PRESIDENTIAL CRISIS RHETORIC AND THE PRESS IN THE POST–COLD WAR WORLD

PRESIDENTIAL CRISIS RHETORIC AND THE PRESS IN THE POST–COLD WAR WORLD

Jim A. Kuypers

Praeger Series in Political Communication

PRAEGER

Westport, Connecticut
London

Library of Congress Cataloging-in-Publication Data

Kuypers, Jim A.
    Presidential crisis rhetoric and the press in the post–cold war
world / Jim A. Kuypers.
        p.   cm.—(Praeger series in political communication, ISSN
1062–5623)
    Includes bibliographical references and index.
    ISBN 0–275–95721–7 (alk. paper)
    1. United States—Foreign relations—1993–   2. Crisis management
in government—United States—History—20th century.   3. Clinton,
Bill, 1946–   —Relations with journalists.   4. Press and politics—
United States—History—20th century.   5. Rhetoric—Political
aspects—United States—History—20th century.   6. Presidents—
United States—Language—History—20th century.   I. Title.
II. Series.
E885.K98   1997
327.73—DC21   97–5588

British Library Cataloguing in Publication Data is available.

Library of Congress Catalog Card Number: 97–5588
ISBN: 0–275–95721–7
ISSN: 1062–5623

First published in 1997

Praeger Publishers, 88 Post Road West, Westport, CT 06881
An imprint of Greenwood Publishing Group, Inc.

Printed in the United States of America

The paper used in this book complies with the
Permanent Paper Standard issued by the National
Information Standards Organization (Z39.48–1984).

10 9 8 7 6 5 4 3 2

To

Andrew Arthur King, my mentor
(ars est celare artem)

Contents

Series Foreword

Those of us from the discipline of communication studies have long believed that communication is prior to all other fields of inquiry. In several other forums I have argued that the essence of politics is "talk" or human interaction.[1] Such interaction may be formal or informal, verbal or nonverbal, public or private, but it is always persuasive, forcing us consciously or subconsciously to interpret, to evaluate, and to act. Communication is the vehicle for human action.

From this perspective, it is not surprising that Aristotle recognized the natural kinship of politics and communication in his *Politics* and *Rhetoric*. In the former, he establishes that humans are "political beings [who] alone of the animals [are] furnished with the faculty of language."[2] And in the latter, he begins his systematic analysis of discourse by proclaiming that "rhetorical study, in its strict sense, is concerned with the modes of persuasion."[3] Thus, it was recognized over 2,300 years ago that politics and communication go hand in hand because they are essential parts of human nature.

Back in 1981, Dan Nimmo and Keith Sanders proclaimed that political communication was an emerging field.[4] Although its origin, as noted, dates back centuries, a "self-consciously cross-disciplinary" focus began in the late 1950s. Thousands of books and articles later, colleges and universities offer a variety of graduate and undergraduate coursework in the area in such diverse departments as communication, mass communication, journalism, political science, and sociology.[5] In Nimmo and Sanders's early assessment, the "key areas of inquiry" included rhetorical analysis, propaganda analysis, attitude change studies, voting studies, government and the news media, functional and systems analyses, technological changes, media technologies, campaign techniques, and research techniques.[6] In a survey of the state of the field in 1983, the same authors and Lynda Lee Kaid found additional, more specific areas of concern such as the presidency, political polls, public opinion, debates, and advertising, to name a few.[7] Since the first study, they also noted a shift away from the rather strict behavioral approach

A decade later, Dan Nimmo and David Swanson argued that "political communication has developed some identity as a more or less distinct domain of scholarly work."[8] The scope and concerns of the area have further expanded to include critical theories and cultural studies. While there is no precise definition, method, or disciplinary home of the area of inquiry, its primary domain is the role, processes, and effects of communication within the context of politics broadly defined.

In 1985, the editors of *Political Communication Yearbook: 1984*, noted that "more things are happening in the study, teaching, and practice of political communication than can be captured within the space limitations of the relatively few publications available."[9] In addition, they argued that the backgrounds of "those involved in the field [are] so varied and pluralist in outlook and approach, . . . it [is] a mistake to adhere slavishly to any set format in shaping the content."[10] And more recently, Swanson and Nimmo called for "ways of overcoming the unhappy consequences of fragmentation within a framework that respects, encourages, and benefits from diverse scholarly commitments, agendas, and approaches."[11]

In agreement with these assessments of the area and with gentle encouragement, Praeger established the "Praeger Series in Political Communication." The series is open to all qualitative and quantitative methodologies as well as contemporary and historical studies. The key to characterizing the studies in the series is the focus on communication variables or activities within a political context or dimension. As of this writing, nearly forty volumes have been published, and there are numerous impressive works forthcoming. Scholars from the disciplines of communication, history, political science, and sociology have participated in the series.

I am, without shame or modesty, a fan of the series. The joy of serving as its editor is in participating in the dialogue of the field of political communication and in reading the contributors' works. I invite you to join me.

Robert E. Denton, Jr.

NOTES

1. See Robert E. Denton, Jr., *The Symbolic Dimensions of the American Presidency* (Prospect Heights, Ill.: Waveland Press, 1982); Robert E. Denton, Jr., and Gary Woodward, *Political Communication in America* (New York: Praeger, 1985, 2nd ed., 1990); Robert E. Denton, Jr., and Dan F. Hahn, *Presidential Communication* (New York: Praeger, 1986); and Robert E. Denton, Jr., *The Primetime Presidency of Ronald Reagan* (New York: Praeger, 1988).

2. Aristotle, *The Politics of Aristotle*, trans. Ernest Barker (New York: Oxford University Press, 1970), p. 5.

3. Aristotle, *Rhetoric*, trans. Rhys Roberts (New York: The Modern Library, 1954), p. 22.

4. Dan Nimmo and Keith Sanders, "Introduction: The Emergence of Political Communication as a Field," in *Handbook of Political Communication*, eds. Dan Nimmo and Keith Sanders (Beverly Hills, Calif.: Sage, 1981), pp. 11-36.

5. Ibid., p. 15.

6. Ibid., pp. 17-27.

7. Keith Sanders, Lynda Lee Kaid, and Dan Nimmo, eds., *Political Communication Yearbook: 1984* (Carbondale: Southern Illinois University, 1985), pp. 283-308.

8. Dan Nimmo and David Swanson, "The Field of Political Communication: Beyond the Voter Persuasion Paradigm" in *New Directions in Political Communication*, eds. David Swanson and Dan Nimmo (Beverly Hills, Calif.: Sage, 1990), p. 8.

9. Sanders, Kaid, and Nimmo, *Political Communication Yearbook*, p. xiv.

10. Ibid., p. xiv.

11. Nimmo and Swanson, "Field of Political Communication," p. 11.

Acknowledgments

The most troublesome aspect of writing an acknowledgment is the irksome sensation that a particular contribution might be overlooked, thus slighting someone who has meaningfully contributed to the project. Moreover, acknowledgments tend to follow an insipid and formulaic path; therefore, most readers, except those expecting to be acknowledged, usually eschew this particular reading experience. Thus, this acknowledgment's brevity.

I offer thanks to all who have helped me with this project, especially the following Louisiana State University professors: Andrew King, Harold Mixon, Kenneth Zagacki, Sally Graham, and Alan Fletcher. Further, I offer distinctive gratitude to my family, Marvin and Joany Floyd, Kristen Copeland, Laser Floyd, and Rebel Kuypers; and to my friends, Elizabeth Barry, David Lambkin, and Lisa Landry.

Dean David Lagomarsino of Dartmouth College deserves recognition for providing funding during the later stages of this project. I wish to add a special thanks to Dick Sheldon of Dartmouth College, for his friendship and encouragement with this project, and to the staff at the Jones Microtext Center at Dartmouth College. Finally, I am deeply obliged to the excellent team at Praeger, especially my production editor, Liz Leiba.

PRESIDENTIAL CRISIS RHETORIC AND THE PRESS IN THE POST–COLD WAR WORLD

Chapter 1

Introduction

In October 1991, President Jean Bertrand Aristide of Haiti was forceful-ly removed from office following a coup d'état led by Haiti's military leader, General Raoul Cedras. In response to this event, President George Bush issued Executive Order 12775, which officially elevated the situation in Haiti to the level of a "national emergency" for the United States. The Bush administration immediately called for eco-nomic sanctions and, in cooperation with the United Nations and the Organization of American States (OAS), initiated an embargo that would last throughout Bush's term as president.

In January 1993, Bill Clinton was sworn in as president and inherited Bush's Haitian policy. Throughout his candidacy, Clinton had derided the Bush administration's policy on Haiti. Yet upon taking office, Clinton essentially left Bush's policies in place, made them his own, and modified them in the ensuing months. Throughout 1993, the situa-tion in Haiti remained unstable, and several key events occurred to which the president and the press responded. On 19 February 1993, the freighter *Neptune* sank, leaving over 800 Haitians dead. On 13 March 1993, the Haitian military arrested a soldier after he had been granted political asylum by the United States. On 15 March 1993, President Aristide visited President Clinton in Washington. On 3 July 1993, the Haitian leaders signed the Governors Island agreement that set a spe-cific time for President Aristide's return to Haiti. Finally, on 11 October 1993, U.S. and Canadian military engineers and trainers were prevent-ed from disembarking in Port-au-Prince.

Although these events prompted criticism of the Clinton administra-tion, they were also used by the Clinton administration to justify increased action. The press focus was primarily upon the legal battle ensuing over the constitutionality of the Clinton administration's re-patriation policy and upon the general plight of Haitian refugees. The administration's focus was bifurcated: one, the return of President Aristide and democracy to Haiti; and two, the prevention of a humanitarian tragedy in the form of a massive refugee flotilla from Haiti. These competing foci produced different discourses about Haiti and the broad divergence of the contending frames through which the president and the press viewed the situation even after significant action had been taken by the chief executive.

Haiti was not, however, the only crisis to face President Clinton during 1993. In March, North Korea announced its withdrawal from the international nuclear nonproliferation treaty that banned the development of nuclear weapons. This was an especially delicate crisis for the fledgling administration. Soon after North Korea's announcement, both North and South Korea had placed their militaries on alert. This situation directly involved the security and interests of the United States. Not only did the United States have mutual defense treaty obligations with South Korea; it also had over 35,000 U.S. soldiers stationed in South Korea. The possibility of North Korea using its enormous military—1.1 million soldiers—let alone developing nuclear weapons, was of immediate importance to the United States; furthermore, nuclear nonproliferation was of early stated importance to the Clinton administration. However, this crisis received little press attention, and the Clinton administration released few public statements concerning the situation. Those statements that were released did not always correspond in content to what the press was reporting about the crisis.

Bosnia was another situation of stated importance to the Clinton administration. The war in Bosnia was well under way when Clinton assumed office, and it was also a situation that seemed to persist throughout the early years of his presidency. However, in November 1995 the Clinton administration announced it would participate in the implementation of the Dayton Accord. The warring Bosnian parties had agreed to this peace plan, and the Clinton administration had agreed to send approximately 20,000 U.S. soldiers to help implement the Accord. This was an issue of great importance to the United States. Questions about the Bosnia mission immediately surfaced, and the press devoted a great deal of attention to the issue. Moreover, the press supported the president by adopting the Clinton administration's assertions about the mission as its own. However, the press also took an oppositional stance to many of the assertions the president and his officials made. These contentions were most notable with the issues of congressional approval for the mission and Bosnian Serb protests over certain provisions of the Dayton Accord.

Using these three cases, this work employs a comparative frame analysis to answer the following questions: (1) How did the Clinton administration frame the situations in North Korea, Bosnia, and Haiti? (2) How did the press, responding to President Clinton, frame the situations? and (3) At what time, if at all, did these frames converge to present a unified contextual whole?

RHETORICAL SITUATIONS, ADMINISTRATIVE RHETORIC, AND CRISES

This work seeks to better understand the interaction of press and presidential discourse in the context of crisis formation. With the Cold War arguably over, President Clinton was the first atomic-age president unable to draw upon the Cold War meta-narrative. This raises the issue of how a president can now frame an international event as a crisis. In the past, it would have been relatively easy for an American President to use North Korea, Bosnia, or Haiti, as a stalking horse for the Soviet Union, thereby justifying almost any level of action/involvement. In the post-Cold War environment, President Clinton appeared unable to do this. He seemed to have lost the authority of unilateral definition, and his assessments were constantly scrutinized and challenged by the national media. This volume analyzes crisis rhetoric at a crucial period in the history of presidential studies. The very nature of how presidents must now frame international events has changed with the demise of the Soviet Union. Thus, this work examines the beginning of the creation of a new and more dialogical method of legitimating international crises. In order to explain how this work will proceed, I will spend the bulk of this chapter describing how I employ the concepts of rhetorical situation, administrative rhetoric, and crisis.

Rhetorical Situations

Bitzer's classic definition of a rhetorical situation entails "a complex of persons, events, objects, and relations presenting an actual or potential exigency which can be completely or partially removed if discourse, introduced into the situation, can so constrain human decision or action as to bring about the significant modification of the exigency."[1] For Bitzer, an "exigence is an imperfection marked by some degree of urgency; it is a defect, an obstacle, something to be corrected."[2] The audience consists of those individuals capable of modifying the exigence. Constraints influence both audience and rhetor(s) and are composed of "persons, events, objects, relations, rules, principles, facts, laws, images, interests, emotions, arguments, and conventions."[3] The above concepts (exigency, audience, and constraints) are interanimated. The three taken together require some type of discourse to fuel their interaction and possible modification. The discourse, or utterance in Bitzer's terminology, "participates naturally in the situation, is in many instances necessary to the completion of situational activity, and by means of its participation with situation obtains its meaning and its rhetorical character."[4]

An important distinction in a situational perspective may be drawn between the concepts of "situation" and "context." Context, a necessary component of human communication, is both more and less than the historical facts surrounding a rhetorical situation. Context is, in part, constituted by the various interpretive communities that apprehend a text. In this vein, Gregory Bateson's definition of context proves illuminating: "a collective term for all those events which tell the organism among what *set* of alternatives he must make his next choice."[5] Thus, contexts have the potential of having broad influences upon our understanding of any particular text. In contradistinction, rhetorical situations are not to be understood at a general level but rather are entered into through the rhetor/text's interaction with audience, exigency, and constraints. Contexts help shape the general level of interpretive precision that produces a text (and its subsequent interpretation); it is this text that enters into the rhetorical situation. Rhetorical situations are a part of the larger context; they "come into existence, then either mature and decay or mature and persist. . . . Situations grow and come to maturity; they evolve to just the time when a rhetorical discourse would be most fitting."[6] Contexts allow for the general interpretation of utterances; rhetorical situations provide moments for a "fitting" utterance through which modification of an exigence may be achieved. For example, consider the destruction of Iran Air flight 655 in 1988. The larger contexts that could have influenced texts entering into the rhetorical situation included the upcoming U.S. presidential election, the Iran-Iraq war, and the historical/cultural understandings of Americans concerning our role in the world. The rhetorical situation, on the other hand, is modified by utterances that are shaped by these contexts. The utterance, however, can have a bearing upon which contexts subsequently wax or wane in influence.

Administrative Rhetoric: Conflation of Role and Text

Many communication scholars view the modern presidency as a *rhet-*

orical presidency.[7] This view of the presidency is justified on three grounds: One, the president sets goals and provides solutions for the nation's problems; two, the mass media dramatize the content of what presidents say, thus moving the emphasis away from what presidents *do* to what they *say*; and three, the continual campaigning by presidents encourages an emphasis upon presidential image and personality, while deemphasizing deliberation on the issue in question.[8] As Denton and Woodward stated: "[T]he presidency is an office, a role, a persona, constructing a position of power, myth, legend, and persuasion. Everything a president does or says has implications and communicates 'something.' Every act, word, or phrase becomes calculated and measured for a response."[9]

What a president or his representatives say, then, is a text. Communication scholars have traditionally associated the term *text* with *rhetor*, but rhetor and text could be conceived in broader terms. A rhetor can range from a lone individual to a collectivity of individuals speaking on behalf of an organization, institution, or presidential administration.[10] A text can consist of several discrete elements/utterances if the set of such elements was conceived as a unified whole (e.g., an advertising campaign) or if all the elements aim to achieve a common purpose. Such a construct does not deny the possibility for members of a collectivity to speak as individuals. It does, however, recognize the tendency of such collectivities to speak with a single voice and permits the analysis of those voices as a collective whole. Furthermore, such a conception recognizes that the discourse situated within rhetorical situations consists of complex episodes: "a conception wherein the entire constellation of rhetoric surrounding a specific event is treated as the rhetorical text."[11] The term *text* in this work refers specifically to the discourse produced by the Clinton administration concerning the situations in North Korea, Bosnia, and Haiti. This "administrative rhetoric" possesses two interacting dimensions. One dimension accounts for the relatively entrenched and stable aspects of administrative systems everywhere, while the other accounts for the "personalities" of various presidential administrations.[12]

A traditional view of presidential roles, based upon the duties described by the Constitution, highlights the stable form of administrative systems. Edward S. Corwin described five roles: chief of state, chief executive, chief diplomat, commander in chief, and chief legislator.[13] Clinton Rossiter described five additional, extra-constitutional roles that have developed since Corwin's listing: chief of party, protector of peace, manager of prosperity, world leader, and voice of the people.[14] These generally agreed upon roles constitute "ideas about what people expect to do in certain situations as well as what others expect them to do in certain situations."[15] They combine presidential and public perception about what a particular role entails. Yet each president's administration adopts its own role(s) to enact. For instance, the Reagan administration viewed itself as working for peace throughout the world, a variation of protector of the peace. This irenic role in international affairs shaped the manner in which the administration could respond to various situations.[16] Roles adopted by administrations act to constrain and foster presidential discourse.

Murray Edelman's early work analyzing the "role-taking" characteristic of administrations is illuminating here: "Factual premises alone are certainly not sufficient to explain administrative decisional choices; but factual premises in conjunction with observable role-taking are: for the role both specifies the value premises operative in a particular instance of decision-making and establishes a probability that these same value premises will be operative in future decision-making in the same policy area."[17] It is the role-taking action that is of importance to this book. The Reagan presidency, for example, had consistently referred to its peacekeeping role in foreign affairs, especially during the Iran-Iraq war. Throughout this conflict, the United States had stressed its role as a neutral third party acting in the capacity of peace broker. This stance in the international arena was a vital one for the Reagan presidency, and it had been used repeatedly to justify various policy decisions.

To be sure, the nature of the threat to the United States posed by the Iran-Iraq war was never truly clear in the mind of the American public; nor was it explained clearly by the Reagan administration. Yet this very ambiguity acted to enhance the image the government hoped to project. The rhetorical potency of ambiguity is explained by Edelman: "Only an intangible threat permits this kind of administrative role taking. In the measure that a threat is clearly observable and subject to systematic study, perceptions of its character and of techniques for dealing with it converge. Polarization and exaggeration become less feasible."[18] In addition, the government's political response to events in the Gulf also highlighted the way that role-taking affects presidential administrations. For example, President Reagan used his administration's role as defender of democracy to justify the United States' invasion of Grenada, and President Bush used his administration's role as world peacekeeper to help justify our early involvement in Kuwait and the Gulf War. By the roles he has highlighted, each president has attempted to "personalize" his administration.

It is in this sense, then, that this work uses the term *administrative rhetoric* to refer to specific governance styles employed by presidential administrations. Through rhetorical grounding of particular actions or policies, each administration will of necessity project the image that it has chosen to highlight and will adopt public roles that are integral to that image. Thus, administrative texts do not necessarily advance procedural aspects of an administration; rather, such texts may function to create and to maintain the roles chosen by a political leader as part of his constituted identity.

Thus, we can begin to see the possible interaction between administrative text, context, rhetorical situations, and crisis formation. I have previously demonstrated elsewhere that crisis situations may begin with no stable means for interpreting the discursive surroundings and that one of the purposes of the administrative text is the creation of a stable contextual frame.[19] The appearance of this frame requires substantial interaction of text and context. Robert J. Branham and W. Barnett Pearce highlighted this reflexivity: "Every communicative act is a text that derives meaning from the context of expectations and constraints in which it is experienced. At the same time, contexts are defined, invoked, and altered by texts. Particular communicative acts simultaneously depend upon and reconstruct existing contexts."[20]

In order for a text to modify an exigency successfully, it must "fit" not only the particular situation into which it enters but also the context in which it is situated. In fact, the creation of a stable context of meaning may be the first step for the successful modification of an exigency that occurs in a situation composed of multiple contexts. Thus, an administrative text (e.g., President Clinton's first utterances about the Haiti situation upon taking office) will act to set the interpretive stage in a crisis drama. These first utterances will draw upon the role(s) that the administration has adopted as well. In President Clinton's case, these first utterances will also be acting to establish the role(s) his administration will enact. This corresponds well with Theodore Windt's first stage of crisis formation—the obligatory statement of facts.[21]

Because they involve interanimation of text and context, are rooted in situations, constrain presidential utterances, and draw upon earlier presidential utterances, international crises may be viewed as rhetorical constructions rooted in material circumstances. Crisis rhetoric occurs when a president chooses to speak on an issue, whether to promote it as a crisis or downplay its perceived significance as a crisis. Thus, presidents act to control the definition of international events. The exigence that the president chooses to address—material condition, the president's credibility, the president's popularity, the perception of crisis itself—is part of the crisis itself and is thus highly unstable and alterable. The president acts to define the context through which the event is viewed.

Crises may develop rapidly, as with the North Korean situation, the KAL 007 and Iran Air 655 (Airbus) shootdowns, or they may slowly evolve, as with Haiti. Either way, text and context interplay alter the situation, eventually providing appropriate moments for "fitting" utterances that can bring the perception of crisis to an end. Utterances in response to crisis situations (or the perception thereof) are historically mandated and culturally based. They draw upon public knowledge; the president's text and the press, however, act as providers of preknowledge (knowledge as yet unassimilated into the public consciousness). Eventually, portions of this preknowledge will evolve into public knowledge. Yet the public's perception of the situation and the initial presidential utterances are viewed through the public's initial knowledge held in general: the historical and cultural knowledge. With no Cold War meta-narrative, however, public knowledge concerning international crisis situations is in flux. The absence of this meta-narrative makes the rhetorical construction of crisis problematic.

Definition of Crisis

Many communication researchers view crises as rhetorical creations of the executive branch of government. Although the declaration of crisis may be unilateral, all subsequent discourse is both coded and rule governed. Theodore Windt argued that a crisis is announced by the president as such and that the situation demands that he "act decisively."[22] By announcing the crisis, the president asks for his decision to be supported, not for debate upon what should be done. According to Windt, so long as the crisis is not one of a military attack upon the United States, it is to be considered a political event "rhetorically created by the president."[23] However, the president is not free to do as he pleases when discursively responding to a crisis. His rhetorical options are limited by "precedent, tradition, and expediency."[24] The discourse of crisis is shaped by the political culture that authorizes it.

An international crisis often appears suddenly and provides no stable means for interpreting the discursive surroundings. Presidential utterances act to create a stable contextual frame from which to interpret the event. As Windt suggested, presidential speeches announcing a crisis "begin with an assertion of the President's control of the facts of the situation and an acknowledgement that the New Facts which occasion the speech constitute a New Situation—crisis for the United States."[25] Windt suggested three basic lines of arguments that distinguish presidential crisis rhetoric from other types of presidential utterances.[26] First, there is the obligatory statement of facts. Second, there is the establishment of a "melodrama" between good (the United States) and evil (traditionally the Soviets). Third, the policy announced by the president and the asked-for support are framed as moral acts. Although this structure may hold true for post-World War II presidents up to Bush, President Clinton was unable to frame his responses to crises in this manner due to the ending of the Cold War. The "Evil Empire," as Ronald Reagan put it, no longer exists. So then, how may a president frame crisis situations?

Outside of military attack, the situation does not create the crisis; the president's response does. The president's perception of the situation and the rhetoric he uses to describe it have the potential to elevate the situation to the status of crisis. D. Ray Heisey argued that the president must build certain images of the "enemy" or must make links with values embedded within American culture and history if he is to mitigate a crisis successfully.[27] In short, "leader[s] must find the acceptable images of political reality suitable for his/her people."[28] Since the dawn of the Cold War, all presidents have been able to call upon the topos of good (the United States) versus evil (the Soviet Union). Yet with the culmination of the Cold War, the Soviet Union is (at least at this writing) in financial, political, and social ruins: the "Evil Empire" is no more. The destruction of the Soviet Union meant the concomitant destruction of the Cold War meta-narrative. This was politically unfortunate for President Clinton; he had to respond to potential crisis situations without the benefit of this action legitimating meta-narrative; and if we grant Windt's stages of presidential crisis rhetoric as necessary criteria, it follows that President Clinton will be unable to define a crisis unilaterally, at least without first redefining how four generations of Americans view the enemy.

THE AGENDA-SETTING AND AGENDA-EXTENSION FUNCTIONS OF THE PRESS

Scholars of mass communication are not certain whether to call agenda-setting a function, a theory, or a hypothesis.[29] Its relevance here, regardless of its status, is to help explain how the press interacts with presidential discourse during crisis situations. Bernard C. Cohen made an early observation that the press "may not be very successful in telling its readers what to think, but it is stunningly successful in telling its readers what to think about."[30] If Cohen's statement is accepted as accurate, then it behooves us to consider presidential crisis rhetoric in relation to the press, not because the press represents public opinion but because it is a good indication of the issues and ideas that informed voters and opinion leaders will be talking about. Thus, the president will be aware of the issues, ideas, and responses that circulate in the press—not because they represent popular opinion but because they are a good indicator of that which still needs to be addressed in his policy or that he should be talking about.

Maxwell E. McCombs and Donald L. Shaw argued that voters learn about an issue "in direct proportion" to the attention given that issue by the press; voters tend to share what the media defines as important.[31] Further, they asserted that the mass media provide voters with the "major primary sources of national political information."[32] This is commensurate with the results of a study by Sheldon Gilberg, Chaim Eyal, Maxwell E. McCombs, and D. Nichols that concluded that the press has the potential to set our government's agenda, even at the highest levels.[33] Michael B. Salwen suggested that policy makers "will address issues only when these issues are perceived as crises by the public."[34] Viewed as a Fourth Estate, the mass media shapes not only what the public "perceives" as "political reality" but also how political elites understand what voters and opinion leaders are thinking about. Thus, a conversation develops among the press, its sources, and the public audience that determines "what is *accepted* as the public agenda."[35]

Gilberg and his colleagues asserted that the president is in a "strategic position to influence the agenda" of the press because he is the major source of news at the national level.[36] Although their study found that the press had a significant influence upon President Jimmy Carter's second State of the Union address, they were unable to determine whether Carter's address influenced subsequent press issues. However, a later study by McCombs, Gilberg, and Eyal found evidence of "presidential influence on subsequent press coverage."[37] The implications of this for the study of presidential crisis rhetoric should be clear, particularly in light of the degree to which the public relies upon the press for information, especially national and international events. These "unobtrusive issues" are not part of an individual's common experience; therefore, the "news media exercise a near monopoly as sources of information and orientation."[38] Although the president surely knows more, the media tell him what we, *the public*, knows.

Agenda-extension occurs when the media move beyond the strict reporting of events, and it is to this concern that we now turn. During the decade of the 1980s, mass media and communication researchers using agenda-setting theory began to discover an evaluative component to media news. They postulated that the media do more than tell us what to think about; they also tell us *how* to think about it. These studies suggested another aspect of agenda-setting as it relates to the public evaluation of presidents; this aspect is described as "priming." These studies also suggested an issue that is germane to the study of presidential crisis rhetoric. They postulated that media provide the contextual cues "by which to evaluate the subject matter" under consideration.[39] In short, the media often "frame" an issue so that it will be interpreted in a specific manner.

Framing involves the relationship between qualitative aspects of news coverage—contextual cues—and how the public interprets the news. William Gamson asserted that a "frame is a central organizing idea for making sense of relevant events and suggesting what is at issue."[40] Facts remain neutral until framed; thus, how the press frames an issue or event invariably affects public understanding of that issue or event. Indeed, Gamson argued that facts "take on their meaning by being embedded in a frame or story line that organizes them and gives them coherence, selecting certain ones to emphasize while ignoring others."[41]

PROCEDURES FOR THIS STUDY

North Korea provides an example of a rhetorical situation that rapidly developed yet persisted for some three months. As such, it allows us the opportunity to examine how the Clinton administration managed the perception of crisis. The Bosnian crisis, on the other hand, emerged from a situation that had persisted prior to the inception of the Clinton presidency. It provides an excellent opportunity to view discourse specifically designed to create a new context through which to view the situation. Finally, the situation in Haiti provides a fine opportunity to analyze the interaction of text, context, and situation over an extended period of time. The situation was inherited by President Clinton upon taking office, and he issued definitive statements early in his term that served to define the situation. The situation exhibited several key events that acted to provide opportunities for fitting utterances. Utterances might have been crafted that would have modified the situation. Yet by the end of 1993, the presidential discourse was inadequate for the situation, and the situation appeared worse than when President Clinton had taken office. Therefore, the Haitian situation provides us with an example of a rhetorical situation that matured and persisted. To fully understand the rhetorical dynamics involved with these situations, I examine in each case the initial situation, the Clinton administration's response, and the framing of the administration's response by the national press. The following research questions are answered through a comparative framing analysis of the Clinton administration's public discursive responses to the situations in North Korea, Bosnia, and Haiti. The *Washington Post* and the *New York Times* (as papers of record) are used to provide the press response to events. There are three specific questions this study answers: (1) How did the Clinton administration frame the situations in North Korea, Bosnia, and Haiti? (2) How did the press, responding to President Clinton, frame the situations? and (3) At what time, if at all, did these frames converge to present a unified contextual whole? For the chapter on North Korea I examine all public administrative utterances made between 12 March and 12 June 1993. I also examine the press reports concerning North Korea during this same time period. For Bosnia I examine all public administrative utterances made between 21 November 1995, the announcement of the Dayton Accord, and 15 December 1995, just after the congressional vote of support on the mission. In the two chapters concerning Haiti, I trace the president/press conversations revolving around President Clinton's formal, public statements about Haiti made during 1993.

The remainder of this work is composed of seven chapters. Chapter Two provides an overview and discussion of presidential crisis rhetoric. Chapter Three provides an overview of agenda-setting and agenda-extension theory. Chapter Four is the analysis of the North Korean crisis. Chapter Five is the analysis of the Bosnian crisis. Chapter Six is the first part of the analysis of the Haitian crisis, specifically the relevant texts from January 1993 through June 1993. Chapter Seven continues the analysis of the Haitian crisis, specifically the relevant texts from July 1993 through December 1993. The book concludes with Chapter Eight which contains a discussion of this study's findings and implications for future studies in presidential crisis rhetoric.

NOTES

1. Lloyd F. Bitzer, "The Rhetorical Situation," *Rhetoric: A Tradition in Transition*, ed. Walter Fisher, (East Lansing: Michigan State University Press, 1974), 252. The initial publication of "The Rhetorical Situation" may be found in *Philosophy and Rhetoric* 1 (1968): 1-14.

2. Lloyd F. Bitzer, "Functional Communication: A Situational Perspective," *Rhetoric in Transition: Studies in the Nature and Uses of Rhetoric*, ed. Eugene E. White, (University Park: Pennsylvania State University Press, 1980), 23.

3. Bitzer, "Functional Communication," 26.

4. Bitzer, "Rhetorical Situation," 215. The conception of rhetorical situation advanced here does not ignore recent revisionist modifications of Bitzer's work. I do, however, advance my own understanding of Bitzer's work as a guide for assessing the very unstable nature of presidential crisis communication. I seek especially to bring out the extreme nature of the interanimation of the components—both discursive and material—within and without rhetorical situations. For two examples of revisionists at work see William L. Benoit, "Genesis of Rhetorical Action," *Southern Communication Journal* 59.4 (1994): 342-355, and Craig R. Smith and Scott Lybarger, "Bitzer's Model Reconsidered," *Communication Quarterly* 44.2 (1996): 197-213.

5. Gregory Bateson, *Steps to an Ecology of Mind: Collected Essays in Anthropology, Psychiatry, Evolution, and Epistemology* (San Francisco: Chandler Publish-

ing Company, 1972), 289.

6. Bitzer, "Rhetorical Situation," 258.

7. Robert E. Denton, Jr., and Gary C. Woodward, *Political Communication in America*, 2nd ed. (New York: Praeger, 1990); Jeffrey K. Tulis, *The Rhetorical Presidency* (Princeton, NJ: Princeton University Press, 1987); James W. Ceaser, Glen E. Thurow, Jeffrey K. Tulis, and Joseph M. Bessette, "The Rise of the Rhetorical Presidency," *Essays in Presidential Rhetoric* ed., Theodore O. Windt and Beth Ingold, (Dubuque, IA: Kendall/Hunt Publishing Company, 1983), 3-22.

8. Judith S. Trent and Robert V. Friedenberg, *Political Campaign Communication: Principles and Practices*, 2nd ed. (New York: Praeger, 1991).

9. Denton and Woodward, 199, 200.

10. See Bernard L. Brock, Robert L. Scott, and James W. Chesebro, *Methods of Rhetorical Criticism: A Twentieth-Century Perspective*, 3rd ed. (Detroit: Wayne State University Press, 1989), 427-446.

11. Marilyn J. Young, "When the Shoe Is on the Other Foot: The Reagan Administration's Treatment of the Shootdown of Iran Air 655," *Reagan and Public Discourse in America*, ed. Michael Weiler and W. Barnett Pearce, (Tuscaloosa: University of Alabama Press, 1992), 205.

12. Denton and Woodward, 111-142.

13. Edward S. Corwin, *The President: Office and Powers*, 3rd ed. (New York: New York University Press, 1948).

14. Clinton Rossiter, *The American Presidency* (New York: Mentor Books, 1962).

15. Denton and Woodward, 204.

16. Murray Edelman, *The Symbolic Uses of Politics* (Urbana: University of Illinois Press, 1964), stressed that "once the pattern of role-taking is established within an administrative agency it becomes self-fulfilling and self-reinforcing" (52).

17. Edelman, 50-51.

18. Edelman, 71.

19. Jim A. Kuypers, Marilyn J. Young, and Michael K. Launer, "Of Mighty Mice and Meek Men: Contextual Reconstruction of the Shootdown of Iran Air 655," *Southern Communication Journal* 59.4 (1994): 294-306.

20. Robert J. Branham and W. Barnett Pearce, "Between Text and Context: Toward a Rhetoric of Contextual Reconstruction," *Quarterly Journal of Speech* 71 (1985): 20.

21. Theodore O. Windt, Jr., "The Presidency and Speeches on International Crises: Repeating the Rhetorical Past," *Speaker and Gavel* 2.1 (1973): 6-14.

22. Theodore Windt, "The Presidency and Speeches on International Crises: Repeating the Rhetorical Past," *Essays in Presidential Rhetoric*, ed. Theodore Windt and Beth Ingold (Dubuque, IA: Kendall/Hunt Publishing Company, 1983), 62.

23. Windt, 62.

24. Windt, 63.

25. Windt, 64.

26. Windt, 68-69.

27. D. Ray Heisey, "Reagan and Mitterrand Respond to International Crisis: Creating versus Transcending Appearances," *Western Journal of Speech Communication* 50 (1986): 325-335.

28. Heisey, 333.

29. Maxwell E. McCombs and Donald L. Shaw consider it a function. See "The Agenda-Setting Function of Mass Media," *Public Opinion Quarterly* 36 (1972): 176-187. McCombs has spent most of his career supporting this assertion, and I borrow freely from his ideas in this area. Also see W. J. Severin and J. W. Tankard, *Communication Theories*, 2nd ed. (New York: Longman, 1988). For a detailed explanation of agenda setting as theory, see R. D. Wimmer and J. R. Dominick, *Mass Media Research*, 2nd ed. (Belmont, CA: Wadsworth, 1987).

30. Bernard C. Cohen, *The Press and Foreign Policy* (Princeton: Princeton University Press, 1963), 13.

31. McCombs and Shaw, 177.

32. McCombs and Shaw, 185.

33. Sheldon Gilberg et al., "The State of the Union Address and the Press Agenda," *Journalism Quarterly* 57 (1980): 584-588.

34. Michael B. Salwen, "News Media and Public Opinion: Benign Agenda-Setters? Opinion Molders? Or Simply Irrelevant?" *Florida Communication Journal* 18.2 (1990): 17.

35. McCombs and Shaw, 152.

36. Gilberg et al., 585.

37. Reported in Maxwell E. McCombs and Sheldon Gilberg, "News Influence on Our Pictures of the World," *Perspectives on Media Effects*, ed. Jennings Bryant and Dolf Zillman (Hillsdale, NJ: Lawrence Erlbaum Associates, Publishers, 1986), 14.

38. McCombs and Gilberg, 11.

39. Trent and Friedenberg, 109.

40. William A. Gamson, "News as Framing: Comments on Graber," *American Behavioral Scientist* 33 (1989): 157.

41. Gamson, 157.

Chapter 2

Presidential Crisis Rhetoric: Review and Extensions

This chapter both reviews and extends upon the scholarly literature most relevant for this study. The two categories reviewed are studies of the origin of Cold War rhetoric and studies of presidential crisis rhetoric (how it is defined and how it is enacted). In addition, this chapter discusses the meaning and significance of these studies for the present work. Thus, it discusses the chief methodological and theoretical issues in presidential crisis rhetoric. In particular, it considers the Cold War itself as a meta-narrative and framing device for presidential crisis rhetoric. Conversely, it discusses the changes in the inventional stature of such rhetoric as a result of the end of the Cold War. Finally, it reviews the limitations of the scholarly literature and the ways in which the present study may extend our knowledge of presidential communication.

STUDIES IN THE ORIGIN OF THE COLD WAR

The Cold War meta-narrative[1] has permeated every aspect of U.S. foreign policy decisions. Its power, its inventional resources, predate the Cold War itself. Robert L. Ivie pointed out that there existed prior to the ending of the Cold War a "contest of force vs. freedom, irrationality vs. rationality, and aggression vs. defense [that permeates] the substance and style of the call-to-arms throughout American history."[2] Cold War rhetoric draws upon this tradition; thus, presidents have been able to construct arguments appealing for public support using the values and cultural myths lived by the American people. Usually, this strategy involved the indirect construction of an image of the enemy through the use of contrasting references: the enemy as "coercive, irrational, and aggressive," attempting to "subjugate a freedom-loving, rational, and pacific victim."[3] For example, the opposition of force versus freedom is exemplified by President Lyndon Johnson's 28 July 1965 news conference concerning American involvement with Vietnam. Johnson stated: "[W]e insist and we will always insist that the people of South Viet-Nam [sic] shall have the right of choice, the right to shape their own destiny in free elections in the South or throughout all Viet-Nam under international supervision, and they shall not have any government imposed upon them by force and terror so long as we can prevent it."[4] Although just one example, the history of how presidents characterize the enemies of the United States, argued Ivie, is replete with such references.

Craig Allen Smith has written on the genesis of Cold War rhetoric. He suggested that Cold War rhetoric developed from three separate lines of foreign policy thought arising immediately after World War II.[5] The first is a *rhetoric of cooperation*. Some politicians "envisioned a world of good and peaceful nations subject to . . . wars caused by . . . outlaws like Hitler and wars caused by conflicting interests."[6] These politicians envisioned many of the world's future conflicts being avoided through the establishment of an international peacekeeping force. The second type of rhetoric is a *rhetoric of red fascism*. Politicians operating within this perspective "explained Soviet expansion with the rhetoric used previously to explain German and Italian fascists."[7] Consquently, the Soviets were cast in the light of a totalitarian police state that was bent upon world conquest. Having just experienced almost a decade of this type of rhetoric, the American public was well familiar with the arguments and characterizations used. The third type of rhetoric is a *rhetoric of power politics*. This rhetoric rejected the "cooperationist and red fascist notions of moral and immoral nations . . . [it instead] depicted Soviet expansion as a powerful nation filling a power vacuum."[8] These three rhetorical strategies were combined in the Truman Doctrine. With the announcement of this new policy, an American foreign policy of containment was established that has carried the country into the 1990s.

It is a well-known American cultural fact that following World War II a forty-five-year Cold War ensued; with each passing year the collective weight of superpower experiences made it easier for presidents to construct foreign policy arguments and take action while concurrently making it more difficult to break the cycle. Martin J. Medhurst commented upon the force that such experience has for American presidents. Since the end of World War II, Soviet-American political interactions have comprised an ever-growing history from which politicians of both sides have drawn arguments, described situations, and predicted the outcomes of superpower struggles. As Medhurst stated, history "'teaches' us how to negotiate with the Soviets. Past 'lessons' constrain the form such negotiations may take."[9] Medhurst illustrated the enormous dimensions of the Cold War meta-narrative:

> Cold War, like its "hot" counterpart, is a contest. It is a contest between competing systems as represented, for example, by the Soviet Union and the United States.
>
> The currency of Cold War combat . . . is rhetorical discourse: discourse intentionally designed to achieve a particular goal with one or more specific audience. Cold War weapons are words, images, symbolic actions, and, on occasion, physical actions undertaken by covert means.[10]

Robert L. Ivie has suggested that the primary inventional resource of Cold War rhetoric lay in its "prevailing image of the Soviet threat."[11] Thus, Cold War rhetoric was used by the U.S. government to characterize antagonist states, most notably the Soviet Union. On this point Ivie stated: "The nation's adversary is characterized as a mortal threat to freedom, a germ infecting the body politic, a plague upon the liberty of humankind, and a barbarian intent upon destroying civilization."[12]

STUDIES OF PRESIDENTIAL CRISIS RHETORIC

Serious research on presidential crisis rhetoric began in the early 1970s, especially with the work of Theodore O. Windt.[13] Since then, crisis rhetoric research has been characterized by epistemic controversies over the definition of the term *crisis rhetoric*, and the relationship between objective situation and rhetorical (discursive) construction in the birth of a crisis. Just what is crisis rhetoric, however? According to Amos Kiewe, crises involve the perception of "immediacy and urgency," as well as the public expectation of "strong leadership qualities."[14] Many rhetorical critics view crises largely or wholly as rhetorical creations. Windt, for instance, argued that a crisis is announced by the president as such and that the situation demands that he "act decisively."[15] By announcing the crisis, the president asks for his decision to be supported, not for debate upon what should be done. Thus, crisis rhetoric is a rhetoric that excludes discussion. It reserves epistemic questions for the president alone. According to Windt, so long as the crisis is not one of a military attack upon the United States, it is to be considered a "political event rhetorically created by the President."[16] However, the president is not free to do as he pleases when discursively responding to a crisis; his rhetorical options are limited by "precedent, tradition, and expediency."[17]

Windt has suggested three basic lines of arguments that distinguish presidential crisis rhetoric from other types of presidential utterances.[18] First, there is the obligatory statement of facts. Second, there is the establishment of a "melodrama" between good (the United States) and evil (traditionally the Soviets). Third, the policy announced by the president and the asked-for support are framed as moral acts. In the sense that these can be framed as normative acts, they are then what everybody already believes to be true. In announcing these lines of arguments, Windt relied upon an analysis of Kennedy's response to the Soviet military buildup in Cuba and upon Nixon's announcement to send American and South Vietnamese forces into Cambodia.

I follow Windt's general line of reasoning in this study. My principal focus is upon those rhetorical resources—interpretation of material sites, epistemic status, the use of various political voices—available for crisis formation and how those forces interact with a particular president's approach to dealing with crises in the post-Cold War world. The constructed nature of presidential crisis rhetoric is thus stressed in this study. As Amos Kiewe suggested, crisis rhetoric "occurs when the president chooses to speak on an issue of critical dimensions, whether to promote or to minimize the perception of a crisis."[19] In short, a crisis—except in cases of military attacks—is initiated when the president chooses to address a situation as a crisis. It can be argued that presidents would want to control the definitions of crises; when others first do so, then presidents may try to downplay the significance. This, too, points to the constructed nature of crisis situations.

Some scholars have argued that crisis responses are not constrained by previous utterances to the same degree; hence, the degree of construction by the president varies from crisis to crisis. Indeed, the basic elements in any rhetorical situation—exigence, audience, and constraints—act in such a manner as to necessitate a variable range of responses from the rhetor, in this case, the president announcing a crisis situation.[20] For example, I have previously argued for understanding crises as situationally bound and as such delimited by context (the discursive and material surroundings) acting upon text, and text upon context, within a limited period of time.[21] This is to say, an inter-animation of text and context occurs. From this point of view, text and context are naturally interacting and evolving elements within any rhetorical situation. Indeed, crisis situations involve a rather violent mix of text/context interaction, often with a demand for quick interpretation from the public. This view supports a reading of crises that views an exigence as highly unstable and mutable. Thus, a conception of a rhetorical situation as presupposing a fixed nature or interpretive pattern—a genre perhaps—is discarded for a more fluid understanding of situational constraints.[22] Indeed, international crisis situations may begin with no stable means for interpreting the discursive surroundings, and one of the purposes of the presidential text is the creation of a stable contextual frame through which to understand the event.[23]

The invention of a stable contextual frame may take some period of time, yet it is the most important criterion for a "fitting response" to the situation. As Windt asserted, presidential speeches announcing a crisis "begin with an assertion of the President's control of the facts of the situation and an acknowledgement that the New Facts which occasion the speech constitute a New Situation—a crisis for the United States."[24] Yet this is not to say that the first utterances of the president create the crisis, nor that it establishes a stable frame. First utterances are first characterizations; they set the tone. As Windt argued, situations "rarely create crises. Rather, Presidents' perceptions of situations and the rhetoric used to describe them mark events as crises."[25] Marilyn J. Young extended this line of thought further by suggesting that as utterances interact with context and antecedent texts, a stability within the situation may occur. As the stability increases, the president will experience both increased freedom to pursue the present course of action and increased limits upon what other options he may enact.[26]

Some scholars have argued that a president's initial response is the most crucial factor in the genesis of rhetorical crises. In short, this response may provide the definition of the event. Dan F. Hahn examined the Ford administration's initial and subsequent descriptions of the *Mayaguez* affair. Hahn argued that the administration's descriptions acted to define the event in a way that legitimated U.S. actions by shutting out any other views of the event. The terminology used by Ford, according to Hahn, "was corrupted by a false description of the situation."[27] For example, by describing the capture of the U.S.S. *Mayaguez* by the Cambodians as an act of "piracy," even though the ship was within the territorial waters of Cambodia, the Ford administration was offering a specific interpretation of the act. This definition, and others offered by the Ford administration, acted to justify future actions—in this case, U.S. forces attacking Cambodian soldiers in order to recapture the vessel. Hahn found evidence for the interpretive power of the president's initial statements: The "president's definition . . . provides the 'terministic screen' through which the population views the event, while at the same time providing him with a 'terministic compulsion' to follow the implications of the terminology to their logical conclusions."[28] Ford's initial utterances on the taking of the U.S.S. *Mayaguez* by the Cambodian government set the stage for future actions. By calling it piracy, Ford legitimated certain actions while he delimited other options—negotiated compromise, for instance: The United States does not negotiate with pirates.

This view of the president's role in defining the situation is commensurate with that expressed by David C. Klope, who argued that the major function of the president's response to a perceived crisis is to redefine the situation in terms that the public can understand or identify with. Klope asserted that the manner in which identification and redefinition occurs is often through "configuring the situation in terms of socially-sanctioned myths."[29] By analyzing Ronald Reagan's response to the Beirut bombing and the invasion of Grenada, Klope discovered that both crises were actually the negative public perception of the events, and thus the president was forced to respond in an attempt to mitigate this negative perception. Reagan used socially accepted American myths to ground his response and ameliorate the ambiguity. Reagan was thus able to bring order to the previously disordered events.

GENERIC CLASSIFICATIONS OF CRISIS RHETORIC

The constructed nature of international crisis situations is agreed upon by most scholars of presidential crisis rhetoric, even though the degree to which an event is constructed is not agreed upon. Be that as it may, even though scholars may agree upon the constructed nature, they are not in agreement on the types of responses that a president makes when responding to the perception of a crisis. Thus, many studies explore a topology of presidential responses. For instance, Richard A. Cherwitz and Kenneth S. Zagacki viewed crises as purposeful rhetorical constructions: "[E]vents become crises, not because of unique sets of situational exigencies, but by virtue of discourse used to describe them."[30] They saw rhetoric as playing a "paramount role in defining, shaping and responding to international crises."[31] In short, discourse is both constrained by and frames the response to the situation. In their analysis of presidential responses to five crises, Cherwitz and Zagacki provided an example of a typological study by distinguishing between consummatory and justificatory responses.

A consummatory response is marked by discourse that initially constitutes the government's official reply to a perceived crisis event. As examples of consummatory replies, Cherwitz and Zagacki used Reagan's response to the Soviet destruction of KAL 007 and Jimmy Carter's reply to the seizure of American hostages in Iran. They posited that consummatory discourse is "circumspect" and stresses the importance of proceeding with "caution" and "patience."[32] This type of discourse calls for the perpetrators to carry out certain (U.S. prescribed) actions to close the crisis. Consummatory discourse is illocutionary in nature; it demands, it seeks to effect a change or induce action. Justificatory discourse, on the other hand, is discourse that is part of a larger, overt military retaliation by the United States. Cherwitz and Zagacki provided for examples Lyndon Johnson's statement after the Gulf of Tonkin retaliation, John Kennedy's statement after the deployment of Soviet missiles on Cuba, and Gerald Ford's response to the seizure of the U.S.S. *Mayaguez*. In each of these cases the president justified U.S. action taken in response to the act of a foreign power. These responses, and justificatory discourse as a whole, are characterized by their irrevocable nature; they are direct, decisive, and announce concrete, definitive military action taken in response to the actions of foreign nations.

According to Cherwitz and Zagacki, both types of discourse are epideictic in nature; they seek to identify and blame adversaries, while concurrently praising U.S. actions. However, consummatory discourse takes on forensic elements since it makes "considerable and concerted efforts . . . to present a prima facie case for [the perpetrator's] guilt to the American public and the world."[33] Justificatory discourse is deliberative in nature: The "official military responses of the U.S. government . . . are explicated and defended."[34]

Not all writers agree, however, with the conception of crisis as rhetorically constructed. For example, Bonnie J. Dow drew a distinction between crises as a result of events and crises as a result of presidential definition. Dow differentiated between presidential crisis rhetoric designed to provide communal understanding (epideictic) and that rhetoric designed for gaining policy approval (deliberative). The former is that which responds to events, and the latter is that which creates or justifies events. Dow argued that epideictic responses function to prevent disparate interpretations of the situation and to "promote continuity, restore communal feeling, and . . . reconcile the audience to a new situation."[35] Deliberative strategies, on the other hand, are those used to demonstrate that the policy being enacted in response to a crisis is "expedient, reasoned and prudent."[36]

LIMITATIONS OF CURRENT VIEWS ON CRISIS RHETORIC

There is an underlying tension within the above studies and others that have crisis rhetoric as their controlling principle. Carole Blair and Davis W. Houck, for instance, have characterized two major weaknesses in the present state of research in presidential crisis rhetoric. They suggested that many crisis rhetoric studies fall into one of two camps of "ambivalences." These ambivalences concern the *generic* quality or the *situatedness* of the rhetoric under consideration.[37] Blair and Houck asserted that many studies often make generic claims and then undermine those very claims. Furthermore, these studies often attempt not to draw the line between a crisis and non-crisis event. They cited several researchers, including James W. Pratt, Theodore Windt, Richard A. Cherwitz and Kenneth S. Zagacki, and Bonnie J. Dow, who produced studies containing examples of generic ambivalence. Drawing upon the work of Thomas C. Conley, Blair and Houck stated that "the particularity of rhetorical events renders their containment in generic categories problematic."[38]

The other view of crisis rhetoric concerns its situated character and how many critics seem to want to delimit the scope of inquiry to international situations only. Richard A. Cherwitz and Klope were cited here.[39] The ambiguous nature of "situatedness" concerns *rhetorical situation* as opposed to *rhetorical invention*. Two problems emerge when crisis rhetoric is viewed as related to situation. First, crisis rhetoric may be applicable to "circumstance other than international discord"; and second, "motivation for 'crisis rhetoric' [may be] more closely related to . . . presidents' desire to maintain political popularity than to the international events themselves."[40] Likewise, two new problems emerge when crisis rhetoric is viewed as rhetorical invention. First, presidents may be viewed as constructing a crisis. As Cherwitz stated, "[P]residential discourse may construct an image of crisis, often regardless of the situational characteristics spawning such discourse."[41] The second problem concerns presidential utterances that respond to a "pre-existing crisis." Blair and Houck cited Dow's analysis of Reagan's response to the downing of KAL 007 as providing an example of this type of situation. The main concern, then, is between viewing crisis rhetoric as constructing the perception of crisis and crisis rhetoric viewed as a response to an event already perceived by some as a crisis.[42]

Blair and Houck argued that the above distinction cannot be proven, nor is it a necessary distinction to understand the nature of crisis rhetoric. They put forward a conception of genre that necessitates a rethinking of how we view crisis rhetoric. Following the literary critic Adena Rosemarin, Blair and Houck suggested that genre should be viewed as a classifying statement, not as a class of discourse: "The critic posits a genre characterization as hypothetical, reads a particular work in terms of that characterization, and concludes with claims about what that work 'is like' when it is read in terms of the hypothesized genre."[43] The purpose is insight, not classification. It is a top-down approach that emphasizes the "recontextualization of the speech" in order to elicit insight.[44] In short, Blair and Houck would have critics of crisis rhetoric ask, "What is the speech like if it is read as a crisis speech?"[45] This approach, however, even while seeming to skirt the genre and situatedness issues, does lead to other abuses. It encourages the removal of rhetoric from the realm of the world in which it is practiced and views it as a stable entity susceptible to outside imposition of theoretical schemata.[46]

Yet even those studies attempting a more practical grounding of the theory used in a particular analysis may fall into the trap of over-determining their typologies. For example, Dow cited the shootdown of KAL 007 as an example of President Reagan using epideictic crisis rhetoric in response to an event "already seen as serious, even critical."[47] Yet with this interpretation we theoretically retrogress to a view of rhetorical situations being deterministic. Dow argued that the Reagan administration's response to the downing is epideictic because there was press coverage prior to the administration's response; this coverage therefore acted to frame the event as a crisis before the President could respond. Yet Secretary of State George Schultz responded to the shootdown on 1 September 1983, only hours after the event, and President Reagan issued a statement the same day saying the plane's destruction was an "appalling and wanton misdeed [that was] inexplicable to civilized people everywhere."[48] These utterances helped to set initially the tone for the administration's response, well before the press made it an issue, or even had reported it. Indeed, the Reagan administration used the shootdown *to create a crisis*; and the excoriation of the Soviet Union was the focus; the loss of American lives was not an issue for the administration, as Dow maintained. Thus, classificatory schema (epideictic, deliberative) may have overdetermined the event to the point that interactions of text and context were overlooked.

Many of the studies reviewed in this chapter have elements that support Windt's contention about the nature of presidential crisis rhetoric. Although some (Dow; Cherwitz and Zagacki; and Klope, for example) have argued from a limited microanalysis and have sought to identify generic elements,[49] they have also pointed to the discursively constructed nature of presidential crises. For example: Klope found that crises are based in part on negative public perception of events; the president must then respond in order to reconstruct this perception. Cherwitz and Zagacki contended that crisis rhetoric is either consummatory or justificatory; yet regardless of which is used to classify the discourse, crisis rhetoric is both constrained by and is a response to the situation; it frames it as a crisis. Kiewe argued that a crisis is constructed as a true crisis by the president's response to an event. Dow argued that presidential crisis rhetoric is of two types: that responding to events (epideictic) and that which creates or justifies events (deliberative).

However, some of these studies suggest disturbing contradictions due to micromanaging theoretical constraints pertaining to the examination of presidential responses to a particular crisis. By listing strategies employed—epideictic, deliberative, justificatory, consummatory, and so on—some researchers have maximized the theoretical discrimination of situational constraints (they have, in fact, been guilty of overdetermining the rhetorical situation; i.e., they have imposed a theoretically generated and rigid framework upon a fluid event). A case in point concerning the theoretical contradictions occurs when we examine the generic classifications espoused by Dow, and Cherwitz and Zagacki when examining Reagan's response to the Soviet downing of KAL 007.

Cherwitz and Zagacki labeled Reagan's response to the shootdown of KAL 007 as "consummatory." This type of discourse demands an action from the adversaries in order to bring the crisis to a close. It is epideictic because it identifies and blames adversaries while concurrently praising U.S. actions. It is forensic because it presents a case to the public for accepting the president's definition of the situation and approving the action taken. Dow, on the other hand, labeled Reagan's response to the shootdown of KAL 007 as epideictic. For Dow, this type of discourse is designed to provide communal understanding of an event. It is a response to an event *already* perceived by the public as a crisis. Micromanaging definitions led these two studies of the same event to come to two oppositional conclusions. Although it has previously been mentioned that Dow is grossly mistaken in her interpretation of the chronology of events, the point remains: Theoretically driven analyses lead to overdetermination of the situational elements. Although the above theoretical "types" were constructed for the purpose of analysis, the above authors have supposed a stable and knowledgeable public audience and that there exists a finite set of rhetorical functions corresponding to their constructed types. This could lead to a limited view of the range of possible communication practices.

PUBLIC KNOWLEDGE AS RESOURCE AND CONSTRAINT

A more useful approach appears in the literature on public knowledge. Marilyn J. Young and Michael K. Launer defined public knowledge as "the accumulated wisdom of the people" that "serves as the authoritative ground for political discourse."[50] In an atmosphere of crisis the public would rely upon this "accumulated knowledge to define the situation."[51] Lloyd Bitzer defined a public as a group of persons "united in interests, aspirations, traditions, and experiences."[52] As a public, these people possess "a fund of truths, principles and values which could only characterize a public."[53] These attributes may include "principles of public life to which we submit as conditions of living together; shared interests and aspirations . . . [and] the accumulated wisdom proffered by our cultural pasts."[54] Such may be called public knowledge. The public and its knowledge act to authorize discourse emanating from rhetors who are acting as representatives for the public—in our case, the president. Although authorization is not always needed, many acts occur within a crisis context and thus require authorization, for "authorization is needed when a proposed act or message might seriously affect the well being of others . . . or when a person or group claims to represent, or stand in for, another person or group."[55]

D. Ray Heisey argued that presidential responses to crises are culturally based and historically mandated.[56] Heisey asserted that the president must build certain images of the "enemy" or must make links with values embedded within American culture and history if he is to successfully mitigate a crisis. In short, "leader[s] must find the acceptable images of political reality suitable for his/her people."[57] Since the dawn of the atomic age, all presidents have been able to call upon the topos of good (the United States) versus evil (the Soviet Union). Yet with the culmination of the Cold War the Soviet Union is in financial and social ruins: The "Evil Empire," as Ronald Reagan put it, is no more. With the destruction of the Soviet Union comes the concomitant destruction of the Cold War meta-narrative.[58] This is politically unfortunate for President Clinton; he must respond to potential crisis situations without the benefit of this action legitimating meta-narrative.

Mark A. Pollock examined President Bush's rhetoric following the Iraqi invasion of Kuwait and provides some insight into the beginnings of post-Cold War crisis rhetoric.[59] Although Pollock believed the study of crises to be a generic endeavor, he did provide insight into the effects of history upon the inventional resources used by the president. Although Pollock did not state that his study emphasized that President Bush was operating in the post-Cold War era, it nevertheless provided us with an example of the move away from constructing crises in the manner described by Windt. Pollock wrote that President Bush

quickly characterized the Iraqi invasion of Kuwait as constituting a new and critical situation. . . . He made repeated references to his efforts to build an international consensus against Iraq. This stress on a search for a peaceful solution fits the pattern of contrasting American good will with the actions provoking the crisis. [This also] framed the crisis as a clear moral issue, transcending the interests of particular nations. [However,] the collapse of the Soviet bloc precluded Bush's use of an ideological call to arms against communism as a way to transform the crisis into an ideological conflict between good and evil.[60]

According to Pollock, President Bush was able to frame the event successfully because he was able to develop an "augmented historical narrative" that drew upon pre-World War II visions of the enemy.[61] In this case, President Bush drew upon America's collective memory about 1938 Munich. The residue of the Cold War meta-narrative and this vision legitimated decisive military action. Pollock rightly pointed out that the 1938 Munich agreement has "great symbolic power" because it is a historical event that has assumed a rhetorical character. Thomas Kane described such transformation as rhetorical events. A rhetorical event is an historical event that has become rhetorical because it "either violates or affirms in some dramatic way those things a culture believes about itself as a collective public. [It becomes] meaningful less from what really happened than [from] the collective set of assumptions and perceptions . . . that have been handed down from previous discourse, arguments, experiences and interpretations."[62]

Young and Launer have provided additional insight into this area. They argued that crisis may be immediate, as with the destruction of Korean Airlines Flight 007, or they may slowly evolve, presenting rhetors with the opportunity to respond to the budding rhetorical situation.[63] In short, they have developed a more subtle analysis than the "either/or" categorizations of Dow, and Cherwitz and Zagacki. They have also provided insight into the relation of the presidential message and the American public: "In clear cases of crisis, the context—and, hence, the [president's] reaction—is less ambiguous. When national interests are not so directly involved, however, the context is more dubious and conflicting perceptions may weaken the parameters of the rhetorical situation. In these instances, the public seeks additional guidance."[64] Furthermore, when the public seeks additional information from the president, seemingly demands it, and it is provided, the overall situation again changes. For with each new round of information disclosures, the amount and primacy of information that constitutes public knowledge change, and with this change comes a change in context. A crisis atmosphere disrupts the usual stability of public knowledge; a state of "flux" ensues. The epistemic status of crisis, by its very transitional nature, generates new knowledge; it subverts or contests old knowledge about the situation.[65]

EXTENSIONS BY PRESENT STUDY

With the Cold War arguably over, it seems that President Clinton is the first atomic-age president who cannot draw upon the continuing Cold War to support his foreign policy actions. The means available to the president for framing an international event as important are no longer obvious. The Cold War has been a common component of American culture since the announcement of the Truman Doctrine in 1947.

Throughout the years following World War II, each president has used the inventional resources of this word-oriented contest in order to justify foreign policy decisions. As Robert L. Scott wrote, "[standing] up to the USSR has been a mainstay in the conduct of U.S. foreign affairs since the end of World War II."[66] Yet standing up to the Soviets is not the only concern. Presidents of the United States have stood up in a specific manner. Their discourse against the Soviets has had a distinct quality, and its nature has permeated American foreign policy for the past forty-five years. Scott pointed out that "U.S. foreign policy generally has been monitored by the rhetoric of the Cold War."[67]

A transformation in superpower Cold War rhetoric began shortly after Mikhail Gorbachev launched his policies of perestroika and glasnost. As the Soviets seemed to move away from the depiction of the enemy that America was accustomed to, President Reagan "was able . . . to preserve domestic unity largely because he transferred the evil empire imagery from Russia to Nicaragua, Libya, and Iran."[68] If we follow this line of reasoning, then Bush may be seen as having worked with the residue of the Cold War imagery in his foreign policy actions, most notably, the Panama invasion and Operation Desert Storm. Thus, the meta-narrative of the Cold War was carried into the 1990s, but it was beginning to unravel. By the time Clinton took office, the Cold War meta-narrative was no more.

This study seeks to identify some of the resources that may be used by the president to frame an international event as a crisis situation in the post-Cold War world. Theoretically speaking, the American public views an international event as important whenever the president is able to frame it as a crisis. Thus, the rhetoric a president employs to address and create crises is different than that used to address non-crisis situations. As Amos Kiewe stated, crisis rhetoric "is distinct from noncrisis rhetoric to the extent that it characterizes a unique and dynamic process."[69]

Although the studies thus far discussed suggest interesting strategies for classifying presidential crisis rhetoric, their most trenchant contribution comes from their implied support for an interpretation of crises as rhetorical constructions. Windt's components of crisis formation are illustrative of this view, yet his structure is premised upon the Cold War meta-narrative—some level of melodrama must be initiated in order for crisis rhetoric to work. The above-mentioned studies support this contention as well. This study, however, advances the proposition that the Soviets are not necessary for the creation of a melodrama that capitalizes upon the topos of good versus evil. The Soviets have been used conveniently for the past forty-five years to fill the "evil" half of the oppositionally structured mythic form, "good versus evil." All that should be necessary for this form to work is something to fill the evil role. As Pollock stated, the "enemy need not be communism—fascism served as well in World War II. But in communism's absence, an ideological substitute must be found."[70] Bush successfully did this during the Gulf War.[71]

Yet Clinton was not successful with Haiti (or with any of his foreign policy crises; e.g., Somalia, Bosnia, and North Korea). So something other than an event and the president's response must account for a successful crisis formation and resolution. As Martin J. Medhurst argued, crisis rhetoric is different with each president; it is, indeed, part of a president's rhetorical biography.[72] Medhurst argued for the examination of crisis rhetoric as part of the president's rhetorical biography; thus, the discourse moves away from a generic classification to a more personal investigation. Indeed, Medhurst put forth a powerful argument that presidents develop their own normative response to a crisis situation. Dwight Eisenhower was shown to have had a well-developed, five-step strategy: One, he attempted to prevent situations from maturing into crises; two, if a crisis developed, he consulted widely; three, he waited for crises to peak before acting; four, while waiting, he told "opponents" that he was ready to take action but conveyed that there was still time to negotiate; and five, when it was time to act, he did so with overwhelming force. Medhurst persuasively argued: "[C]rises, by definition, bring into play matters of personal values, political philosophy, strategic theory, and psychological predisposition, not to mention the peculiar exigencies of the historical moment."[73] James W. Pratt examined the crisis rhetoric of Presidents Eisenhower, Kennedy, and Johnson and found that the three presidents used a variety of strategies in responding to the crises. This lends support for this study's view of crises as defying generic classification; furthermore, Pratt's inquiry suggested presidential style is a factor in the handling of crises: It "appears that the speaking characteristics of the president involved and the specific nature for the crisis setting combine to determine the type of speech which will result and that this contention is more important than the simple presence or absence of the crisis."[74]

This work takes the position that the study of presidential crisis rhetoric should not primarily approach an event as an example of crisis (Cherwitz and Zagacki) or examine a speech/text through a genre of crisis (Blair and Houck) or suggest a situation is already perceived as a crisis (Dow). Rather, this study suggests that researchers would be more productive of knowledge by examining the interplay of various texts and contexts that act to alter the situation and public perception of the situation. Thus, criticism of presidential crisis rhetoric should be a blend of discursive and material conditions. Questions that might be asked are many. For example: How are the perceptions of crises formulated? How are contexts/situations developed so that a "fitting" utterance may be created to bring a crisis to resolution successfully?

We must now consider the initial situation, the president's response, and presidential style. These three elements are conveyed to the public via the press; thus, it follows that we should ask what role the press plays in crisis development. It seems logical that the press plays a considerable role in disseminating the message of the president to the American public and international audiences. It is also true that presidents "can depend on tremendous public support for whatever policy they pursue in situations they deem 'critical.'"[75] Yet Clinton was unable to marshal this broad support, even though he continually stressed the importance of the situations in Bosnia and Haiti. Since the public receives its information from the press, it follows that the role of the press in the development of this crisis needs to be examined. What role, if any, did the press play in keeping a crisis from formulating in North Korea, Bosnia, and Haiti?

Although the structure suggested by Windt may hold true for post-World War II presidents up to Bush, President Clinton was unable to frame his responses to crises in this manner owing to the end of the Cold War and the demise of the "Evil Empire." In its absence exists an inventional vacuum where the Cold War meta-narrative once existed; presidents must now rethink ways of framing their crisis responses. This work asserts that in this time of flux President Clinton would have been unable to successfully frame his utterances about Haiti in such a manner that the public and the press accepted it as true. Thus, the press will report the president's response but, in the post-Cold War confusion, advance its own conception of the situation. This study thus contributes to our understanding of presidential crisis rhetoric in three ways. First, it advances a little-studied notion of crisis rhetoric as an inter-animation of text and context within situational constraints. Second, it examines crisis rhetoric occurring in the wake of the Cold War. Finally, it examines the role of the printed press in presidential crisis rhetoric.

NOTES

1. I view the period between 1947 and 1991 as constituting the discernible Cold War phase of the American/Soviet relationship. The combined totality of all U.S./Soviet communication interactions during this period I call the Cold War meta-narrative. This narrative involved the general American cultural perception of the Soviets as "evil" or "bad" as opposed to the United States being identified with "good" or "moral." It is a narrative that is found to underlie almost all U.S. government communication about the Soviets—thus, its "meta" nature. In "Images of Savagery in American Justifications for War," *Communication Monographs* 47 (1980): 279-294, Robert L. Ivie stated that the "enemy [in our case, the Soviets] is

portrayed as savage, i.e., as an aggressor, driven by irrational desires for conquest, who is seeking to subjugate others by force for arms" (281). This image is juxtaposed to an image of the United States as a "representative of civilization . . . rational, tolerant of diversity, and pacific" (281).

2. Ivie, "Images," 281.

3. Ivie, "Images," 284.

4. Lyndon B. Johnson, "The President's News Conference of July 28, 1965," *Public Papers of the Presidents of the United States* (Washington, D.C.: Office of the Federal Register, National Archives and Records Service, 1963-1969; 1965), 796-797. Quote found in Ivie, 284.

5. Craig Allen Smith, *Political Communication* (San Diego: Harcourt Brace Jovanovich, Publishers, 1990).

6. Smith, 200.

7. Smith, 201.

8. Smith, 201.

9. Martin J. Medhurst, "Rhetoric and Cold War: A Strategic Approach," *Cold War Rhetoric: Strategy, Metaphor, and Ideology*, ed. Martin J. Medhurst, Robert L. Ivie, Philip Wander, and Robert L. Scott (Westport, CT: Greenwood Press, 1990), 21.

10. Medhurst, "Rhetoric," 19.

11. Robert L. Ivie, "Metaphor and the Rhetorical Invention of Cold War 'Idealists,'" *Cold War Rhetoric: Strategy, Metaphor, and Ideology*, ed. Martin J. Medhurst, Robert L. Ivie, Philip Wander, and Robert L. Scott (Westport, CT: Greenwood Press, 1990), 103.

12. Robert L. Ivie, "Cold War Motives and the Rhetorical Metaphor: A Framework of Criticism," *Cold War Rhetoric: Strategy, Metaphor, and Ideology*, ed. Martin J. Medhurst, Robert L. Ivie, Philip Wander, and Robert L. Scott (Westport, CT: Greenwood Press, 1990), 72.

13. Theodore O. Windt, Jr., "The Presidency and Speeches on International Crises: Repeating the Rhetorical Past," *Speaker and Gavel* 2.1 (1973): 6-14.

14. Amos Kiewe, ed., *The Modern Presidency and Crisis Rhetoric* (Westport, CT: Praeger, 1994), xvii.

15. Theodore O. Windt, "The Presidency and Speeches on International Crises: Repeating the Rhetorical Past," *Essays in Presidential Rhetoric*, ed. Theodore Windt and Beth Ingold, 2nd ed. (Dubuque, IA: Kendall/Hunt Publishing Company, 1987), 125-134.

16. Windt, "Presidency and Speeches," 126.

17. Windt, "Presidency and Speeches," 127. The constrained nature of presidential utterances is reaffirmed by Windt in *Presidents and Protesters: Political Rhetoric in the 1960s* (Tuscaloosa: University of Alabama Press, 1990). Windt stated: Presidents "are free to define issues within the context of their political beliefs, traditions, circumstances, past history, and political affiliation. Once having spoken for the public record, they have to defend their words and the policies that issued from them. Other politicians, journalists, and the public . . . demand consistency" (4).

18. Windt, "Presidency and Speeches," 68-69. Karlyn Kohrs Campbell and

Kathleen Hall Jamieson, *Deeds Done in Words: Presidential Rhetoric and the Genres of Governance* (Chicago: University of Chicago Press, 1990), argued that there are distinct genres of presidential discourse. Among these are inaugural addresses; State of the Union addresses; veto messages; war rhetoric; rhetoric to forestall impeachment; pardoning rhetoric; and farewell addresses. These genres help to provide "structural supports for the edifice of the presidency" (4). Of interest to this study is Campbell and Jamieson's conception of war rhetoric as genre. They believe that war rhetoric usually assumes the form of justifying military action already taken and then calling for public and congressional support. There are five pivotal characteristics of war rhetoric: One, a deliberate decision is produced through thoughtful consideration; two, "forceful intervention is justified through a chronicle or narrative from which argumentation claims are drawn"; three, unanimous commitment and united purpose (a united audience and community); four, justification of the use of force and request to Congress to legitimate actions; and five, strategic misrepresentation of facts in order to "preempt dissent through misrepresentation, for example, by transforming the dramatic narrative justifying the use of force into a melodrama" (105, 119). Campbell and Jamieson used the similarities between these characteristics of war rhetoric and the characteristics of crisis rhetoric espoused by Windt to argue for a conception of crisis rhetoric as generic category. They state that the above characteristics help "presidents [to] recast situations of conflict in terms that legitimate their initiatives." (105).

19. Kiewe, xxiii.

20. For a detailed explanation of how a rhetorical situation works, see Lloyd F. Bitzer, "The Rhetorical Situation," *Philosophy and Rhetoric* 1 (1968): 1-14. The copy used for this book is reprinted in *Rhetoric: A Tradition in Transition*, ed. Walter Fisher (East Lansing: Michigan State University Press, 1974), 247-260. Also see Lloyd F. Bitzer, "Political Rhetoric," *Handbook of Political Communication*, ed. Dan D. Nimmo and Keith R. Sanders (Beverly Hills, CA: Sage Publications, 1981), 225-248; Lloyd F. Bitzer, "Functional Communication: A Situational Perspective," *Rhetoric in Transition: Studies in the Nature and Uses of Rhetoric*, ed. Eugene E. White (University Park: Pennsylvania State University Press, 1980), 21-38.

21. Jim A. Kuypers, Marilyn J. Young, and Michael K. Launer, "Of Mighty Mice and Meek Men: Contextual Reconstruction of the Shootdown of Iran Air 655," *Southern Communication Journal* 59.4 (1994): 294-306.

22. This view runs contrary to that espoused by Jeff D. Bass in "The Rhetorical Opposition to Controversial Wars: Rhetorical Timing as a Generic Constraint," *Western Journal of Speech Communication* 43 (1979): 180-191. Bass views situations generically in his study. He presupposes that rhetorical situations are, as a rule, "highly structured and dominated by a controlling exigency" (181). Although Bass does admit that on "rare occasions" situations may come into existence that are of a "longer duration than is usually the case . . . [thus having] fewer antecedent rhetorical forms" to shape audience expectations, he still argues for a generic reading of situations because those of "longer duration" exhibit "strong internal structure." (181).

23. Kuypers, Young, and Launer, 294-306.

24. Windt, "Presidency and Speeches," 128.

25. Windt, *Presidents and Protesters*, 5.

26. Marilyn J. Young, "When the Shoe Is on the Other Foot: The Reagan Administration's Treatment of the Shootdown of Iran Air 655," *Reagan and Public Discourse in America*, ed. Michael Weiler and W. Barnett Pearce (Tuscaloosa: University of Alabama Press, 1992), 203-224.

27. Dan F. Hahn, "Corrupt Rhetoric: President Ford and the *Mayaguez* Affair," *Essays in Presidential Rhetoric*, ed. Theodore Windt and Beth Ingold, 2nd ed. (Dubuque, IA: Kendall/Hunt Publishing Company, 1987), 317.

28. Hahn, 324. Ivie predates Hahn in this assessment of terministic screens: "[T]he vocabulary manifests a severely delimited set of ideal purposes and agencies that, presumably, should be adhered to by all men in all places." See Robert L. Ivie, "Presidential Motives for War," *Quarterly Journal of Speech* 60 (1974): 344.

29. David C. Klope, "Defusing a Foreign Policy Crisis: Myth and Victimage in Reagan's 1983 Lebanon/Grenada Address," *Western Journal of Speech Communication* 50 (1986): 348.

30. Richard A. Cherwitz and Kenneth S. Zagacki, "Consummatory versus Justificatory Crisis Rhetoric," *Western Journal of Speech Communication* 50 (1986): 307.

31. Cherwitz and Zagacki, 318.

32. Cherwitz and Zagacki, 310.

33. Cherwitz and Zagacki, 313.

34. Cherwitz and Zagacki, 314.

35. Bonnie J. Dow, "The Function of Epideictic and Deliberative Strategies in Presidential Crisis Rhetoric," *Western Journal of Speech Communication* 53 (1989): 301.

36. Dow, 303.

37. Carole Blair and Davis W. Houck, "Richard Nixon and the Personalization of Crisis," *The Modern Presidency and Crisis Rhetoric*, ed. Amos Kiewe (Westport, CT: Praeger, 1994), 91-118.

38. Blair and Houck, 95. Thomas C. Conley, review of *Form and Genre: Shaping Rhetorical Action*, ed. Karlyn Kohrs Campbell and Kathleen Hall Jamieson, *Communication Quarterly* 26 (1978): 74.

39. Richard A. Cherwitz, "Masking Inconsistency: The Tonkin Gulf Crisis," *Communication Quarterly* 28 (1980): 27-37.

40. Blair and Houck, 95.

41. Cherwitz, 34.

42. Such a view is based on a misreading of Bitzer's work concerning the properties of the rhetorical situation. This misreading allows for a tidy division between rhetoric as a response to an event or rhetoric as constructing an event. The former views the exigence as demanding or necessitating a fitting response to an exigence already materially in place (rhetoric as situated). The latter view, linked to Richard Vatz, holds that the utterance, as situation generating, calls into being the exigence; hence, the rhetoric constructs the event. See Bitzer above; for

examples of Bitzer misread, see Blair and Houck; Dow; Carolyn R. Miller, "Genre as Social Action," *Quarterly Journal of Speech* 70 (1984): 151-167; and Richard E. Vatz, "The Myth of the Rhetorical Situation," *Philosophy and Rhetoric* 6 (1973): 154-161.

43. Blair and Houck, 98. Adena Rosemarin, *The Power of Genre* (Minneapolis: University of Minnesota Press, 1985).

44. Blair and Houck, 98.

45. Blair and Houck, 98.

46. Indeed, what Blair and Houck advocate sounds suspiciously similar to Edwin Black's description of "etic" criticism. Certainly Blair and Houck's suggestion is liable to the same types of abuses. See Edwin Black, "A Note on Theory and Practice in Rhetorical Criticism," *Western Journal of Speech Communication* 44 (1980): 331-336.

47. Dow 296.

48. U.S. Department of State, *KAL Flight #007: Compilation of Statements and Documents, September 1-16, 1983* (Washington, D.C.: Bureau of Public Affairs, 1983), 1-2.

49. Although Cherwitz and Zagacki stated that their "study of presidential messages is not intended to be a genre analysis . . . [they] are in agreement with previous writers that crisis rhetoric is constitutive of a genre of presidential discourse" (308-309). I would argue, however, that their analysis is about generic classification. They have their elements—consummatory and justificatory—and with these elements they set out to discover "presidential messages [that] contain discernable and recurring features that shape public expectations regarding crisis management" (308).

50. Marilyn J. Young and Michael K. Launer, "KAL 007 and the Superpowers: An International Argument," *Quarterly Journal of Speech* 74 (1988): 272.

51. Young and Launer, "KAL 007," 289.

52. Lloyd F. Bitzer, "Rhetoric and Public Knowledge," *Rhetoric, Philosophy, and Literature: An Exploration*, ed. D. M. Burks. (West Lafayette, IN: Purdue University Press, 1978), 74.

53. Bitzer, "Rhetoric and Public Knowledge," 68.

54. Bitzer, "Rhetoric and Public Knowledge," 87.

55. Bitzer, "Rhetoric and Public Knowledge," 75.

56. D. Ray Heisey, "Reagan and Mitterrand Respond to International Crisis: Creating versus Transcending Appearances," *Western Journal of Speech Communication* 50 (1986): 325-335.

57. Heisey, 333.

58. This might be an opportunity to view the demise of the Soviet Union as the "emptying" of the ideograph "Soviets." No longer can it be used as the antithesis to "America," "Freedom," and the like.

59. Mark A. Pollock, "The Battle for the Past: George Bush and the Gulf Crisis," *The Modern Presidency and Crisis Rhetoric*, ed. Amos Kiewe (Westport, CT: Praeger, 1994), 203-224.

60. Pollock, 207-208.

61. Pollock, 220.

62. Thomas Kane, "Rhetorical Histories and Arms Negotiations," *Journal of the American Forensic Association* 24 (1988): 144.

63. Marilyn J. Young and Michael K. Launer, Flights of Fancy, Flight of Doom: KAL 007 and Soviet-American Rhetoric (Lanham, MD: University Press of America, 1988); Young and Launer, "KAL 007"; Marilyn J. Young and Michael K. Launer, "Superpower Role Reversals: Political Rhetoric Following the Destruction of KAL 007 and the Iranian Airbus" (paper presented at the annual meeting of the World Communication Association Singapore, 1989); and Young, "When the Shoe Is on the Other Foot."

64. Young and Launer, "KAL 007 and the Superpowers" 289.

65. Andrew A. King, *Power and Communication* (Prospect Heights, Il: Waveland Press, Inc., 1987).

66. Robert L. Scott, "Cold War and Rhetoric: Conceptually and Critically," *Cold War Rhetoric: Strategy, Metaphor, and Ideology,* eds. Martin J. Medhurst, Robert L. Ivie, Philip Wander, and Robert L. Scott (New York: Greenwood Press, 1990) 2.

67. Scott 11.

68. Smith 213.

69. Kiewe xvi.

70. Pollock 205.

71. Karen Rasmussen and Sharon D. Downey, "The Rhetoric of the Persian Gulf War: Imperialism and American Mythology of War." Paper presented to the annual meeting of the Speech Communication Association, New Orleans, 1994. Yet Bush could have successfully drawn upon the Western mechanisms of the Cold War that remained in place immediately following the dissolution of the Soviet Union. NATO, the Warsaw Pact, and the Middle Eastern Alliances were still operating during the Gulf war. Indeed, Charles W. Kegley, Jr. and Eugene R. Wittkopf as late as 1991 stated that "it would be premature to assert that the anticommunist impulse has been exorcised from the American polity or from American foreign policy" (548). Furthermore, they stated that a "Cold War orientation continues to shape American leaders' interpretation of unrest in the Third World" (548). See, Charles W. Kegley, Jr. and Eugene R. Wittkopf, *American Foreign Policy: Pattern and Proscess,* 4th ed. (New York: St. Martin's Press, 1991). These researchers argued that America's long standing foreign policies of containment, globalism, and anticommunism were just beginning to be rethought during the Bush administration. President Clinton may be said to be the first American President to truly form a foreign policy in the absence of the Cold War meta-narrative.

72. Martin J. Medhurst, "Eisenhower, Little Rock, and the Rhetoric of Crisis," *The Modern Presidency and Crisis Rhetoric*, ed. Amos Kiewe. (Westport, CT: Praeger, 1994) 19-46.

73. Medhurst, "Eisenhower" 41.

74. James W. Pratt, "An Analysis of Three Crisis Speeches," *Western Speech* 34 (1970): 202.

75. Windt, *Presidents and Protesters* 5. Original in italics.

Chapter 3

Agenda-Setting, Agenda-Extension, and Framing Analysis

Because presidential communication is mediated communication for the vast majority of American citizens, any study of presidential discourse must deal with the media. The print media have long functioned as presidential conduit, interpreter, and adversary. Accordingly, this chapter examines the agenda-setting and agenda-extension functions of the press in contemporary presidential politics. Moreover, this chapter will outline the procedures used for the framing analysis used in Chapters Four, Five, Six, and Seven. This chapter concludes with a brief assessment of the meaning of this research for the present study.

"The public's right to know" is a common phrase today. It represents the perspective underpinning the social responsibility theory of the media.[1] This view of the press demonstrates the strong movement away from Libertarian theory in that it underscores the common person's right to know and the editor's moral responsibility to ensure that the requirements for the public's knowing occur. There are six basic functions of the press under social responsibility theory: One, provide service to the political system by providing information, discussion, and debate; two, help to enlighten the general public so that it might self-govern; three, act as a defender of civil rights by assuming a role as government watchdog; four, act as a conduit through which the economic sector might be served by bringing together buyers and sellers through advertisements; five, provide entertainment; and six, maintain financial independence so that reporting will not be influenced by special interests.[2]

Whereas Libertarian theory rests upon a negative conception of liberty and press freedom ("freedom from"—that is, freedom from government control and censorship), social responsibility theory rests upon a positive notion of liberty and freedom of the press: "freedom for" "achieving the goals defined by its ethical sense and society's needs."[3] As previously noted, the Commission on Freedom of the Press, the so-called Hutchins Commission, reported on the workings of the press and advanced the idea of viewing press functions through the lens of social responsibility. Subsequent emendations of the commission's report speak to the complex interplay of three aspects of contemporary media: one, communication technology; two, economic pressures; and three, societal change. Social responsibility theory attempts to come to grips with the problems of the press by taking into account all three of these important considerations.

Practically speaking, freedom for achieving certain societal goals necessitates that certain requirements be set for those who constitute the media in this country. The Hutchins Commission, anticipating this need, listed these standards for press performance. First, the press must provide "a truthful, comprehensive, and intelligent account of the day's events in a context which gives them meaning."[4] Second, the press must serve as a "forum for the exchange of comment and criticism."[5] Third, the press must project "a representative picture of the constituent groups in society."[6] Fourth, the press must assume responsibility for "the presentation and clarification of the goals and values of the society" in which it operates.[7] Finally, the press must provide "full access to the day's intelligence."[8] It is the first of these responsibilities that I intend to highlight when discussing agenda-setting theory.

The above accoutrements of social responsibility theory underpin the functions of the press as defined by communication and political science scholars. Doris A. Graber has maintained that there exist four basic functions of the press: one, surveillance; two, interpretation; three, socialization; and four, manipulation. Surveillance corresponds to the "information and news providing function of mass communication."[9] Interpretation corresponds to what Dominic A. Infante, Andrew S. Rancer, and Deanna F. Womack have called correlation, "how the mass media select, interpret, and criticize the information they present to the public."[10] Socialization "involves the learning of basic values and orientations that prepare individuals to fit into their cultural milieu."[11] Finally, manipulation refers to "the deliberate manipulation of the political process."[12] This final function reported by Graber corresponds to what Infante, Rancer, and Womack called mobilization: "the ability of the media to promote national interests and certain behaviors, especially during times of national crisis."[13]

Yet Graber's conception of manipulation is more complicated than that espoused by Infante and coworkers. It posits that the media maintains an agenda; her conception suggests an active role for the media in shaping the news. Manipulation, for Graber, involves two distinct forms. The first of these involves writing "stories that expose misconduct in government and produce reforms."[14] The second involves presenting "sensational information that attracts large media audiences and enhances profits."[15] I am primarily concerned with the first form of manipulation in this study. By deciding what needs to be changed or fixed in our society, the press has distinctly moved away from a traditional notion of objective news reporting. However, this mode of operating stills falls within the realm of social responsibility theory. We must remember, however, that the "mass media are an important influence on politics because they regularly and rapidly present politically crucial information to huge audiences."[16] Like Graber, I maintain that agenda-setting/building is a "widely used strategy for manipulating politics."[17] If this thought is kept paramount, then we must examine the agenda-setting role of the press.

THE AGENDA-SETTING FUNCTION OF THE PRESS

Scholars of mass communication are not certain whether to call agenda-setting a function, a theory, or a hypothesis.[18] Whatever its true designation, as Infante, Rancer, and Womack pointed out, "the concept has received considerable attention from mass communication theorists."[19] Indeed, as a theory, it affirms that the media "do have a great deal of influence" upon political decision making and that the media are especially influential in telling the general population what to think about.[20] Its relevance here, regardless of its status, is to help explain how the press interacts with presidential discourse during crisis situations. Bernard C. Cohen observed that the press "may not be very successful in telling its readers what to think, but it is stunningly successful in telling its readers what to think about."[21] Agenda-setting researchers following Cohen have used similar phraseology to describe the agenda-setting function of the press.

Maxwell E. McCombs and Donald L. Shaw found that voters learn about an issue "in direct proportion" to the attention given that issue by the press.[22] The question central to their study was whether or not the key issues in a political campaign, as reported by the general public, correlated with actual media content. They found that voters tended to share what the media defined as important. Moreover, they asserted that the mass media provide voters with the "major primary sources of national political information."[23] This is commensurate with the results of a study by Sheldon Gilberg et al. that asserted that the press has the potential to set our government's agenda, even at the highest levels.[24] Michael B. Salwen took the above position to the extreme and suggested that policy makers "will address issues only when these issues are perceived as crises by the public."[25] However, if everyday issues can be elevated to the status of major importance by mere frequency of occurrence in the media, then how much more important the role of the press becomes when examining those events the *President* deems as crisis events. If Cohen's assertion of the power of the media to establish the relevance of particular issues and thus control the width of public discussion, if not the content, is true, then it behooves scholars to consider presidential crisis rhetoric in relation to the press, not because the press represents public opinion but because it is a good indication of the issues and ideas that informed voters and opinion leaders will be talking about. Thus, the president will be aware of the issues, ideas, and responses that circulate in the press, not because they represent popular opinion but because they are a good indicator of that which still needs to be addressed in his policy or which he should be talking about.[26]

The contribution of the press in this regard is highlighted by McCombs and Shaw:

As a Fourth Estate, the press is an independent force whose dialogue with other elements of society produces the agenda of issues considered by political elites and voters. Witness the major role of the elite press as a source of information among major decision makers. Through its winnowing of the day's happenings to find the major events, concerns, and issues, the press inadvertently plays an agenda-setting influence role.[27]

Thus, it follows that the mass media shape not only what the public "perceives" as "political reality" but also how political elites understand what voters and opinion leaders are thinking about. A relationship therefore develops between the press, its sources, and the public audience that determines "what is *accepted* as the public agenda."[28] Moreover, Roy L. Behr and Shanto Iyengar provide us with evidence that suggests this relationship is unidirectional; that is to say, press content affects public concern, but public concern does not affect that which the news focuses upon.[29]

Gilberg et al. have asserted that the president is in a "strategic position to influence the agenda" of the press because he is the major source of news at the national level.[30] In addition, they found that the press had a significant influence upon President Carter's second State of the Union address but could not determine if Carter's address influenced subsequent press issues. This notwithstanding, a subsequent study by McCombs, Gilberg, and Eyal found evidence of "presidential influence on subsequent press coverage" of an event.[31] The implications of this for the study of presidential crisis rhetoric suggests that the president does have an influence upon the content of news items but that the press may also influence the issues the president discusses and how they are discussed. These influences take on more importance when we consider the degree to which the public rely upon the press for information, especially national and international events. These "unobtrusive issues" (i.e., not affecting the day-to-day community involvement) are not part of an individual's common experience; therefore, the "news media exercise a near monopoly as sources of information and orientation."[32] Although the president surely knows more, the media tell him what we, the public, know.

FROM AGENDA-SETTING TO AGENDA-EXTENSION: CONSIDERATION OF PRIMING AND FRAMING

The basic theme expressed by the studies listed above is cogently summed by Judith F. Trent and Robert V. Friedenberg: "[T]he media set public priorities just by paying attention to some issues while ignoring others. They determine what issues are important and in this way play an important role in structuring our social reality."[33] Yet the media also move beyond the strict reporting of facts, and it is to this concern that we now turn. During the decade of the 1980s, mass media and communication researchers using agenda-setting theory began to discover an evaluative component to media news. They postulated that the media do more than tell us what to think about; they also tell us how to think about it. These studies suggested another aspect of agenda-setting as it relates to the public evaluation of presidents; this aspect is described as "priming." These studies also suggested a germane issue for this study; they postulated that media provide the contextual cues "by which to evaluate the subject matter" under consideration.[34] In short, the media often "frame" an issue so that it will be interpreted in a specific manner.

According to Graber, this type of "manipulative journalism raises philosophical, ethical, and news policy questions."[35] This manipulative aspect to media functions is called agenda-building by Graber and is defined by her as the "process whereby news stories influence how people perceive and evaluate issues and policies."[36] This clearly moves beyond agenda-setting. It involves the influencing of public opinion. I call it agenda-extension to distinguish it from the agenda-building theory discussed by Michael B. Salwen, as well as by Roger W. Cobb and Charles D. Elder.[37] Anne Johnston has written that recent work in agenda-setting research has uncovered this agenda-extension process.[38] The public becomes primed to evaluate the president, for example, by how well he handles the issue covered by the press. The more the press covers an issue, the more the public will evaluate the president's success or failure in relation to the content of media coverage. The public, then, become primed to "evaluate the president . . . by his apparent success in dealing with this issue."[39] Another way the media participate in policy making is through muckraking. Journalists try to focus the public eye upon those aspects of society that, in the opinion of the *journalist*, need change. They are "sensational exposes of corruption usually involving high status individuals."[40] The press may also "manipulate the political scene by creating a climate for political action."[41] It is at this point that agenda-extension helps to explain the influence of the press in policy making.

Shanto Iyengar and Adam Simon have studied the effects of network news coverage during the Gulf War, which provides an example of the differences between agenda-setting, priming, and framing. They defined priming as the "ability of news programs to affect the criteria by which political leaders are judged."[42] Specifically, priming involves the correlation among patterns of news coverage and the manner in which the public evaluates the performance of politicians. These effects are strongest in the area of performance and weakest in the area of affecting judgment on personality. This aspect of news coverage is intimately linked with agenda-setting because the "more prominent an issue in the national information stream, the greater its weight in political judgments."[43] In analyzing the news coverage of the Gulf War, Iyengar and Simon found that the "amount of coverage accorded to the Gulf's situation and the proportion of respondents nominating it as the nation's most important problem were highly correlated" (agenda-setting).[44] In terms of the role that priming played, they found foreign policy "performance assessments tended to override economic assessments in their impact on . . . ratings of George Bush during the Gulf crisis."[45]

These findings are significant in that they show dramatic shifts in the criteria used to evaluate the president during times of crisis and increased coverage of an event. Before the Gulf crisis, Americans were overwhelmingly concerned with domestic issues (the economy and crime); after the Gulf War, Americans evaluated President Bush more with general foreign policy considerations than with his domestic performance. These findings lend support to the studies on crisis rhetoric discussed in the previous chapter by highlighting the relationship between issues the president announces as important and the perceived importance of those issues/events to the American people. Iyengar and Simon spoke to this point: "Print and broadcast news coverage of world events involving the use of U.S. military force have propagated the world view and policy preferences of the incumbent administrations."[46] This may in part be due to the lack of available information from sources other than the administration during crisis events, but Iyengar and Simon suggested that this practice "of 'official' journalism . . . ensures that the public's and the President's understanding of . . . international crisis would be congruent."[47] According to Iyengar and Kinder, priming works because "by calling attention to some aspects of national life while ignoring others, network news programs determine the standards by which presidents are judged."[48] Iyengar and Kinder drew from basic psychological theory to explain how this works. They argued that public attention is highly selective and that the public relies upon information that is most easily accessible. Judgments about political matters, or the performance of a president, are in part due to what standards come to individuals' minds but also are due to those "considerations that are, for whatever reason and however briefly, accessible."[49] In terms of presidential performance, news coverage that implies a president's responsibility for a problem at the national level encourages viewers to attach more importance to his performance on that particular problem when evaluating his overall performance as president. Iyengar and Kinder suggested that this "effect appears to be stronger for problems that are relative newcomers to the American political agenda, problems for which the public's understanding is still in formation."[50] Thus, in situations of crisis, where public knowledge is in flux and preknowledge is constantly being injected into the public's evaluative consciousness, the effects of priming could be considerable. As the public's need for information increases, and media provide focused coverage on a particular event, evaluation of the president's performance during the event comes under greater scrutiny than is otherwise expected. During the Cold War, presidents were able to frame an event using the Cold War meta-narrative. Since Clinton is unable to use the narrative to give events coherence, salience, and direction, he may experience greater difficulty in framing at a time when media power is undiminished.

Framing

Johnston stated that news stories not only provide their audiences with the important subjects to think about, but they also provide "contextual cues or frames in which to evaluate those subjects."[51] Issues are often framed by station managers, producers, or editors by how they tell the story of the issue. Gladys Engel Lang and Kurt Lang discovered this type of agenda-extension to be operating during the Watergate hearings. They demonstrated that agenda-extension begins when media gatekeepers decide to publish a particular story.[52] Although this is the first step in all news reporting, the move toward agenda-extension occurs when a second step is taken, the decision concerning how much attention to give to the story. As pointed out by Graber, it is at this "point where ordinary agenda-setting activities can most readily turn into deliberate agenda-building [agenda-extension]."[53] By continually focusing on an issue, the media may thrust it into the fore-front of national thought. And at the point when an issue emerges, its media context becomes crucially important. Lang and Lang noted that the Watergate coverage was first put into the framework of the elec-tion campaign, thus leading the public to think of it as part and parcel of partisan politics. But as soon as the media switched contextual frames, moving from the framework of the 1972 presidential campaign to the framework of continual Washington corruption, the nation became obsessed.

In their analysis of the Gulf War coverage, Iyengar and Simon pro-vided an example of framing effects:

[C]ontent data (showing that network news coverage was preoccupied with military affairs and highly event oriented) and survey data are coupled to show that respondents reporting higher rates of exposure to television news expressed greater support for a military as opposed to a diplomatic response to the crisis, because the news media framed the events in the Gulf episodically as a series of military actions.[54]

Framing thus involves the relationship between qualitative aspects of news coverage—contextual cues—and how the public interprets the news. William Gamson asserted that a "frame is a central organizing idea for making sense of relevant events and suggesting what is at issue."[55] He noted that facts remain neutral until framed. Indeed, Gamson argued that facts "take on their meaning by being embedded in a frame or story line that organizes them and gives them coherence, selecting certain ones to emphasize while ignoring others."[56]

Although it can be successfully argued that providing contextual cues for interpretation is a necessary part of media responsibility, when the media place their own partisan context over that of the people or government, the potential for public manipulation increases. Graber conducted a content analysis of television news coverage of the 1984 presidential campaign that sheds light upon this media manipula-tion.[57] Her focus was on how the news was framed. She found that there was a ratio of three to one of bad over good news for the United States during this period. This news primarily focused on foreign policy and economic concerns. Graber posited that this overwhelming bad-news coverage should have derailed Reagan's reelection bid but did not. The networks had framed the news so as to stress the bad aspects of Ameri-can news; they also primed the population to evaluate President Rea-gan's performance on foreign policy and economic considerations. Taking the context in which the news is reported as a frame leads us to consider the probability of frames being potentially broad in their inclusion of possibilities. Graber noted: "[V]arious media effects are modulated by the sensitivity of audiences to particular issues, and that effects vary with background, demographic characteristics, and experiences of individual audience members."[58] Reagan was able to overcome the negative effects of priming because there were good stories mixed in with the bad that had a "leavening" effect. Graber, like Iyengar and Simon, also noted that priming effects are linked with policy and not with personality.

Day, discussing the first of the requirements of the press (providing "a truthful, comprehensive, and intelligent account of the day's events in a context which gives them meaning"), suggested that reporters must "clearly distinguish between fact and opinion."[59] Furthermore, news stories must be put into "perspective" by providing "relevant back ground."[60] These journalistic norms described by Day include social responsibility, objectivity, fairness, and truth.[61] Yet agenda-extension suggests that something other than these idealized norms are operating. Instead of a Fourth Estate, the media seem to be part of a partisan effort at persuading the public to accept the media's interpretation as truth. According to Mitchell Stephens, objectivity involves both impartiality and the reflection of the "world as it is, without bias or distortion of any sort."[62] In short, the news as a true image of the world. A laudable goal but difficult to put into practice. Yet by framing an issue, the media has a decision to make: one, frame it according to the needs of the readers; two, frame it according to the needs of the media; or three, frame it so as to accurately impart the meaning of those speaking/writing upon it. The last of these choices seems to adhere best to the requirements of a socially responsible press.

According to Day, media practitioners should "strive to keep their personal preferences and opinions out of news stories. . . . [They should be] concerned with facts and impartiality in the presentation of those facts."[63] Self-reflective writing should help to assure this. Yet this goal is often ignored for various reasons (economic, political, institutional). Be that as it may, by not striving to be objective, by establishing an agenda, the press steps out of its socially mandated role of a responsible Fourth Estate and instead assumes its own political persona in opposition to the elected government and the will of the people. In so doing, it removes itself from the confines of the norms of social responsibility and sets itself up as an independent self-advocate.

IMPLICATIONS OF FRAMING FOR THE PRESENT STUDY

This chapter has thus far provided a brief overview of relevant agenda-setting and agenda-extension theory. The literature in agenda-setting theory has demonstrated the force of Cohen's statement: The power of the media to establish the relevance of particular issues and thus control the width of public discussion and content is great. This chapter also highlighted those studies examining agenda-extension. This function of the press primes readers to evaluate presidents in light of a specific issue that the press has focused on. Agenda-extension also includes framing, the central organizing principle of continued news coverage; in short, how the press organizes the context through which the public will view the news.

It is the potential power of framing that concerns the present study. I posit that in the vacuum created by the ending of the Cold War meta-narrative, the press, picking up on Clinton's inability to quickly and effectively frame crises, began to frame them in their own manner. As Gamson suggested, by "analyzing news content in terms of the frames presented, the manifest-latent distinction is partially bridged."[64] This is to say that some facts are emphasized by certain frames and others are not; it is this presence or absence of certain facts that may reveal the implicit aspects of the news coverage. In order to better understand this process, the remainder of this chapter advances a conception of framing as a rhetorical process for both the president and the media; it proposes a tentative theory of press and presidential roles; and finally, an exposition of the scope, procedures, and materials of this study is provided.

Framing as Rhetorical Process

Robert M. Entman stated that to frame is to take "some aspects of a perceived reality and make them more salient in a communicating text, in such a way as to promote a particular problem definition, causal interpretation, moral evaluation, and/or treatment recommendation for the item described."[65] Frames define problems, diagnose causes, make moral judgments, and suggest remedies. They operate by making some information more salient than other information; therefore, they "highlight some features of reality while omitting others."[66] Frames are located in the communicator, the text, the receiver, and the culture at large.

The tremendous power of frames to shape the manner in which the public interprets certain issues and situations is readily discernable in a study by Paul M. Sniderman, Richard A. Brody, and Philip E. Tetlock.

For these researchers, who used mandatory testing for HIV (human immunodeficiency virus) as the controlled frame, the results were instructive: The effect "of framing is to prime values differentially, establishing the salience of the one or the other. [A] majority of the public supports the rights of persons with AIDS [acquired imuno-deficiency syndrome] when the issue is framed to accentuate civil liberties considerations—and supports . . . mandatory testing when the issue is framed to accentuate public health considerations."[67] The power of framing is great indeed, especially considering the pervasiveness of the mass media in the country. Framing becomes even more powerful when concerning international events, because of the limited, firsthand access Americans have to foreign affairs information. For example, Entman and Page found that during the prewar stage of the debate about U.S. policy toward Iraq the media frame had only two remedies for the situation: war now or sanctions now and war later.[68] Any "critique transcending the remedies inside the [media] frame breached the bounds of acceptable discourse, hence was unlikely to influence policy."[69]

Zhongdang Pan and Gerald M. Kosicki advanced one way of using frame analysis for the analysis of news stories. They suggested that each news story will have a theme that "functions as the central organizing idea" of the story.[70] Themes provide readers with signifying elements that prompt them to comprehend a news story in a particular manner. The signifying elements of themes are "structurally located lexical choices of codes constructed by following certain shared rules and conventions."[71] These codes and lexical choices are the tools that news makers use to construct news discourse and the psychological stimuli the audience processes when reading the news. For Pan and Kosicki, themes function as frames, and the signifying elements within themes may be likened to framing devices. In examining a single news story about a pro-life rally in Wichita, Kansas, Pan and Kosicki advanced four framing devices that helped to establish the presence of a particular frame within a news story: syntactical structure, script structure, thematic structure, and rhetorical structure.

At the syntactical level of analysis, one looks for stable patterns of arrangement of words and phrases into sentences; headlines and lead sentences are particularly important. At the script level, one looks for how news stories are conceived of as stories. This involves an action or event orientation; the five W's and one H of journalism. At the thematic level, one looks for elements of causality within the news item. Often this causality is implied by presenting "actions in a context in which one may be seen as an antecedent and another as a consequence."[72] Thematic structure consists of a summary—the headline, lead, or conclusion—and a main body of text—the evidence: events and sources.

At the rhetorical level, one looks for any of five rhetorical framing devices: metaphors, exemplars, catchphrases, depictions, and visual images.

For Pan and Kosicki, the framing of news stories is reduced to lexical choices made by the journalists—words in a vocabulary. The words chosen by a news reporter reveal the way that reporter categorizes that which he is reporting upon. Word choice often "signifies the presence of a particular frame."[73] For example, Pan and Kosicki cited the descriptions of Saddam Hussein given by American reporters during the Gulf War. Hussein was described as the "Iraqi dictator," a description that placed him in the same category, in the minds of Americans, as Hitler, Stalin, and perhaps Manuel Noriega. If, on the other hand, one were to describe him as the "Iraqi leader," "Iraqi president," or the "Iraqi commander in chief," the connotations would be quite different. The lexical choices made within the various framing devices—syntactic, script, thematic, rhetorical—act to frame the news story to engender a dominant reading of that story.

Pan and Kosicki conducted an empirical analysis of news stories that took place on a microlevel of analysis; that is, they examined each sentence of a news story for the lexical choices made at each of the four framing levels. They sought to "describe the varying functions between the identified structural and lexical features of news stories and the predictable mental representations of the story on the part of audiences."[74] In their brief analysis of a single news story, Pan and Kosicki found that the story framed the pro-life rally in confrontational terms. Sentence by sentence they proceeded through each of the four levels of analysis and found aggregate evidence that supported the confrontational theme. They pointed out that framing analysis allows researchers to provide information about how an issue is discussed in the news and "how the ways of talking about the issue [are] related to the evolution of the issue in political debates."[75] However, given the nature of their study—a single news story—it would appear that making such inferences would be difficult at best. Moreover, if one were to cover numerous stories over a period of time, attempting to discern the relationship of the issue and frame relationship, one would surely find the microlevel of Pan and Kosicki's analysis belaboring to the point of impossibility.

To overcome the limitations of a microanalysis, and validly make generalizations concerning a frame's influence upon political debates, one must find a way of identifying frames at a more general level of analysis. Robert M. Entman comparatively analyzed the narratives within news stories about the KAL and Iran Air shootdowns.[76] Entman chose these particular incidents because they could have been reported on in a similar fashion; thus, any differences in the information that comprised the frames would be easier to detect. For Entman, "frames reside in the specific properties of the news narrative that encourage those perceiving and thinking about events to develop particular understandings of them."[77] The specific properties reside in the narrative accounts of events and are composed of key words, metaphors, concepts, symbols, and visual images. Accordingly, frames are fashioned by particular words and phrases that consistently appear within a narrative and "convey thematically consonant meanings across . . . time."[78] Thus, framing makes some ideas more salient than others, while making some ideas virtually invisible to an audience.

For Entman, the initial framing process is set in motion by the interaction of sources and journalists. Once initiated, the established frame guides audience and journalist thinking. Entman called this type of frame an "event-specific schema." Once in place, an event-specific schema encourages journalists to "perceive, process, and report all further information about the event in ways supporting the basic interpretation encoded in the schema."[79] In his study of the coverage of the two shootdowns, Entman used news items appearing in *Time*, *Newsweek*, *CBS Evening News*, the *Washington Post*, and the *New York Times*. The results are instructive. Entman found that the KAL shootdown was framed as a moral outrage, whereas the Iran Air shootdown was framed as a technical problem. This was accomplished in several ways. For example, during the two-week period following the KAL shootdown, the *New York Times* printed 286 stories and the *Washington Post* printed 169 stories. During the two-week period following the shootdown of Iran Air 655 the *New York Times* printed 102 stories and the *Washington Post* printed 82 stories. Thus, the frame—actual coverage, in this case—helped to determine the importance of the event.

For another example, during the two-week period following the KAL shootdown the *New York Times* used the term "attack" ninety-nine times, and the *Washington Post* used the term sixty-six times. However, during the two-week period following the shootdown of Iran Air 655, the *New York Times* used the term "attack" only thirty times, and the *Washington Post* used the term twenty-four times. These and other findings reported by Entman demonstrated how frames represent dominant event-specific schemata. They have the capacity to obscure contrary information that may be presented in a particular case. On this point, Entman found that "for those stories in which a single frame thoroughly pervades the text, stray contrary opinions . . . are likely to possess such low salience as to be of little practical use to most audience members."[80] So although it was perfectly acceptable for political elites to describe the KAL shootdown as a brutal attack, it was far less likely for them to describe it in terms of a tragedy; the frame had been set: the

Soviets were evil and at fault. To think of the shootdown in terms of tragedy runs against the frame and would mitigate the culpability of the Soviets.

Entman focused on those frames he considered politically important—that is to say, those elements within frames that would be most likely to "promote a common, majority response to the news events as measured in public opinion polls."[81] According to Entman, the process of framing is a reciprocal process between political elites and journalists. In established frames, political elites often find it difficult, if not foolhardy, to resist the frame's pervasive influence; however, in the development of *new* event-specific schemata elites have great influence in establishing the initial frames. This is particularly true with breaking foreign affairs items. This supports the conclusions of the literature on crisis rhetoric that point out the "rally-'round-the-president" stance of the press during times of crisis.

The Role of News Media

Since 1947, all presidential responses to perceived crisis events have been uttered under the constraining and growing influence of the Cold War meta-narrative, if the Cold War meta-narrative is seen as a frame. After so long, the removal of this frame might lead to confusion about how to view the role of the United states in international situations. Presidents throughout this period have also enjoyed some degree of cooperation from the press during times of crises. Brigitte Lebens Nacos has analyzed the relationship of the press and presidents during six crisis periods.[82] Her study spanned domestic and foreign crises, serious (Cuban Missile) to "middle-level" (Reagan assassination attempt), four different presidents (Kennedy, Johnson, Carter, and Reagan), and a twenty-one-year period. Nacos argued that during periods of crisis the media abandoned an adversarial role with the president, and as a result, "news coverage during crises periods reflects the tendency of political actors to support a crisis-managing President or, at least, to refrain from expressing criticism."[83]

The results of Nacos's work are important to the present study; with the loss of the Cold War meta-narrative, presidents might now be forced to compete with the press over how to frame international crisis situations.[84] Nacos found "distinctive patterns" in the manner in which the press covered the various crises. First, no fundamental changes were revealed in the way that newspapers covered crisis episodes between 1962 and 1983. Second, a strong relationship exists between editorial positions and the content of political news coverage. This suggests that editors exert a greater degree of control over news items during times of crises. Nacos highlighted the consistency of coverage by the national press during the studied period: "[N]ews coverage reflected a rally-'round-the-president reaction by domestic political actors and/or an unwillingness to criticize the president's crisis-related policies. [However, in] those instances [in] which presidential policies related to an upcoming crisis were articulated, the coverage of pre-crisis periods revealed the conflicting views one would expect in American politics."[85] This same pattern was found during the crises of the Kennedy administration by Montague Kern, Patricia W. Levering, and Ralph B. Levering. Kern and colleagues analyzed six foreign and domestic policy crises and discovered certain limitations upon the president's control over the facts: Despite "the strong impact of presidential leadership on press treatment of crisis issues, the overall generalization emerges that the president dominates press coverage primarily in situations where competing interpretations of events are not being espoused by others whom the journalists consider important."[86]

Presidents thus have enjoyed some degree of cooperation from the press during times of crises. At least in part, this has been a result of the legitimating influence of presidential authority and the perennial influence of the Cold War meta-narrative. During precrisis periods of discussion about a particular policy (the days and weeks before the Iran Airbus shootdown, for example), there exists a general level of debate over the administration's policies. This discussion period would end once a given president spoke out definitively in response to a situation perceived as a crisis. The ending of the Cold War, however, seems to have changed this. The Cold War meta-narrative and the role(s) it created and legitimated for the president depended on the "degree of anxiety the myth [of Soviet evil rationalized and], the intensity with which the particular expectation that forms the central premise [is] held."[87] The meta-narrative acted to frame or contextualize a president's utterances in crisis situations. With the ending of the Cold War, the public no longer automatically cocontextualizes presidential utterances in response to a perceived crisis. In this vacuum, then, a space exists available for the variable framing of presidential utterances in response to international crisis situations.

The general hypothesis undergirding this work suggests that President Clinton's utterances and assumed roles in North Korea, Bosnia, and Haiti will not coincide with how the press framed his utterances. This is to say, Clinton will provide the American public with a particular frame through which to interpret the events (trying to establish a stable contextual frame to legitimate his actions), and the press will provide competing frames for the public to evaluate Clinton's actions. Thus, there exists no stable frame through which to view the utterances and proposed actions of the president. I am not asserting that the press is intentionally ignoring responsible norms of objectivity; that is something we may not know without asking members of the press. Be that as it may, the media may attempt some objectivity but still frame in such a manner that prevents readers from making a "balanced assessment" of a particular event.[88]

Procedures and Materials

The press facilitates public perception of the context in which a particular situation resides. In the past, the Cold War meta-narrative has helped to establish this context in foreign affairs; it was common, public knowledge. Now the way the press frames international events takes on an even greater importance and may even contend against the president's frame. For this study, then, I perform a comparative analysis of the rival frames used by the Clinton administration and the printed press when discussing North Korea, Bosnia, and Haiti. Specifically, I analyze how the Clinton administration framed the situations and how the press framed the situations as a response to the administrative text. For North Korea I examine those comments given by President Clinton and his administration officials between 12 March and 12 June 1993; I also examine the press reports, represented by the *Washington Post* and the *New York Times*, concerning North Korea during this same time period. For Bosnia I examine all public administrative utterances made between 21 November 1995, the announcement of the Dayton Accord, and 15 December 1995, just after the congressional vote of support on the mission. I also examine the press reports concerning Bosnia during this same time period. For Haiti I examine those comments given by President Clinton and his administration officials between 14 January of 1993 and 20 December 1993, the first and last comments by President Clinton during 1993.[89] I examine the *Washington Post* and the *New York Times* during a ten-day period following each of President Clinton's public statements.[90] The Haiti analysis proceeds in two sections: January through June and July through December. Period one covers the Clinton administration's first statements about Haiti and ends just prior to the July signing of the Governors Island agreement. The second period begins with the July signing of the Governors Island agreement that set the date for Aristide's return to Haiti and ends in the period following the October incident in Port-au-Prince. These times were selected because they reflect those periods during the crisis in which the majority of administrative utterances upon Haiti were made.

I proceed by analyzing the administrative texts for narratives.[91] In this I follow Entman and look for the various framing devices that may have been used by the Clinton administration: key words, metaphors, concepts, and symbols. Having accomplished this, I next repeat the analysis on news stories and editorials contained in the *New York Times* and the *Washington Post*. Having done this, I then answer the following questions: How did the Clinton administration frame the situations in North Korea, Bosnia, and Haiti? How did the press, responding to President Clinton, frame the situations? And at what time, if at all, did these frames converge to present a unified contextual whole?

In summation, this chapter has reviewed the concepts of agenda-setting, agenda-extension, and framing as rhetorical processes. This study posits that administrative utterances interact with the rhetorical situation and affect the manner in which the public perceives a crisis. The press plays a role in the transmission of presidential utterances. Since 1947, most, if not all, international crises have been framed by U.S. presidents with the Cold War meta-narrative; once presidential utterances enacted this frame, dissenting voices were made virtually unnoticeable. With the Cold War over, it would seem logical that initial presidential utterances would have a more difficult time developing new event-specific schemata. This study, then, is about the interaction of the president and the press in framing the crisis situations in North Korea, Bosnia, and Haiti.

NOTES

1. Today, the press in America is viewed as having operated under a Libertarian perspective, a perspective that grew out of the Enlightenment. Humans were viewed as rational, enlightened beings who could discern between truth and falsehood. The press was conceived as "a partner in the search for truth" and was used to provide the public with the necessary information to "make up their own minds as to policy." See Fred S. Siebert, Theodore Peterson, and Wilbur Schramm, *Four Theories of the Press* (Urbana: University of Illinois Press, 1956), 3. This position stressed minimal or no government control, and it is through this perspective that we have come to view the press as a Fourth Estate in this country. The primary characteristic of this perspective is one that rests upon a concept of language as a transparent vehicle of thought. With the first concerns over press ownership—influence by the source or control by the source—we find a concomitant weakening of Libertarian theory.

We see concerns about source control emerge by the mid-1920s, when the media of this country had come to be dominated by a few wealthy and powerful people. This may in part be explained through economic necessity, yet the potential for abuses remains. Shortly after World War II, the Commission on Freedom of the Press, the so-called Hutchins Commission, took up the issue of press ownership and responsibility. The report of the commission, entitled *A Free and Responsible*

Press, represented the growing trend in American media toward a theory and practice of the press advocating social responsibility. The basic premise of the commission was that "the power and near monopoly position of the media impose on them an obligation to be socially responsible" (Siebert, Peterson, and Schramm, 5). The idea behind the commission's report, according to Louis Day, underpins a contemporary notion of social responsibility. See, Louis A. Day, *Ethics in Media Communication* (Belmont, CA: Wadsworth Publishing Company, 1991), 35. This idea of social responsibility is summed by Theodore Peterson: "Freedom carries concomitant obligations; and the press, which enjoys a privileged position under our government, is obliged to be responsible to society for carrying out certain essential functions of mass communication in contemporary society" (Siebert, Peterson, and Schramm, 74).

2. Siebert, Peterson, and Schramm, 74.

3. Siebert, Peterson, and Schramm, 94.

4. Siebert, Peterson, and Schramm, 87.

5. Siebert, Peterson, and Schramm, 89.

6. Siebert, Peterson, and Schramm, 91.

7. Siebert, Peterson, and Schramm, 91.

8. Siebert, Peterson, and Schramm, 91.

9. Doris A. Graber, *Mass Media and American Politics*, 3rd ed. (Washington, D.C.: Congressional Quarterly Press, 1989), 11.

10. Dominic A. Infante, Andrew S. Rancer, and Deanna F. Womack, *Building Communication Theory*, 2nd ed. (Prospect Heights, IL: Waveland Press, 1993), 397.

11. Graber, *Mass Media*, 11.

12. Graber, *Mass Media*, 12.

13. Infante, Rancer, and Womack, 399.

14. Graber, *Mass Media*, 12.

15. Graber, *Mass Media*, 12.

16. Graber, *Mass Media*, 29.

17. Graber, *Mass Media*, 277.

18. Maxwell E. McCombs and Donald L. Shaw consider it a function. See "The Agenda-Setting Function of Mass Media," *Public Opinion Quarterly* 36 (1972): 176-187. McCombs has spent most of his career supporting this assertion, and I borrow freely from his ideas in this area. Also see W. J. Severin and J. W. Tankard, *Communication Theories*, 2nd ed. (New York: Longman, 1988). For a detailed explanation of agenda-setting as theory, see R. D. Wimmer and J. R. Dominic, *Mass Media Research*, 2nd ed. (Belmont, CA: Wadsworth, 1987).

19. Infante, Rancer, and Womack, 399.

20. Judith S. Trent and Robert V. Friedenberg, *Political Campaign Communication: Principles and Practices*, 2nd ed. (New York: Praeger, 1991), 107.

21. Bernard C. Cohen, *The Press and Foreign Policy* (Princeton: Princeton University Press, 1963), 13.

22. McCombs and Shaw, 177.

23. McCombs and Shaw, 185.

24. Sheldon Gilberg et al., "The State of the Union Address and the Press Agenda," *Journalism Quarterly* 57 (1980): 584-588.

25. Michael B. Salwen, "News Media and Public Opinion: Benign Agenda-Setters? Opinion Molders? Or Simply Irrelevant?" *Florida Communication Journal* 18.2 (1990): 17.

26. There have been numerous detailed studies of the relationship of the press and presidents during periods of crises. These studies tend to be descriptive, analyzing how the press reports crises, whether or not the press supports a particular president's policy decisions, and the like. Thus, they compliment my study but do not seek to discover how the press functions in concert with the president to construct rhetorically crisis situations. For three excellent studies see, Brigitte Lebens Nacos, *The Press, Presidents, and Crises* (New York: Columbia University Press, 1990); Dan Nimmo and James E. Combs, *Nightly Horrors* (Knoxville: University of Tennessee Press, 1985); and Montague Kern, Patricia Levering, and Ralph Levering, *The Kennedy Crises* (Chapel Hill: University of North Carolina Press, 1983).

27. Maxwell E. McCombs and Donald L. Shaw, "Agenda-Setting and the Political Process," *The Emergence of American Political Issues: The Agenda-Setting Function of the Press*, ed. Donald L. Shaw and Maxwell E. McCombs (St. Paul, MN: West Publishing Co., 1977), 151.

28. McCombs and Shaw, "Agenda-Setting and the Political Process," 152.

29. Roy L. Behr and Shanto Iyenger, "Television News, Real-World Cues, and Changes in the Public Agenda," *Public Opinion Quarterly* 49 (1985): 38-57.

30. Gilberg et al., 585.

31. Maxwell E. McCombs, Sheldon Gilberg, and C. H. Eyal, "The State of the Union Address and the Press Agenda: A Replication" (paper presented at the annual meeting of the International Communication Association, Boston, 1983). Results reported in Maxwell E. McCombs and Sheldon Gilberg, "News Influence on Our Pictures of the World," *Perspectives on Media Effects*, ed. Jennings Bryant and Dolf Zillman (Hillsdale, NJ: Lawrence Erlbaum Associates, Publishers, 1986), 14.

32. McCombs and Gilberg, 11.

33. Trent and Friedenberg, 108.

34. Trent and Friedenberg, 109.

35. Graber, *Mass Media*, 278.

36. Graber, *Mass Media*, 287.

37. Michael B. Salwen, drawing from the work of Roger W. Cobb and Charles D. Elder, described agenda-building as a theory that explains how the "public can participate in the democratic process in a limited way by influencing national agendas." This theory essentially stresses grassroots genesis of political ideas and change. See Salwen, 16-23; see also Roger W. Cobb and Charles D. Elder, *Participation in American Politics: The Dynamics of Agenda-Building* (Baltimore: Johns Hopkins University Press, 1983).

38. Anne Johnston, "Trends in Political Communication: *A Selective Review of Research in the 1980s*," *New Directions in Political Communication: A Resource Book*, ed. David L. Swanson and Dan Nimmo (Newbury Park, CA: Sage Publications, 1990), 329-362.

39. Johnston, 337.

40. Graber, *Mass Media*, 281.

41. Graber, *Mass Media*, 287.

42. Shanto Iyengar and Adam Simon, "News Coverage of the Gulf Crisis and Public Opinion: A Study of Agenda-Setting, Priming, and Framing," *Communication Research* 20.3 (1993): 368.

43. Iyengar and Simon, 368.

44. Iyengar and Simon, 375-376. They found r = .85. This is a very high degree of correlation. Not to belittle their results, it must be mentioned, however, that America was at war. It makes sense that the majority of Americans would consider an event involving the lives of American soldiers as being among the nation's most important problems.

45. Iyengar and Simon, 376.

46. Iyengar and Simon, 381.

47. Iyengar and Simon, 382.

48. Shanto Iyengar and Donald R. Kinder, "More than Meets the Eye: TV News, Priming, and Public Evaluations of the President," *Public Communication Behavior*, ed. George Comstock, Vol. 1 (Orlando, FL: Academic Press, 1986), 136.

49. Iyengar and Kinder, 139.

50. Iyengar and Kinder, 162.

51. Johnston, 337.

52. Gladys Engel Lang and Kurt Lang, "The Media and Watergate," *Media Power in Politics*, ed. Doris A. Graber (Washington, D.C.: Congressional Quarterly Press, 1984), 202-209.

53. Graber, *Mass Media*, 288.

54. Iyengar and Simon, 365. Italicized in original.

55. William A. Gamson, "News as Framing: Comments on Graber," *American Behavioral Scientist* 33 (1989): 157.

56. Gamson, 157.

57. Doris A. Graber, "Framing Election News Broadcasts: News Context and Its Impact on the 1984 Presidential Election," *Social Science Quarterly* 68 (1987): 552-568.

58. Graber, "Framing Election News," 566.

59. Day, 35.

60. Day, 35.

61. Day, 8.

62. Mitchell Stephens, *A History of News: From the Drum to the Satellite* (New York: Viking Penguin, 1988), 264.

63. Day, 32.

64. Gamson, 158.

65. Robert M. Entman, "Framing: Toward Clarification of a Fractured Paradigm," *Journal of Communication* 43 (1993): 52. Italicized in original.

66. Entman, "Framing: Toward Clarification," 53.

67. Paul M. Sniderman, Richard A. Brody, and Philip E. Tetlock, *Reasoning and Choice: Explorations in Political Psychology* (Cambridge, England: Cambridge University Press, 1991), 52.

68. Robert M. Entman and B. I. Page, "The News before the Storm: The Iraq War Debate and the Limits to Media Independence," *Just Deserts: The News Media, U.S. Foreign Policy, and the Gulf War,* ed. W. Lance Bennet and D. L. Palentz (Chicago: University of Chicago Press, 1994). See also Kathleen M. German, "Invoking the Glorious War: Framing the Persian Gulf Conflict through Directive Language," *Southern Communication Journal* 60.4 (1995): 292-302.

69. Entman, "Framing: Toward Clarification," 55.

70. Zhongdang Pan and Gerald M. Kosicki, "Framing Analysis: An Approach to News Discourse," *Political Communication* 10.1 (1993): 55-75.

71. Pan and Kosicki, 59.

72. Pan and Kosicki, 61.

73. Pan and Kosicki, 62.

74. Pan and Kosicki, 64.

75. Pan and Kosicki, 65.

76. Robert M. Entman, "Framing U.S. Coverage of International News: Contrasts in Narratives of the KAL and Iran Air Incidents," *Journal of Communication* 41.4 (1991): 6-27.

77. Entman, "Framing U.S. Coverage," 7.

78. Entman, "Framing U.S. Coverage," 7.

79. Entman, "Framing U.S. Coverage," 7.

80. Entman, "Framing U.S. Coverage," 21.

81. Entman, "Framing U.S. Coverage," 8.

82. Nacos, *The Press, Presidents, and Crises.*

83. Nacos, 8.

84. This view is commensurate with that found in Robert M. Entman, *Democracy without Citizens: Media and the Decay of American Politics* (New York: Oxford University Press, 1989). See also, Robert M. Entman and Andrew Rojecki, "Freezing Out the Public: Elite and Media Framing of the U.S. Anti-Nuclear Movement," *Political Communication* 10.2 (1993): 155-173.

85. Nacos, 183, 184.

86. Kern, Levering, and Levering, 195.

87. Murray Edelman, *Politics as Symbolic Action* (Chicago: Markham, 1971), 55.

88. Entman, "Framing: Toward Clarification," 56.

89. The primary documents of concern will be those containing comments made by the president; secondary sources will also be examined, notably those made by administration officials. Many of the comments made are in the form of press conferences. This study will not examine the interaction of the president and press during a press conference. The focus will be on what the president or administration official actually said and what the press reported was said and how the press response is framed. For those readers interested in the rhetorical dynamics of presidential press conferences, see Carolyn Smith, *Presidential Press Conferences* (New York: Praeger, 1990).

90. For all three case studies, I analyze all relevant news items in the political sections of the *New York Times* and the *Washington Post*. These generally appear

in section A. These news items included editorials. Excluded were stories appearing in other sections of the paper such as the magazine section, travel, sports, and so on. These two papers were chosen because they "are the foremost leaders and agenda setters for the rest of the print and electronic news media and that they influence the news judgment of other news organizations heavily. These newspapers are most widely read by the Washington community of political elites and are recognized as intragovernmental means of communication" (Nacos, 12). See, too, Michael Baruch Grossman and Martha Joynt Kumar, *Portraying the President* (Baltimore: Johns Hopkins University Press, 1981); Ben H. Bagdikian, *The Effete Conspiracy* (New York: Harper & Row, 1972); and Kern, Levering, and Levering, who describe the *New York Times* and the *Washington Post* as "politically significant papers that had substantial national impact [during the Kennedy administration and today]" (13). I am especially indebted to the excellent study by Nacos for insight into delimiting the nature of the news items employed for analysis.

91. These include all written, verbatim Clinton administration texts produced during the three periods. Since the focus in this study is domestic, the sources used were the *Weekly Compilation of Presidential Documents* and documents procured from the White House, Office of the Press Secretary, and the U.S. State Department.

Chapter 4

North Korea and Nuclear Nonproliferation

In February 1993, North Korea refused to allow representatives from the International Atomic Energy Agency (IAEA) to inspect its nuclear sites suspected of concealing materials that could be part of a covert operation to develop nuclear weapons. On 12 March 1993, North Korea, responding to IAEA demands for access to the suspect sites, announced its decision to withdraw from the international nuclear nonproliferation regime (Npt). Within a week, both North and South Korea had placed their militaries on alert. This was an event of special importance to the security and interests of the United States, for North Korea represented the last vestige of Cold War fronts. Indeed, the demilitarized zone separating North and South Korea spans some 150 miles. North Korea possesses one of the largest standing army in the world, some 1.1 million soldiers—and a full two thirds are reported as being stationed within 60 miles of the demilitarized zone that divides the Korean peninsula. These troops are positioned against approximately 650,000 South Korean and 35,000 U.S. troops.[1] The possibility of North Korea using its military, let alone developing nuclear weapons, is of immediate importance to the United States; furthermore, nuclear nonproliferation was of early stated importance to the Clinton administration. Nevertheless, in stark contrast to the importance of this event and the possible negative consequences of it not being successfully resolved, the reactions of both the press and the Clinton administration appear surprisingly laconic. Indeed, this incident received little attention in the press and even fewer public comments from the Clinton administration.

In this chapter, I will examine the public utterances of the White House from 12 March 1993 through 12 June 1993. I will then examine the press response to the administrative utterances. Finally, I will summarize how the Clinton administration and the press framed the North Korean situation.

INITIAL WHITE HOUSE FRAME

During a White House press briefing on 15 March 1993, Dee Dee Myers was asked about the situation concerning North Korea's announced withdrawal from the Npt. Myers responded that "it's quite serious, and obviously, the administration is very unhappy with that decision by North Korea, and we'll work toward getting them to agree to nuclear inspections again."[2] Later that same day, George Stephanopoulos held a press briefing in which the first question asked concerned the situation in North Korea. Stephanopoulos replied, "[I]t's a situation of great concern to the President and the entire administration. We're watching it very closely."[3] During a press conference that same day, President Clinton spoke about North Korea's announced withdrawal from the Npt. The potential gravity of the situation was not underscored, nor was any sense of urgency imparted. The president expressed "concern" and "disappointment," especially in light of the progress made by North and South Korea in the areas of commerce, communication, and contact. However, the president did make it clear that the United States "simply cannot back up on the determination to have the IAEA inspections proceed there."[4]

Even in the face of direct questions from the White House press corps, the administration's calm was apparent. For example, on 16 March 1993, one reporter asked: In light of alleged reports that North Korea may have developed missles that could hit Japan, is "it acceptable to the United States for North Korea to have nuclear weapons?" Myers's answer relayed only that which had been stated before by White House officials: "I think we are hopeful that they would continue to abide by the terms of the nonproliferation treaty, and we'll do everything we can to get them to agree to reenter the terms of the treaty."[5] Thus, with North and South Korean troops on alert, North Korea beginning its withdrawal from the Npt and strongly suspected of building a nuclear bomb, and the very real possibility of an Asian nuclear arms race, the Clinton administration managed to convey a calm and deliberate manner. Moreover, it publicly imparted no substantial information about the incident to the media.

INITIAL PRESS RESPONSE

The *New York Times* and *Washington Post* published few articles detailing North Korea's decision to refuse IAEA inspections and to withdraw from the Npt. However, those articles published report North Korea's refusals in a manner that heightened the potential negative consequences of the withdrawal. For example, the *Washington Post* reported that North Korea's refusal "may lead to a confrontation with widespread repercussions in Asia."[6] The *New York Times* reported that Central Intelligence Agency (CIA) Director R. James Woolsey (Bush administration) believed that "North Korea has made enough material for at least one nuclear weapon but is hiding the production from international inspectors."[7] Woolsey was further quoted as stating that North Korea is the U.S. government's "most grave current concern."[8]

One might well expect, given the importance of the nonproliferation issue, a great deal of discussion after North Korea announced that it would withdraw from the nonproliferation treaty. Such was not the case, however. It has already been noted that the Clinton administration publicly commented little on this matter, and the press followed suit. Indeed, during the week following North Korea's announcement, the *New York Times* published only ten articles (two of which were editorials) and the *Washington Post* published four news articles.[9] However, the papers did report the event, and the initial reporting was somewhat similar for each paper. The *Washington Post* basically framed the event as a confrontation between the North Korean government and the IAEA. Both "sides" were given detailed coverage of their respective assertions. The *New York Times* attempted to cover the major aspects of the withdrawal but with heavy reliance upon South Korean sources. However, in marked contrast to the *Washington Post*, the *New York Times* attempted to invest the North Korean action with some degree of drama: "The abrupt decision [of the North Koreans to withdraw], which took American officials in Asia by surprise, adds urgency to the Clinton Administration's biggest security challenge in the region."[10] Also, "Expressing alarm at North Korean defiance, the United States sought allied agreement today [on taking action against North Korea]."[11] The act of withdrawal was described as a "surprise," as "unnerving," and as "alarming."[12]

Of note, however, was that no sources were provided for these "alarming" assertions. Furthermore, very few direct administrative quotes were included in these initial reports. Those source quotations included did report what the administrative texts demonstrated—that the White House had little to say publicly: "'We are monitoring the situation carefully and have no further comment.'" For the most part, however, hearsay was the standard reportorial practice during this time: "In recent weeks, American officials have conceded they have little leverage over North Korea. The country is already deeply isolated, so economic sanctions would have little impact."[13] The earliest *New York Times* editorial also makes a sourceless assertion: "Pyongyang's pullout from the nonproliferation treaty raises the nuclear nightmare anew."[14] These statements, so often ascribed to "administrative officials," are not reflected in the administration's public utterances. Throughout the incident, the majority of reports were ascribed to "U.S. officials," "U.S. sources," and "Clinton administration sources." There were very few specific sources provided for quotes and extremely few direct references to White House statements.

In addition to the media-generated drama of the confrontation between the two parties, the *Washington Post* and the *New York Times* engaged in speculation about the motives behind North Korea's withdrawal. A plethora of different views from concerned parties was presented here: Japanese officials, IAEA officials, U.S. officials, and UN officials all had their stories to tell. The result of this speculative collage of various sources was a media-created picture of "tense and confusing" days, an alarmed United States and a fearful Asia.[15] Indeed, the speculative reasons provided for North Korea's withdrawal were highlighted in great detail: One, the Koreans had built or were close to building a bomb; two, it was a gambit to test the reactions of two new presidents: Kim Young Sam (South Korea) and Bill Clinton; three, it was the result of political maneuvers as part of an internal power struggle; four, it was a deliberate effort to generate an international crisis to draw attention away from North Korea's domestic economic problems; and five, it was a genuine protest over U.S.-South Korea war games.[16] Along these same lines, possible reactions to North Korea's action were also allowed the full range of speculation. For example, the UN Security Council was reported as stating that it could retaliate in three ways: one, with "strong public statements"; two, with "economic sanctions"; or three, with "U.N. sponsored military actions."[17] With speculations in place, the *Washington Post* assumed the mind of the President, stating that it was "difficult for a president to know what to do."

The *New York Times* initially placed a heavy reliance upon South Korean reports of North Korean actions, as well as reactions to U.S. diplomatic activity. South Korea was reported as having placed its troops on alert, halting all economic investment in North Korea, and asking China to intervene and pressure North Korea to rejoin the nonproliferation treaty. However, the South Korea actions were relayed in such a manner as to minimize the potential negative impact of the moves. For example, the South Koreans were quoted as saying,

"'We never want North Korea to be isolated internationally, nor do we want to inflict suffering on them.'"[18] Even the impact of South Korea's military alert was minimized: "Military alerts for South Korea's 650,000 troops are relatively common."[19] In contrast to the confusing but subdued account provided by "news" articles, an editorial for the *New York Times* painted a very different picture: "North Korea Trifles with Doomsday" and "for the past few days Pyongyang has been flirting with diplomatic suicide and scaring a lot of people."[20] This particular editorial called for sanctions if diplomacy failed.[21] A later *New York Times* editorial took the same approach and stated that North Korea was in "defiance of the world" and that because "America, as a Pacific power, still needs to play a central role in keeping Asian peace," the Clinton administration should have "strong encouragement in taking on a more active, constructive role" in moving toward collective security agreements in Asia.[22]

Throughout the first few days, one finds examples of analysis mixed with news reports, although this was limited in most cases to the *New York Times*. For example, this *New York Times* account: "For the United States . . . the announced withdrawal from the accord represents a substantial setback. It followed North Korea's abrupt refusal this year to allow inspections of two secret sites."[23] An earlier *New York Times* editorial engaged in the same type of analysis when it reported that the North Koreans had placed their troops on alert and withdrew from the Npt in reaction to U.S. and South Korea joint military exercises. It then went on to say: "The Team Spirit exercises are not needed to reassure Seoul of Washington's rock-solid commitment to its defense."[24]

CONTINUATION OF THE ADMINISTRATION'S FRAME

On 24 March 1993, Dan Rather asked President Clinton the following question: "North Korea, nuclear proliferation: one of those things people's eyes glaze over. Important of course, but is it something that consumes a lot of your time?"[25] The President responded that it was a "very sad and troubling development" but that he did not "want to overreact to it."[26] The president chose, instead, to highlight the recent warming of relations between North and South Korea and to suggest that reunification had entered the minds of many Koreans. Furthermore, the North Koreans still had two months to change their minds. (A three-month waiting period was granted to any member state wishing to leave the nuclear nonproliferation regime.)

The same day, George Stephanopoulos was asked about China's opposition to UN action against North Korea to force compliance with the Npt protocol. Stephanopoulos included in his reply that the administration had asked China to use its influence with North Korea to coax them back into the nonproliferation regime: "We understand China's position. They think that the best way to achieve this goal is through patient diplomacy rather than sanctions, and we're in touch with them and have urged them to use their influence with North Korea to change its mind about withdrawing from the Npt and to comply fully with the nonproliferation obligations."[27] Administrative utterances were consistent throughout the remainder of the month of March. The administration portrayed itself as concerned but hopeful and as considering asking the UN Security Council to impose sanctions. However, little was said about the situation, and no details were provided concerning what actions were being taken.

CONTINUATION OF THE PRESS FRAME

Throughout March and into early April, the frames of the press gradually expanded. Both the *New York Times* and the *Washington Post* increased the inclusion of analysis in news stories, and the *Washington Post* engaged in derogation of the North Korean government. For example, North Korea was depicted as a "Third World state that is still primitive"; its government was said to "actually [work] more like a cult than a country"; and its "government [uses] its captive media to put out endless statements that sound like bad parodies of communist propaganda at the height of the Cold War."[28]

The mild attempt at drama building continued as well, although the bulk of this type of reporting was confined to the *New York Times*. Drama building usually took the form of more or less benign literary description: "a major blow to international efforts," a "menacing nuclear challenge," "the international equivalent of a Stephen King horror plot," "a nightmare," and "a last ditch effort."[29] Although few in number, the *Washington Post* used such literary flourishes as well: "alarmed the United States and aroused new fears . . . in Asia" and "a tense and confusing day on the Korean Peninsula."[30] These dramatic embellishments were primarily employed early in the event. Near the end of March, articles exhibited a more composed nature, even to the point of one article stating, "[T]he initial air of crisis surrounding the withdrawal has partially calmed."[31]

Analysis, speculation, and hearsay were all regular features of articles during March, especially those contained in the *New York Times*. For example: "China may be applying quiet pressure on North Korea"; China's foreign minister's "opposition to international pressure on North Korea is almost certainly linked to China's discomfort with the idea that international bodies can tell sovereign nations what they can and cannot do."[32] Subtle examples existed as well: "Taking a more conciliatory line than the United States has, a top South Korean official said today . . ."[33] More obvious examples existed as well: "In the clearest signal yet that North Korea is in the midst of a transition of power during its nuclear standoff with the West . . . the son and heir apparent of the nation's founder . . . had been appointed chairman of the National Defense Committee."[34] Editorial hearsay also existed: "Some in Washington are urging more forceful steps [against North Korea]. But attacking Iraq's nuclear facilities failed to put it out of the bomb making business."[35] An opinion piece by a staff reporter exhibited the same type of speculation contained within news articles: "The fact that North Korea has proceeded this far with its nuclear weapons project, despite Chinese opposition, is an indication of China's limited leverage over the Kim family."[36] Although the *Washington Post* had few instances of rank speculation, they were still apparent: "Whatever North Korea's reasons for rebuffing the nuclear agency inspectors, it is not going to be easy to punish Pyongyang for its move. The nation is so isolated already that economic sanction will not make an enormous difference. That leaves two other approaches to gain access for nuclear inspectors: the route of diplomacy and the tougher option, military action."[37]

Still peculiar to the *Washington Post* was the framing of the event as a confrontation between the IAEA and North Korea. In fact, specific strategies used by the IAEA to "confront" North Korea were often relayed. Indeed, one article went so far as to describe the confrontations as a game of hide-and-seek: "North Korea was hiding something; the IAEA was searching for it; and Washington was standing on the sidelines letting inspectors know when they were getting warm or cold."[38]

THE ADMINISTRATION'S FRAME AND MFN TRADE STATUS FOR CHINA

The administration's framing of the situation with North Korea was well established by mid-April 1993. Any utterances made were essentially a continuation of the earliest public statements. However, the question of China's influence with North Korea had been raised by the press, and now the administration had to contend with the relationship of renewal of Most Favored Nation (MFN) trade status for China and China's political influence over North Korea. The initial administrative framing elements can be traced back as far as then-candidate Clinton's statements about the Bush administration renewal of MFN for China in 1992. On 3 June 1992, candidate-Clinton released a statement critical of the Bush administration's handling of China's MFN renewal. The statement was especially critical of President Bush's decision not to impose penalties for China's alleged violation of Western standards of human rights: "[R]ather than leading an international effort to pressure the Chinese government, the Bush administration has coddled the regime, pleading for progress [in the area of human rights] but failing to impose penalties for intransigence."[39]

It was shortly after Clinton assumed office that China's MFN status became a subject of press interest. During a 26 February 1993 press briefing, George Stephanopoulos was asked about MFN for China. The secretary replied that the United States would "go forward with renewal subject to conditions—on improvements in human rights and respect for democracy in China."[40] Stephanopoulos reiterated at a later press briefing that President Clinton's approach would be the same as that stated in the presidential campaign—there would be conditions on the renewal of MFN: "The President believes that we should extend [MFN] subject to conditions on progress in human rights and opening up toward democracy and release of political prisoners."[41] The relationship of MFN renewal and China's influence over North Korea remained in the background until 8 April 1993, when the administration was asked about China's possible influence over North Korea and whether or not the administration was asking China to help influence North Korea. State Department spokesman Richard Boucher reiterated the administration's position that missile proliferation was an important concern and went on to say, "I'll see if we can give you some sort of listing [of countries that have influence over North Korea] and tell you if it includes China."[42] However, on 16 April 1993, the administration was again confronted with this sensitive issue: "Was China perhaps one of those countries that Clinton seemed to refer to on the issue of North Korea, possible influence on North Korea with the Npt?"[43] The administration's response was characteristically brief but also included the first admission that China was playing a role in the matter: "China is an important player."[44] Be that as it may, on 26 May 1993, George Stephanopoulos stated that the administration was going to make certain that "we have the toughest conditions ever imposed [on China for renewal of MFN]."[45] However, the reasoning of the *New York Times* on this matter was somewhat different: "Senior administration officials say they have little options but to seek Chinese help. But other Government officials have expressed concern that relying on Beijing to help cajole Pyongyang could cause the White House to feel obligated to reward China by expanding trade, despite widespread criticism of its human rights record."[46]

Throughout April and early May, the administration said little about North Korea. However, there was talk about MFN for China. The administration was consistent in stating that MFN for China would be linked to progress in human rights. Yet this was never a definitive statement. For example, George Stephanopolous stated that "the general approach of conditioning MFN to progress towards human rights and democracy is something the President is consistently supporting."[47] Indeed, as May approached, the White House seemed to highlight conditionality in the few statements made about China and MFN: "[T]he President . . . continues to support the idea of conditionality and will continue to demand progress from China on human rights and other issues before he approves MFN."[48] By 5 May 1993 the situation with North Korea had all but faded from public view. Although no resolution to the crisis had been achieved, there was minimal progress to report upon. When asked about the "status" of North Korea and its nuclear program, administration officials were rather quiescent, as this reply of George Stephanopoulos illustrates: "I don't have any new update on that today. I can take the question and see if there's been any change in the situation."[49]

The end of May revealed the unconditional renewal of China's MFN status. Conditions were, however, attached to the following year's renewal review. The president's basic argument for such an approach was that denying MFN would not facilitate progress in human rights in China. In short, President Clinton "concluded that the public interest would be served by a continuation of the waiver of the application of [certain sections of the Trade Act of 1974] on China's MFN status for an additional 12 months with renewal thereafter subject to . . . conditions."[50] The administration's justification for the continuation of MFN was linked to China's recent "significant progress" in the areas of human rights, prison labor reform, and emigration reform.[51] Assistant Secretary of State Winston Lord stated that the President's MFN policy was a "fulfillment of [Clinton's] campaign promise."[52] However, all of the noted advancements were made under the Bush administration, which had never linked MFN with progress in the areas highlighted by Lord. This fact was noticed by a member of the press during the Lord press briefing: "[T]his sounds a lot like President Bush's argument for not wanting to sign bills imposing conditions on China. What's the real difference, you know, 12 months before the deadline [for compliance]?"[53] The exchange is interesting in that the press contended that there were no conditions, and Lord asserted that there were conditions placed upon MFN for China. At this point, however, the facts were simply this: China had its MFN status renewed for one year, subject to conditions for renewal the following year. The secretary of state would be required to determine if progress had been made in the specified areas and then give his recommendation to the president.[54] Close on the heels of the renewal of China's MFN status came this 11

June 1993 presidential statement: North Korea had agreed not to withdraw from the Nonproliferation Treaty.

THE PRESS REPLY

From late March through early June 1993 the press said much about China's possible influence over North Korea. As early as 26 March 1993 the *New York Times* linked renewal of China's MFN and its willingness to help bring North Korea back into the Npt family: "As a permanent member of the [UN] Security Council, China has veto power over any United Nations sanctions."[55] In an opinion piece, the *New York Times* clearly linked MFN status with helping deter North Korea: "Since Beijing wants to preserve its most-favored nation trade status, the question is, Would it drop opposition to sanctions?"[56] On 30 March 1993 the White House was reported as seeking China's help, and this line of reporting continued throughout April and May. It was even reported that the White House was "pressing China . . . to persuade the [North Korean] Government to permit a 'special inspection' of two buildings [suspected of harboring illegal nuclear materials]."[57] On 9 May 1993 the *New York Times* reported what was heretofore only reported in opinion editorials: "At the request of China, State Department officials have met with North Korean diplomats, and further meetings are planned. Some American officials have expressed concern that if Washington increases its reliance on Beijing to put pressure on North Korea, the Clinton administration will have to ease its stand on China's human rights record and agree to expand trade."[58] This same connection was again made in a *New York Times* editorial the next day.

The *Washington Post* reported on the connection of MFN for China and China's influence with North Korea; however, it was limited to an opinion article in which the association was made quite clear.[59] Although the *New York Times* seemed to focus on China as a hinderance, the *Washington Post* reported that China was also involved in a manner consistent with UN efforts: "China, which has argued for moving slowly before punitive action against North Korea is considered, nonetheless made clear . . . its own opposition to any nuclear weapons effort on the Korean peninsula."[60] The *Washington Post* described President Clinton's decision concerning MFN for China in the following manner: "Clinton's decision amounted to a compromise between his tough campaign rhetoric and the economic realities of U.S. relations with the world's most populous country. Of the three potential MFN conditions, human rights had attracted the most support on Capitol Hill."[61]

The White House announcement that North Korea agreed not to withdraw from the Npt produced minimal press coverage. President Clinton's announcement was succinct and did not attempt to overstate his role in the matter. Indeed, the president merely stated that North Korea would not withdraw, that progress was being made, and that he was happy with the direction the negotiations were taking. The *Washington Post* described the administration's success in a subdued manner: "The accord removes the atmosphere of crisis surrounding the matter but without resolving a key issue that several months ago heightened . . . suspicions of North Korea's intentions and capability to produce a nuclear bomb."[62] The *New York Times* described the return of North Korea to the treaty in a similar manner: "The North Korean agreement to honor the treaty for a bit longer fell short of the complete acceptance demanded by the United States. American diplomats said the agreement was the best they could obtain, but warned that more pressure would be necessary before North Korea opens sensitive sites to international inspectors."[63]

SUMMARY

White House Frames

The Clinton administration was laconic concerning the North Korean incident. However, even in dearth there existed the beginning of framing devices. First, the administration helped to facilitate an atmosphere of calm by the very lack of information it conveyed to the public. Statements made by administration officials were few and were usually brief and bereft of any detailed information concerning U.S. or North Korean actions. Those statements made by President Clinton were also brief, yet the focus was slightly different than statements made by his officials. President Clinton often stressed the improvement in the relationship between North and South Korea and how he hoped this could continue. Calm reconciliation, not nuclear confrontation, was an implied administrative frame.

Another administrative frame can be summed up with the simple statement: The United States "cannot back up on determination to have . . . IAEA inspections [in North Korea]."[64] This simple declarative statement often served as explanation for U.S. actions that were neither detailed nor explained. What did emerge was a three-part stance that carried the administration to the conclusion of the confrontation. First, the administration was committed to seeing that North Korea abided by the terms of the Npt. Second, the administration wanted international pressure and was not interested in working alone. Department of State spokesman David Boucher stated that the Clinton administration had "consistently said that the issue is between North Korea and the international community. Our task is to support the efforts of the appropriate international bodies as they work to resolve the situation."[65] Finally, the administration consistently stressed that it was working to keep North Korea in the treaty in conjunction with international efforts but that no new information was available to give to the public. This 3 May 1993 statement by State Department spokesman Joe Snyder is illustrative of a common response: "As we've said all along, we think that North Korea ought to reconsider its decision to withdraw from the NPT and its cooperation with the IAEA. There is a date coming up [the end of the three month waiting period for final withdrawal], and we hope that the North Koreans will reconsider and change their minds on that."[66]

The third framing device that emerged concerns the administration's view of the role that China played in the incident. The administration was slow to publicly recognize China's importance, but when it finally did, it was done in a brief yet clear manner: "China is an important player"on the international scene. Although seemingly reluctant to announce it, the administration did state that it had sought help from China in attempting to convince North Korea to return to the Npt. When discussing China, the administration was careful not to allow its request for Chinese assistance and the issue of MFN to intermingle. For the administration, the questions of MFN and asking for Chinese help with North Korea were two separate events.

The Press Framing of Administrative Utterances

The press framed the situation with North Korea differently than the administration had. Although what little was said by the administration was reported, the overall feeling imparted was different than that imparted when viewing only administrative statements. Both the *New York Times* and the *Washington Post* shared one framing element but possessed framing elements peculiar to each individual paper as well. In addition, both papers exhibited two general strategies—as opposed to developed frames—for reporting on the situation.

The primary framing element shared by both papers was to view China both as a hindrance and as a help. This is to say, China was viewed as hindering the efforts of the United States and United Nations because it wanted to employ diplomacy, not sanctions, and threatened to use its Security Council veto if sanctions were sought against North Korea. To be fair, this line of reasoning was blatant early on in the incident, and later China's possible veto was usually implied by the press; this was especially true after China announced its opposition to a nuclearized Korean peninsula. China was viewed as a help in that it was the only nation politically close enough to North Korea to have an influence. Following the initial disclosure of the North Korean withdrawal, it was often pointed out by the press that the White House would seek Chinese help. Later, it was reported that the White House had sought Chinese help. There were several instances of the media linking this help with renewal of China's MFN in the coming year, but no connection was made to White House sources in order to substantiate this claim beyond speculation.

The *Washington Post* used a unique framing strategy in its coverage of the situation. The event was often depicted as a confrontation between North Korea and the IAEA. Many of the stories published, especially during the first weeks of the incident, detailed the investigations of the IAEA and also the North Korean response to the findings of the investigations. The reporting was generally balanced, with North Korea's position being presented side by side with that provided by the IAEA.

Particular to the *New York Times* were two framing strategies. Although the first was evident to a limited degree in the *Washington Post*, it was generally the *New York Times* that most frequently employed it. This framing device consisted of investing the situation with drama and highlighting the nature of possible repercussions of North Korean actions. This, however, did not last long, and by the end of the third week following the North Korean announcement, this framing device had all but vanished from view. The second device involved an extreme focus on South Korean reactions. The *New York Times* used a great deal of South Korean sources, thereby removing the situation from the American homeland. This strategy of using South Korean sources continued throughout the incident and was reflected in the large number of non-U.S. sources used by the *New York Times*.

One of two general reportorial strategies employed by both papers involved the noticeable use of anonymous sources. This was especially true of the *New York Times*. Both papers relied heavily on "U.S. officials," "unnamed officials," "White House sources," "administration sources," and even simply "sources." The extreme reliance on anonymous sources may be linked with the second general reportorial strategy, the use of speculation. Both papers included broad speculation, analysis, and hearsay in their regular news stories. Of fifty-five articles used for this case study, only five were editorials, and no stories were labeled as "news analysis." Yet as the above examples have shown, there were numerous instances of reporters engaging in speculation, analysis, and at times, hearsay—and this often with ascription only to "sources."

NOTES

1. The total investment of U.S. military personnel during 1993 has been listed as high as 73,000, with an estimated annual maintenance cost of $2 billion. See R. Jeffrey Smith, "North Korea's Strongman: Canny or 'Crazy'?" *Washington Post National Weekly Edition* 4-10 October 1993: 18.

2. White House, Office of the Press Secretary, "Press Briefing by Dee Dee Myers" (15 March 1993): 9.

3. White House, Office of the Press Secretary, "Press Briefing by George Stephanopoulos" (15 March 1993): 1.

4. U.S. Department of State, "The President's News Conference with Prime Minister Yitzhack Rabin of Israel (March 15, 1993)," *Weekly Compilation of Presidential Documents* 29 (22 March 1993): 436.

5. White House, Office of the Press Secretary, "Press Briefing by Dee Dee Myers" (16 March 1993), 4.

6. Don Oberdorfer, "Nuclear Inspectors to Demand Access to N. Korea Sites," *Washington Post* 11 February 1993: A31.

7. Douglas Jehl, "U.S. Outlines Concerns over North Korean A-Arms," *New York Times* 25 February 1993: A7.

8. Jehl, "U.S. Outlines Concerns," A7.

9. From 1 February 1993 to 13 June 1993 the *New York Times* published a total of forty-four articles and the *Washington Post* published a total of twenty-three. Figures found in *The Washington Post Index 1993*, Vol. 5 (Ann Arbor, MI: UMI, 1994); and the *New York Times Index 1993*, Vol. 81 (New York: New York Times Company, 1994).

10. David E. Sanger, "North Korea, Fighting Inspection, Renounces Nuclear Arms Treaty," *New York Times* 12 March 1993: A1.

11. Douglas Jehl, "U.S. Seeking U.N. Pressure to Compel North Korea to Honor Treaty," *New York Times* 13 March 1993: A3.

12. Sanger, "North Korea, Fighting Inspection," A1; Jehl, "U.S. Seeking U.N. Pressure," A3; David E. Sanger, "The Nonproliferation Treaty Bares Its Toothlessness," *New York Times* 14 March 1993: E18.

13. Sanger, "North Korea, Fighting Inspection," A8.

14. "The Korean Peninsula Heats Up," Editorial, *New York Times* 12 March 1993: A28.

15. R. Jeffrey Smith, "N. Korea Quitting Arms Pact," *Washington Post* 12 March 1993: A16; R. Jeffrey Smith, "U.S. Denounces N. Korea for Quitting Nuclear Pact," *Washington Post* 13 March 1993: A1; T. R. Reid, "Overtures Made to N. Korea," *Washington Post* 17 March 1993: A25.

16. See, for example, David E. Sanger, "West Knew of North Korea Nuclear Development," *New York Times* 13 March 1993: A3.

17. Don Oberdorfer, "U.S. Steps Up Pressure on N. Korea," *Washington Post* 18 March 1993: A33.

18. David E. Sanger, "North Korea Hit by First Sanctions," *New York Times* 16 March 1993: A3.

19. David E. Sanger, "Citing Caution, South Korea Puts Troops on Alert," *New*

York Times 14 March 1993: A6.

20. "North Korea Trifles with Doomsday," Editorial, *New York Times* 16 March 1993: A20.

21. Of note is that on this same day a guest editorial called for an even tougher approach to dealing with North Korea: "[T]ry to take out its [North Korea] nuclear weapons capacity as the Israelis did to the Iraqis in 1981." See A. M. Rosenthal, "Facing the Risks," *New York Times* 16 March 1993: A21.

22. "Old Alliances, New Asia," Editorial, *New York Times* 19 March 1993: A28.

23. Jehl, "U.S. Seeking U.N. Pressure," A3. Of interest here is the implication that not having North Korea in the nonproliferation regime is of such grave concern. As of 1993 three other nations suspected of having nuclear weapons had not even joined the regime: Pakistan, India, and Israel.

24. "The Korean Peninsula Heats Up," A28.

25. U.S. Department of State, "Interview with Dan Rather of CBS News," *Weekly Compilation of Presidential Documents* 29 (29 March 1993): 484.

26. U.S. Department of State, "Interview with Dan Rather," 484.

27. White House, Office of the Press Secretary, "Press Briefing by George Stephanopoulos" (24 March 1993): 15.

28. T. R. Reid, "North Korea's New Nuclear Deadline Nears," *Washington Post* 30 March 1993: A16.

29. Nicholas D. Kristof, "China Opposes U.N. over North Korea," *New York Times* 24 March 1993: A10; David E. Sanger, "Neighbors Differ on How to Chasten North Korea," *New York Times* 31 March 1993: A9; Nicholas D. Kristof, "China and North Korea: Not-So-Best of Friends," *New York Times* 11 April 1993: E4; Douglas Jehl, "U.S. and North Koreans Press Nuclear Talks," *New York Times* 11 June 1993: A9.

30. Smith, "U.S. Denounces N. Korea," A1; Reid, "Overtures Made to N. Korea," A25.

31. Reid, "North Korea's New," A14.

32. Kristof, "China Opposes," A10.

33. Douglas Jehl, "Seoul Eases Stand on Nuclear Inspections of North," *New York Times* 30 March 1993: A13.

34. David E. Sanger, "North Korean Chief's Son Gains Military Post," *New York Times* 10 April 1993: A4.

35. "In North Korea, Try Diplomacy First," Editorial, *New York Times* 8 April 1993: A20.

36. Kristof, "China and North Korea," E4.

37. Reid, "North Korea's New," A16.

38. R. Jeffrey Smith, "N. Korea and the Bomb: High-Tech Hide-and-Seek," *Washington Post* 27 April 1993: A11. The analogy was ascribed to an anonymous White House official.

39. Bill Clinton, "Statement on China," 3 June 1992 (Press Release: Clinton for President). Available from Internet [Gopher] north america/politics/clinton/china

40. White House, Office of the Press Secretary, "Press Briefing by George

Stephanopoulos" (26 February 1993): 12.

41. White House, Office of the Press Secretary, "Press Briefing by George Stephanopoulos" (4 March 1993): 18.

42. Department of State, Office of the Spokesman, Daily Press Briefing: DPC#50 (8 April 1993): 10.

43. White House, Office of the Press Secretary, "Background Briefing by Senior Administration Official" (16 April 1993): 10.

44. White House, Office of the Press Secretary, "Background Briefing by Senior Administration Official," 10. See, too, U.S. Department of State, "The President's News Conference with Prime Minister Kiichi Miyazawa of Japan," *Weekly Compilation of Presidential Documents* 29 (19 April 1993): 602.

45. White House, Office of the Press Secretary, "Press Briefing by George Stephanopoulos" (26 May 1993): 7. This statement, however, should not be overstressed. No presidential administration had ever before imposed conditions on China's MFN renewal, thus rendering this statement's force anemic. On the other hand, that conditions would be imposed at all signaled a new direction in China policy.

46. Douglas Jehl, "U.S. Agrees to Discuss Arms Directly with North Korea," *New York Times* 23 April 1993: A10.

47. White House, Office of the Press Secretary, "Press Briefing by George Stephanopoulos" (22 April 1993): 13.

48. White House, Office of the Press Secretary, "Press Briefing by George Stephanopoulos" (27 April 1993): 9.

49. White House, Office of the Press Secretary, "Press Briefing by George Stephanopoulos" (5 May 1993): 7.

50. White House, Office of the Press Secretary, "Executive Order #12850" (28 May 1993): 1-2.

51. White House, Office of the Press Secretary, "Statement by the President on Most Favored Nation Status for China" (28 May 1993). See also White House, Office of the Press Secretary, "Report to Congress Concerning Extension of Waiver Authority for the People's Republic of China" (28 May 1993).

52. White House, Office of the Press Secretary, "Press Briefing by Assistant Secretary Winston Lord" (28 May 1993): 1.

53. White House, Office of the Press Secretary, "Press Briefing by Assistant Secretary Winston Lord," 3.

54. U.S. relations with China being what they are, the president has found it difficult to do this. On 10 July 1996 National Public Radio reported that the Clinton administration had renewed China's MFN status for another year with no conditions attached.

55. "Sanctions on North Korea May Get Tighter," *New York Times* 26 March 1993: A13.

56. William J. Taylor, "Cool Off Korean Tension," *New York Times* 27 March 1993: A21.

57. David E. Sanger, "North Korea Stirs New A-Arms Fears," *New York Times* 6 May 1993: A16.

58. Frank J. Prial, "U. N. Weighs Plea to North Korea," *New York Times* 9 May

1993: A12.

59. Jim Hoagland, "China Policy: Back to Bush?" *Washington Post* 1 April 1993: A23.

60. R. Jeffrey Smith, "N. Korea Censure Seen as Turning Point in Arms Control," *Washington Post* 7 April 1993: A23.

61. Daniel Williams and R. Jeffrey Smith, "Clinton to Extend China Trade Status," *Washington Post* 28 May 1993: A34.

62. R. Jeffrey Smith, "N. Korea Won't Quit Nuclear Ban Treaty," *Washington Post* 12 June 1993: A1.

63. Douglas Jehl, "North Korea Says It Won't Pull Out of Arms Pact Now," *New York Times* 12 June 1993: A1.

64. U.S. Department of State, "The President's News Conference with Prime Minister Yitzhack Rabin," 436.

65. U.S. Department of State, Office of the Spokesman, "Daily Press Briefing: DPC#58" (22 April 1993): 6.

66. U.S. Department of State, Office of the Spokesman, "Daily Press Briefing: DPC#64" (3 May 1993): 7.

Chapter 5

The Bosnian Crisis: 21 November 1995 to 15 December 1995

The conflict in Bosnia-Herzegovina had been ongoing for approximately three and one-half years when President Clinton announced that he would be sending U.S. troops to the former Yugoslavia as part of a NATO peacekeeping effort. The crisis in Bosnia had heretofore been just that, a crisis in Bosnia; it had been but background noise in the daily lives of most Americans. However, with President Clinton's announcement, it became consequential in the minds of Americans and a crisis for his administration. Reflected in the U.S. Senate and House of Representatives was the divided national opinion concerning U.S. involvement. The most important exigency faced by the President was to gain national and congressional approval for commitment of U.S. troops to promote the budding Bosnian peace. This was especially important since his administration had committed not only to the Bosnians but also to America's European allies, NATO, and even Russia. The credibility of the Clinton administration and the United States was on the line. The Clinton administration had forged the Bosnian peace, and now it had to convince the American public that this peace was worth the possible loss of American lives.

Although the history of the Bosnian conflict is extremely complex, some key events are important to keep in mind when reading the press responses to the administration's utterances on the event. The roots of the conflict in the former Yugoslavia began in June 1991 when Croatia and Slovenia proclaimed independence. In March 1992, Bosnian Muslims and Croats voted for independence from Yugoslavia. This action was not supported by Serbs living in Bosnia. In April 1992, after the European Union officially recognized Bosnia's independence, the Bosnian Serbs, with Serbia's support, declared war on the independence-minded Bosnian government. In January 1993, war broke out between Bosnian Muslims and Croats. At this time, then, a three-way civil war was raging in Bosnia. In March 1994 the Bosnian Muslims and Croats formed a Federation, thereby combining their forces against those of the Bosnian Serbs. In March 1995 Croatia entered the fray, siding with the Croats and Muslims. In October 1995 a cease-fire was negotiated between the Bosnian Serbs (the Bosnian Serb Republic) and the Muslim/Croat Federation (the Republic of Bosnia-Herzegovina). On 21 November 1995 a peace agreement was reached in Dayton, Ohio.

I do not intend to examine all of the intricate nuances of the conflict in Bosnia, nor do I intend to cover the full range of U.S. involvement. Instead, I will focus on a limited period of time: 21 November 1995 through 15 December 1995. This period covers the initial Clinton announcement of the peace plan and U.S. troop involvement and ends shortly after the congressional vote of support for U.S. troop deployment. The focus of this chapter will be on the public utterances of the Clinton administration and the press responses made during this important period and not on the conflict itself. Toward this end this chapter is divided into three sections. The first period of time to be examined will be 21 November 1995 through 28 November 1995. The second period examined will cover President Clinton's European visit, 29 November 1995 through 4 December 1995. The final period examined will be 5 December 1995 through 15 December 1995, two days after the congressional vote of approval.

PERIOD ONE: 21 NOVEMBER 1995 THROUGH 28 NOVEMBER 1995

Initial White House Frame

For several weeks in November 1995, President Slobodan Milosevic of Serbia, President Alija Izetbegovic of Bosnia-Herzegovina, President Franjo Tudjman of Croatia, and senior members of the U.S. Department of State met in Dayton, Ohio, to negotiate peace for the Balkans. On the morning of 21 November 1995 Presidents Milosevic, Tudjman, and Izetbegovic initialed a comprehensive peace plan—thereafter referred to by the administration as the Dayton Accord. President Clinton announced the Bosnia-Herzegovina peace agreement later this same day. In doing so, he initiated the frames for three key issues his administration would advance throughout the period leading up to congressional approval for the mission. These issues were composed of the peace plan, the mission, and U.S. leadership and values. Two other issues were framed later that day by the administration, the question of congressional support and Bosnian Serb resistance to the Dayton Accord, but these were entirely in response to press questions.

The President's Announcement. President Clinton declared the Dayton Accord as ending the "worst conflict in Europe since World War II."[1] The president was generous with his praise and explained that this peace was a result of the Bosnian, Croatian, and Serbian leaders listening to the will of their people; furthermore, it was a direct result of American, European, and Russian negotiation team involvement. The president listed the major components of the Accord and also highlighted that all three Presidents had asked for an international force to supervise the implementation of the peace plan. President Clinton also explained a key component of his argument for American troop involvement:

Only NATO can do that job. And the United States as NATO's leader must play an essential role in this mission. Without us, the hard-won peace would be lost, the war would resume, the slaughter of innocents would begin again, and the conflict that already has claimed so many people could spread like poison throughout the entire region.[2]

The NATO implementation force, one third of which would be composed of U.S. troops, was known as IFOR (Implementation Force). According to the president, the mission would be "clear and limited."

The mission itself constituted another of the initial subjects carefully framed by the president. The mission was very carefully described as possessing distinct goals and limited objectives; moreover, the administration emphasized that it was designed to pose the least possible risk to U.S. soldiers. Also stressed was that IFOR would be there to keep the peace, not stop the war. Indeed, much of future White House utterances to the subject of the mission can be traced to this initial Clinton announcement:

The NATO military mission will be clear and limited. Our troops will take their orders from the American general who commands NATO. They will have authority to meet any threat to their safety . . . with immediate and decisive force. And there will be a reasonable timetable for their withdrawal.

I am satisfied . . . that the risks to our troops are minimized.[3]

Although not detailed, the president did initiate the perception that the peace plan and the mission were linked with American values and interests: "Our leadership made this peace agreement possible. . . . Our values, our interests, and our leadership all over the world are at stake."[4]

The last issue for which the president initiated framing devices concerned congressional approval for the Bosnia mission. This issue was the topic of the one question allowed to be asked during the "Exchange with Reporters" section of the president's announcement of the Dayton Accord. The president responded that the Congress should have the time to review the peace agreement and that he had placed calls to the leaders of both parties and Houses of Congress. Essentially, Congress would be notified and given a chance to have its concerns heard. Indeed, President Clinton went so far as to say that a schedule for future consultations would be made and that "there would be no deployment until they [Congress] have a chance to be heard on this issue."[5]

Administration Officials Expand and Reiterate. These four issues were publicly reiterated in various forms three other times during this day. White House Press Secretary Mike McCurry stated that the president was committing the United States to the peace plan for the people of Bosnia. He also made a point of stating that the need to win the approval of Congress was a bipartisan issue; this is to say, that Congress as a whole needed to have a case made for full deployment. The administration wanted congressional support and was willing to brief and consult with congressional leaders on the issue. McCurry went beyond President Clinton's announcement in several areas, however. The president's constitutional authority as commander in chief was mentioned, as was a more detailed operational plan for the mission that would have President Clinton approving NATO plans twice before submitting them for final congressional approval.

McCurry brought up the issue of American leadership as well. According to the White House, the President had the authority as commander and chief to deploy the troops. Furthermore, it

also remains his very strong view that given the importance of this settlement to the people of the United States of America, given our interest in peace and security and stability throughout Europe, and given the importance of our long-lasting treaty commitments to our Nato allies, that the case for American participation in helping make this peace will be clear to the American people and, thus, also clear to the American Congress.[6]

Perhaps the best summary of the administration's framing of the issues may be found in Secretary of State Warren Christopher's remarks following the initialing of the peace accord. Christopher made two public appearances following the signing. During the first appearance he outlined the principles followed in drafting the peace agreement: a single Bosnian state; a unified federal government; free democratic elections; and strong guarantees of human rights.[7] Secretary Christopher's second appearance was with the presidents of Serbia, Croatia, and Bosnia-Herzegovina. During this public announcement, Secretary Christopher summarized the framing elements generated during this day well. His words merit careful reading since they contain the seeds of all future administrative framing elements concerning these issues:

Today's agreement certainly does not erase the stark memories of the past nor does it guarantee that the fabric of the society of Bosnia will be easily restored. But still, it is a victory for all of us.

It is a victory for people of every heritage in the former Yugoslavia. It offers tangible hope that there will be no more days of dodging bullets, no more winters of freshly dug graves, no more years of isolation from the outside world.

The agreement is a victory for all of those who believe in a multi-ethnic democracy in Bosnia-Herzegovina.

The agreement was a victory for all those in the world who believe that with determination a principled peace is possible.

But the victory achieved here will not be secure unless we all get to work to ensure that the promise of this moment is realized.

The United States and the international community will have to work hard to help them succeed. It is profoundly in our self-interest to do so.

As we move forward, we must be both realistic and clear-eyed. We should not assume that the people of the former Yugoslavia have resolved all of their historic differences. But we should also remember that we have now an opportunity to put behind them the horrors of the last four years. The war in Bosnia has been a challenge not only to our interests but to our values. By our leadership here, we have upheld both.[8]

Administrative Framing Continued. The days following the initial administrative utterances witnessed a reiteration of the four issues outlined by President Clinton and his officials and also a continuation of the particular manner in which they were framed. For example, on 22 November 1995, Department of State Spokesman Nicholas Burns reiterated the major points of the peace plan. After describing the technical aspects of the peace plan, which paralleled those given by Warren Christopher the day before, Burns provided important clues for how the administration viewed the Dayton Accord: "This peace agreement at Dayton doesn't solve all the problems of Bosnia-Herzegovina. It's not an ideal or perfect peace in any way. But then again no peace is. No peace can be. We had to deal with the situation as it was given to us and to the parties. What is most important is that we have stopped the war."[9]

A new issue emerged during discussion of the peace plan and was a direct response to media questions about Serbian resistance to implementation of the Dayton Accord. Nicholas Burns responded to these questions by highlighting that Serbian President Milosevic had initialed and committed for the Bosnian Serbs and that the war was not favoring the Bosnian Serbs at the time of the initialing of the agreement.[10] Burns also highlighted that the agreement had been initialed by the leaders of the Bosnian Serbs and that no organized resistance was expected. Negative comments were to be expected but were not to be construed as walking away from the agreement. As Burns later stated: "They [the Bosnian Serb leaders] had said formally they will comply with the Dayton Accords [sic]. We fully expect that will be the case."[11] Secretary Christopher later reiterated these points and stated that it would be normal to expect some complaints. Indeed, according to the secretary, the "situation in Dayton was really as difficult as I've ever seen it; the tensions were overt, really the hostility was very deep-seated—so it's not surprising when an agreement is reached, compromises are made, that some of the people in Bosnia are going to be unhappy about it."[12]

Descriptions of the mission continued as well, and like the statements about the peace plan, these utterances were well defined and consistent from day to day. Along with President Clinton, both Mike McCurry and Secretary Christopher spoke about the impending mission on 21 November 1995, but it was not until the following day that Nicholas Burns provided more than cursory details. Burns highlighted that this mission would be the greatest undertaking in NATO's history, then proceeded to detail various aspects of the mission. For example, concerns about U.S. troop safety were addressed: "As NATO draws up its military plans, it will do so in a way that will allow the NATO forces the capability to be able to push back and defend themselves in an aggressive way if they're challenged."[13] Even more details were provided by the president during his "Radio Address" to the nation on 25 November 1995. During this address, President Clinton announced that the United States would be sending approximately 20,000 troops to Bosnia—about one third of the anticipated force. The president described the mission as limited, achievable, and "the right thing to do"; in essence, it was the "responsibility [of the United States] to see this achievement through."[14] Two days later, during a formal "Address to the Nation," the president again detailed his conception of the mission and, in so doing, solidly set the framing elements that his administration would use to describe the mission for the next several weeks. The mission would be "precisely defined with clear, realistic goals that can be achieved in a definite period of time."[15] The president went on to say that the risk to U.S. troops would be "minimized" but that "no deployment of American troops is risk-free."[16] In short, the president attempted to demonstrate the care with which his administration was undertaking the plans; however, a pragmatic vein was opened in which truthful presentation of possible risk to U.S. soldiers was presented to the American people.

Closely linked to the mission was the issue of importance. Indeed, the administration usually emphasized its view of the importance of the mission whenever mission dynamics were discussed. Mike McCurry on 21 November 1995 stated that the United States had an interest in peace, security, and stability throughout Europe; furthermore, the United States had treaty commitments with its NATO allies. On this same day Secretary Christopher stated that the "international community, led in this case by the United States," felt this to be an important mission.[17] State Department Spokesman Nicholas Burns linked the mission's importance with the leadership role the United States played in world affairs when he stated that the United States had a "moral obligation" to the people of Bosnia "to stop the war forever, to provide conditions for them of peace and of stability and conditions where they can heat their homes."[18] Burns continued and reiterated the heart of the administration's arguments for deploying in Bosnia:

The only military force that can ensure the peace that was made in Dayton . . . is NATO. The only leader of NATO is the United States. This effort . . . will not succeed without the United States, and the United States must assume the obligations of leadership. [T]o walk away now . . . would be an abdication of American leadership in Europe. It would be a moral abdication because we would be throwing away the opportunity to relieve suffering in a region that has seen hundreds of thousands of people killed and made homeless. Americans should not walk away when everyone is counting on us, when we are the world's great power and the heart and soul of NATO."[19]

These same sentiments were echoed in President Clinton's "Radio Address" on 25 November 1995. Indeed, the president's radio address was a precursor to the main arguments to be presented during the president's "Address to the Nation." The president linked U.S. values clearly with the situation in Bosnia: "The violence done to those innocent civilians does violence to the principles on which America stands." The president continued, saying that only by securing this peace could the killing be stopped. Furthermore, by taking the steps we already have, we now "have a responsibility to see this achievement for peace through. Our values, our interests, and our leadership are at stake."[20] By the president's 27 November 1995 "Address to the Nation," the values, interests, and leadership that the administration meant had solidified. The president mentioned all of these ideals in his address, and whether clear or not, the manner in which the administration had framed these ideals was now set. For example, the president addressed the issue of American interests: "[W]e will have the chance to help stop the killing of innocent civilians, especially children, and at the same time, to bring stability to Central Europe, a region of the world that is vital to our national interests. It is the right thing to do."[21] Perhaps most important, however, the president detailed his conception of American leadership:

With the cold war over, some people now question the need for continued active leadership in the world.

As the cold war gives way to the global village, our leadership is needed more than ever because problems that start beyond our borders can quickly become problems within them.

But nowhere has the argument for our leadership been more clearly justified than in the struggle to stop or prevent war and civil violence.

There are times and places where our leadership can mean the difference between peace and war, and where we can defend our fundamental values as a people and serve our most basic, strategic interests.

The terrible war in Bosnia is such a case.

Implementing the agreement in Bosnia can end the terrible suffering of the people, the warfare, the mass executions, the ethnic cleansing, the campaigns of rape and terror. Let us never forget a quarter of a million men, women, and children have been shelled, shot, and tortured to death.

American leadership created the chance to build a peace and stop the suffering. Securing a peace in Bosnia will also help to build a free and stable Europe. [For] Bosnia lies at the very heart of Europe. . . .

If we're not there, NATO will not be there; the peace will collapse; the war will reignite; the slaughter of innocents will begin again.

And America's commitment to leadership will be questioned. . . .

The people of Bosnia, our NATO allies, and people all around the world are now looking to America for leadership. So let us lead. That is our responsibility as Americans.[22]

These identical framing elements were used by Secretary Christopher on the same day during an interview on PBS-TV's *News Hour with Jim Lehrer*. However, the secretary extended the president's explanation of American interests in Bosnia:

European problems are very important to the United States. We have economic and political and social interests in Europe. Twice before in this century, we have been drawn into European wars with tens of thousands of casualties, hundreds of thousands of men.

This commitment of 20,000 men into a peacekeeping endeavor is a good investment to prevent us from being drawn into, once again, a majop war in Europe.[23]

Moreover, the secretary underscored the framing of the President during an interview on National Public Radio's *All Thing's Considered* on 27 November 1995. At this time the secretary stated that Bosnia "involves some of our most vital interests." These were simply and succinctly enumerated: "First, our leadership as the superpower remaining, we have a very strong interest in vindicating our leadership." Second, it is in the interest of the United States to see the peace agreement through "so we don't have a broader war in Europe." Finally, the horrors of the war, the concentration camps, starvation, and mass graves involve American values in the decision.[24]

The issue of congressional support for the Bosnian mission continued to be raised through media questioning during the days following the announcement of the Accord. This issue had to do with congressional support for the deployment of American soldiers to help ensure that the conditions of the Dayton Accord were seen through. Immediately following the Dayton announcement the administration addressed the issue of congressional support in an open and inviting manner. For example, Nick Burns stated on 22 November 1995 that the administration "had an obligation to Congress, to give Congress enough time to study the peace accord reached at Dayton."[25] Furthermore, he also stated that the administration was "very glad to see that Speaker [of the House Newt] Gingrich yesterday at least left the door open. He said that all members of Congress should have an open mind."[26] President Clinton framed the congressional approval question as an issue involving questions that the American people might have: "I know that there are many questions, and good questions, that have to be answered to the Members of Congress and on behalf of the American people coming through the Members of Congress."[27] Furthermore, in response to a reporter's question that attempted to frame the issue in terms of Republican contentiousness, the president clearly made it an issue for both political parties to contend with: "We had . . . a meeting . . . with the Republican and Democratic leadership of the Congress to discuss scheduling of hearings, debate, and vote. And we had a very constructive meeting. I . . . was very pleased with the meeting."[28]

The Press Response: Support and Alternate Framing

The initial press response to the Dayton Accord was tepid, although support for troop involvement was quickly provided. Initial press criticism focused not on the president but on the Dayton Accord, and this solely along multicultural grounds: The plan allowed the Bosnian Serbs to have a separate state within a unified Croat-Muslim/Serb Federal state. To the press, the separation of warring ethinic factions was considered a betrayal of sorts. The criticism quickly abated after the first day of coverage, and thereafter support for the president's decision was consistently provided. Framing of issues did occur, however, and the manner in which the press framed the issues did not always coincide with the manner in which the administration had framed them. The press advanced frames involving four broad areas during this initial period: the mission, Congress, Bosnian Serb resistance to the Dayton Accord, and press ideals of ethnic diversity.

The Mission. Both the *New York Times* and *Washington Post* offered early support for involvement of American troops to help enforce the Dayton Accord, while at the same time criticizing what it viewed as serious faults in the plan. For example, the *New York Times* editorial of 22 November 1995 stated that Americans should "take justified pride in Washington's leading role in bringing about a settlement. . . . [And that] the Clinton Administration has reclaimed leadership in Atlantic affairs."[29] The *New York Times* editorial went on to say that President Clinton now needs to convince both the American people and Congress that the mission was necessary and prudent. "It is both," stated the *New York Times*, thereby providing unequivocal editorial support.[30] This particular editorial listed the very assertions that the president had given just the day before: Washington negotiated the peace; it can't walk away now; NATO will secure the peace; an American general will lead the NATO mission; the rules of engagement would be clear and permit proactive and forceful retaliation to any threat; and the mission would last only one year. Yet with this praise came criticism as well. The *New York Times* clearly stated that the Dayton Accord "represents the imperfect political resolution of a conflict that, while launched by cynical politicians, quickly brought into play ancient ethnic animosities. As such, it is a fragile peace."[31]

Less than a week later the *New York Times* was making another statement of editorial support for the president's Bosnia mission. Although entitled "Making the Case on Bosnia," no argumentative case was advanced. The editorial was primarily a reiteration of administrative assertions about the mission: "[The] mission the President has defined is limited, achievable and in accordance with American national interests. [He has] negotiated a workable Bosnian peace agreement, the United States cannot honorably evade responsibility for enforcing it. President Clinton has defined a reasonable mission for American troops. He deserves the country's carefully considered support."[32] The *Washington Post* also gave qualified editorial support to the president's plan: "[T]he obstacles and worries do not necessarily amount to reasons to back off peace enforcement. [I]n long-suffering Bosnia, there is an opportunity at least to ameliorate a horrific situation; it should be taken."[33]

Support was not limited to editorials, however. The mission was discussed in news articles as well. For example, the *Washington Post* often paraphrased the president's assertions in a positive manner, then would reiterate by providing a quote from an administrative source. For example, on 22 November 1995: "Clinton said the Americans would take orders only from the U.S. general commanding the NATO operation, and would have authority to respond with force to any threat." And then the reiteration of the central administrative contention: "[The president said] the U.S. military will have 'a clear, limited, achievable mission' and with a 'reasonable' timetable for withdrawal."[34] Advancing the administration's assertions as right and true was a common press practice. For instance, on 25 November 1995 the *Washington Post* reported that the secretary of defense "told his commanders that the United States has 'vital political, economic and security interests in Europe' and that continued war in Bosnia 'threatens these interests.'"[35] The *New York Times* frequently paraphrased the administration's assertions in a positive manner: "Mr. Clinton would argue that America has a moral obligation to stop the killing in Europe and a strategic interest both in remaining the leader of the NATO alliance and in keeping the Balkan conflict from spreading in Europe."[36] On 26 November 1995 the *New York Times* stated that "Mr. Clinton won a diplomatic triumph"with the initialing of the Dayton Accord.[37] On 29 November 1995, the president's assertion concerning the mission was again relayed: "'[O]ur mission will be clear, limited and achievable and that the risks to our troops will be minimized.'"[38]

Descriptions of Congress. During this period, the press was intent on portraying Congress as divided on the issue of supporting the troop deployment and as also being hostile to President Clinton. Although multiple congressional opinions regarding troop deployment were reported, the overall framing of the responses was such as to cast Congress in a bipartisan and hostile light. For example, on 26 November 1995 the *New York Times* reported that the president faced "a critical test as he attempts to convince a skeptical public and a hostile Congress. . . . Senator Bob Dole, the majority leader, and Newt Gingrich, the Speaker of the House, both said . . . that Mr. Clinton had yet to make a solid case."[39] Another article relayed much the same impression: "Mr. Clinton will face a wary public and an openly skeptical Congress."[40] In a news analysis article on 28 November 1995, the *New York Times* reported on the Republicans' promise not to make the issue of supporting the mission a partisan battle but then gave a critical rejoinder: "But keeping partisanship out will be a heroic task in the environment of mutual denunciation and distrust that the intense budget battle is generating. It is hard to invite international statesmanship from someone you have just called a hard-hearted destroyer of Medicare."[41]

The *Washington Post*, as early as 22 November 1995, began framing the Congress as hostile to the president's plan; indeed, "Congress challenged President Clinton . . . to make his best case on why American ground forces should be deployed to Bosnia."[42] Reporting on the president's publicly stated optimism concerning congressional approval for the mission, the *Washington Post* wrote that "the Republican-controlled Congress, which has been deeply skeptical of the idea of sending U.S. troops to Bosnia" would, in President Clinton's mind, support the mission.[43] Moreover, despite President Clinton's words to the contrary, the *Washington Post* reported that mission approval had been linked to budget considerations: "[T]he Bosnia agreement quickly became part of the budget dispute between Clinton and the GOP-led Congress."[44] After the president's 27 November 1995 "Address to the Nation," the *Washington Post* reported on congressional reaction. Republican leaders were reported as saying that President Clinton had failed to answer "some important questions" but that a few "key senators" had offered praise and a receptive attitude. However, this was quickly followed by a stark statement: "House members were far more skeptical, even hostile."[45]

Bosnian Serbs as Dissenters and Rebels. Both the *New York Times* and *Washington Post* focused extensively on the Bosnian Serb reaction to the Dayton Accord—almost to the complete exclusion of reactions from Muslims and Croatians. Reports usually framed the Serbs as being rebels and dissenters and as generally disagreeing with the provisions of the Dayton Accord. For instance, on 22 November 1995 the *New York Times* reported that the Serbs were "enraged by the map of . . . Sarajevo" and that it was not clear whether or not Serbian President Milosovic had "the power to force the Serbs of Bosnia to do what he says."[46] Reaction to the Dayton Accord was usually given in the form of Serbian protests over the provisions of the agreement, especially those concerned with the capital, Sarajevo. Of the plan it was reported that the "decision of President Slobodan Milosevic of Serbia to sign the agreement on behalf of the Bosnian Serbs was met by protest from many in the Serbian-held portions of Bosnia. These Serbs had nothing but complaints about the Ohio agreement. . . . That, they said, assures that Bosnia will become the flash point of World War III."[47] Bosnian Serb leaders were described as "bellicose" and as "strongly opposed to the presence of any NATO troops in Bosnia."[48] Furthermore, the press preoccupation with Sarajevo helped to keep the focus on the Serb reactions as this byline suggests: "Serbs of Sarajevo May Offer Resistance."[49]

Both papers routinely and harshly condemned the Serbs, yet the *Washington Post* provided the more extreme examples of this practice. Indeed, the *Washington Post* clearly framed the Serbs as rebels against a fledgling Bosnian government trying to promote ethnic harmony. For example, on 22 November 1995, it was the "objections of the Bosnian Serb leaders to the peace accord" that suggested "that the international implementation force will face an uphill struggle to ensure respect for the accord."[50] Too, territorial gains made by the Serbs were at times described in a hostile manner, as "the Serbs' brutal capture of . . . Srebrenica" illustrates.[51] Failure for the collapse of prior peace agreements was given to the Serbs to bear as well: "Twice before, the Bosnian Serbs have wriggled out of peace agreements, and criticism by Bosnian Serb leaders of the Dayton accord began soon after it was signed [initialed]."[52] Although little was presented in the way of Bosnian Croat/Muslim temperament and culpability, quotes were provided that condemned the Serbs, such as this by U.S. Ambassador Madeleine K. Albright: "'The world has had enough of Bosnian Serb arrogance and brutality. Their compliance must be demanded . . . by every civilized person on earth.'"[53]

During the same time that the *Washington Post* was actively deploring Serb resistance to the Dayton Accord, it was also framing the Bosnian Serbs as rebels. Indeed, common language used to describe the Bosnian Serbs included "separatist Serbs" and "rebel Serbs"; the government that the Bosnian Serbs had set up was described as the "self-proclaimed Bosnian Serb State," the "self-styled Bosnian Serb State," and the "rebel Serb State"; the capital and Parliament were described as "Pale, the Bosnian Serbs would-be capital" and the "self-proclaimed Bosnian Serb Parliament."[54] By 28 November 1995, the frame establishing the Serbs as the "bad guys" had been well established:

Of the many potential traps to the NATO forces as they roll into Bosnia, none could be more deadly than the Bosnian Serbs.

[NATO] and other power brokers in the region must clarify the position of the people largely responsible for what have been called the worst war crimes in Europe since World War II.

Throughout the war, the Serbs have proved themselves masters at prevarication, at agreeing to deals and never implementing them, at misinterpretation and at stonewalling.[55]

In addition, it "was the Bosnian Serbs who started the war in 1992 when they rebelled against efforts by Bosnian Muslims and Croats to withdraw from Serbia-dominated Yugoslavia."[56]

Ethnic Diversity. This particular framing device was employed primarily, but not exclusively, by the *Washington Post*. Multiethnicity (multiculturalism) was seen as a universal good, and thus the Serbs were destroying that possibility, as was the Dayton Accord, which essentially divided Bosnia between the Croat/Muslim and Serbian forces. For example, a 22 November 1995 news analysis article heralded the above notion through its headline: "Plan Legitimizes Years of 'Ethnic Cleansing.'" In this particular article the lands of the former Yugoslavia were described as having "once had richly diverse populations."[57] This same article continued, "What appears to have won at Dayton is the concept of an ethnically homogenous state. What is lost is the belief that groups that once made up Eastern Europe's richest nation can live together in peace."[58] Although a news analysis article, it does foreshadow much of what is to come in many articles in the *Washington Post*; the primary difference is that this article is more forward in advancing its conception. For example, on the same day, an article detailing the principal American Dayton Accord negotiators stated that some "supporters of the Bosnian cause in the United States argue that he [Assistant Secretary of State Holbrooke] has led the way in sacrificing the ideal of a multiethnic Bosnian state in his relentless pursuit of a peace settlement."[59]

On 27 November 1995 an article lamented the destruction of Sarajevo but expressed no concerns about its terrified Serb inhabitants: "Sarajevo, whose blackened, mortared [sic] landscape came to symbolize the death of its people's ideal of a multi-cultural society, will fall under the control of the Muslim-Croat federation, along with its Serb-held suburbs."[60] Another article charged that the Dayton Accord drew Bosnia's new borders along ethnic lines, thereby ignoring military territorial control and land swaps that gave Croat-dominated lands to the Bosnia Serbs and Bosnian Serb-dominated lands to the Muslim-Croat Federation: "[T]he zones amount to new borders, drawn along ethnic lines, that partition Bosnia between [the warring parties]."[61] In a *New York Times* article on 30 November 1995, the potential exodus of Bosnian Serbs from Sarajevo after the Muslim takeover was described as not only creating another refugee crisis, "but it would also negate the ideal of Sarajevo becoming a multiethnic, multicultural city again."[62]

PERIOD TWO: THE PRESIDENT'S EUROPEAN VISIT, 29 NOVEMBER 1995 THROUGH 4 DECEMBER 1995

Continuation of the White House Frame

In late November 1995, President Clinton visited several European nations. The visit began with the United Kingdom, included Ireland and Germany, and ended with Spain. While touring Europe, the president spoke many times about the impending Bosnian operation. Overwhelmingly, these comments addressed the substance of the mission, although there were comments addressed toward the peace plan, U.S. leadership and values, and the question of congressional support for U.S. participation.

During a dinner hosted by England's Prime Minister John Major, President Clinton addressed the peace plan and, seemingly, those who would attack it as imperfect: "We will support those who take risks for peace. We will not attempt to tell people what peace they should make but only to urge on them the need to make peace at the soonest possible date in a fair and honorable and decent way."[63] Secretary Christopher, still in Washington speaking before the House Committee on International Relations, also raised the issue of the peace plan and seemed to reiterate the president's defense: "[O]n every important issue, it meets the principled and practical standards on which my negotiating team and I insisted. It is an agreement not just of goals, but of means."[64] While in Spain, both President Clinton and Secretary Christopher spoke in defense of the peace plan. The president stated in response to alleged Serbian resistance to the treaty that he did not think the treaty was in trouble or that it should be renegotiated. Moreover, the president was frank in stating that all parties—Serbs, Croats, and the Muslims—had made concessions that they were unhappy about. To this point the president stated: "That's what—when you make a peace agreement, not everybody is happy with it."[65] In short, grumbling was expected, but the administration fully expected the terms of the Dayton Accord to be carried out. Secretary Christopher said it best while being interviewed in Spain by ABC-TV's *This Week with David Brinkley*: "I suppose it's not surprising that in any kind of peace settlement there are certain things that one side or another is unhappy about. But each of the three Presidents have committed themselves to carry out this agreement, and we expect them to do so."[66]

By far the largest topic of discussion during the president's European visit was the mission itself. The president spoke extensively about the mission, and any comments of his administration officials simply reiterated his words. During a news conferences with Prime Minister John Major, the president stated that the mission was "not to fight a war in Bosnia but to help secure a peace."[67] Secretary Christopher reminded reporters that the United States needed to do its share and that "we should remember that other nations, including nearly all our NATO allies, Russia, and many of our new partners in Central Europe, will contribute 2/3 of the troops in IFOR."[68]

While in Ireland the president was confronted with charges of "mission creep," a term used by the press to describe incremental upward adjustments to troop numbers, costs, and activities. The president insisted that U.S. participation would still remain at 20,000 troops and about 5,000 support personnel. The president also provided the White House perspective on any numbers being "bandied around here" when he stated: "[T]his is an appropriate level of contribution. This is no more than a third. . . . You heard the British Prime Minister say . . . that he expected Great Britain, a country with a population . . . less than a fourth of ours, is going to send 13,000 troops to the theater. So the

Europeans are going to take the major load, and we should support them."[69] The president also underscored the importance of the mission to the United States: "Our Nation . . . has a vital stake in a Europe that is stable, strong, and free. . . . But we know that such a Europe can never be built as long as conflict tears at the heart of the Continent in Bosnia. [I]t also breaks our heart and violates our conscience."[70]

In Germany the president addressed U.S. troops. The issue of the mission was of special importance during this appearance and reflected well the reasons given to the Congress and the American people for U.S. involvement. During his remarks to U.S. troops in Germany, the president touched upon each of the major elements that would fill his comments throughout his remaining days in Europe: the mission, its importance, and American leadership and values:

It is in our Nation's interest and consistent with our values to see that this peace succeeds and endures.

[The Bosnians need help to rebuild] and they have asked America and our NATO allies . . . to provide it.

Each side wants NATO to help them live up to the commitments they've made . . . [and] to maintain the cease-fire so that the war does not start again. . . .

I pledged to the American people that I would not send you to Bosnia unless I was absolutely sure that the goals we set for you are clear, realistic, and achievable in about a year. This mission meets those essential standards.

You will take your orders from General Joulwan [an American], who commands NATO. There will be no confusing chain of command. You are superbly prepared. You will be heavily armed.

[You] will have very clear rules of engagement that spell out the most important rule of all in big, bold letters: If you are threatened with attack, you may respond immediately and with decisive force.

Your presence will help to create the climate of security Bosnia needs.

Without you the door will close, the peace will collapse, the war will return, the atrocities will begin again. The conflict then could spread throughout the region, weaken our partnership with Europe, and undermine our leadership in other areas critical to our security.[71]

The president also detailed the importance of Europe in a new fashion, one that was designed to bring the importance from abstract principles espoused since 21 November 1995 to concrete images with which Americans could identify: "Europe can be our strongest partners in fighting the things that will threaten the security of your children: the terrorism, the organized crime, the drug trafficking, the spread of weapons of mass destruction. We have to work with Europe [on Bosnia] if we're going to work on all those problems that will be the security problems of the future."[72]

The issue of U.S. leadership and values was rarely mentioned while the president was in Europe. However, the president's 2 December 1995 "Radio Address," played to an American audience, stands out as an exception to this; furthermore, it demonstrates that the case was still being made at home for the Bosnian mission. The president summarized his exchanges with European leaders in such a manner as to show the importance of American leadership in this area:

[T]he message to me was the same: American leadership for peace matters. American leadership is welcome in Europe. American leadership is necessary in Europe, whether to achieve peace in Northern Ireland or join in implementing the peace in Bosnia.

The mission is clear and so are the stakes, for the Bosnian people, for the security of Europe, and for America's leadership around the world.[73]

The issue of congressional support for the mission was raised several times while the president was in Europe. In keeping with earlier comments, the president and his officials clearly made this a bipartisan congressional issue and were generous with positive comments and acknowledgment of support. Indeed, on 29 November 1995 Mike McCurry stated that the Clinton administration was "gratified both by the public and the private remarks of the Republican leadership of Congress. They are clearly keeping an open mind and encouraging members to keep an open mind."[74] McCurry later gave thanks again to Republican members of Congress: The president is "gratified for the way that both the Senate Majority Leader [Dole] and the Speaker [Gingrich] have encouraged members of Congress to keep an open mind and have worked with the administration to address our serious responsibilities to participate in the implementation of a new and fragile peace in the Balkans."[75] The president even publicly stated that he was "very gratified" by Senator Dole's support. Indeed, the president stressed the bipartisan nature of the issue: "I think that the decision by Senator Dole and Senator McCain will help immeasurably . . . to build the kind of bipartisan support that we need to make this an American effort."[76]

Continuation of the Press Frames

During the period the president was in Europe, the press continued the frames and strategies that it used during the first period covered in this chapter. However, several changes in coverage did occur. Although the *New York Times* continued coverage concerning the mission, the *Washington Post* reduced its coverage in this area. Also, whereas the *Washington Post* had included many references to ethnicity, during this period there is comparatively little in the way of ethnic framing. What resulted was a focus on three elements: the mission (primarily *New York Times* coverage), Congress, and the Bosnian Serbs, the most copious coverage of all.

The Mission. The *New York Times* reported essentially what the president stated about the mission. Indeed, the President was often quoted, with this statement either followed or preceeded by a positive paraphrase in the words of the reporter. Thus, even when criticism of the president's plan was offered, it was usually sandwiched in between the words of the president and the paraphrase of the reporter. For example, on 3 December 1995, the *New York Times* reported on the president's Baumholder, Germany, speech:

Mr. Clinton went out of his way to emphasize that the American mission in Bosnia was peacekeeping, not war-making, that it would be limited to about a year and that all efforts would be taken to minimize risks to American life.

"Your mission is clear," he said in the speech to the troops. "You are strong, you are well prepared, and the stakes demand American leadership that you will provide."

"You will also have very clear rules of engagement that spell out the most important rule in big, bold letters: If you are threatened with attack, you may respond immediately, and with decisive force."[77]

The *Washington Post* had little to say about the mission during this period, although those articles that did seemed to follow the same general pattern as that used by the *New York Times*: extend the president's assertions. For example, on 3 December 1995, an article reporting on President Clinton's speech before U.S. troops in Baumholder, Germany essentially "sandwiched" the president's remarks in between positive descriptions of the president's words: "[The president] tried to reassure thousands of American soldiers today that their mission is clearly defined, limited and 'safe as it can be.'" Later in the same article the president was reported as having made "the case that the United States has a responsibility to enforce the peace agreement it helped broker in Bosnia and a moral responsibility to end the killing and brutality there."[78]

Congress. Although the *New York Times* had much to report concerning the mission, it had comparatively little to say during the president's European trip concerning the discussion of Bosnia by Congress. In contrast, although the *Washington Post* had little to say regarding the mission during this period, it did have a great deal to report concerning Congress during this time. In general, Congress was framed in much the same manner as before the president's European visit. Congress—meaning the Republicans—was opposed to the deployment of troops to

Bosnia. For instance, on 30 November 1995, the *Washington Post* reported that many "Republican senators and House members, as well as some Democrats, have complained that the administration lacks a coherent 'exit strategy' from Bosnia. . . ."[79] Although it appears that the article is providing criticism of the administration, the remainder of the article is essentially devoted to presentation of administrative claims as to why this is not so: "A partial response to these [congressional] questions is contained in the military annex to the peace agreement."[80] The article then devotes the remaining eleven (of a total of sixteen) paragraphs to explaining away the complaints of a suspect "exit strategy."

The "battle" over congressional approval of the Bosnia mission was linked by the *Washington Post* to the ongoing White House/congressional budget battle. It was implied that the "Republican led" Congress was strong-arming the president of the United States into signing a Defense appropriations bill he did not want to sign: "In the end, the White House decided that it didn't have the leverage to veto the bill. House Republicans, already deeply skeptical of the Bosnian mission, could have tried to limit the mission or block it outright through restrictive language in a new defense bill."[81] Another aspect of the focus on Congress involved focusing on Bob Dole, the Senate majority leader. About a week after President Clinton announced the Dayton Accord, Senator Dole announced that he would support the president's plan. The *Washington Post* reported this as the first step in making the mission a bipartisan effort, even though the administration had consistently stressed the bipartisan nature from the very first day of the announcement of the peace plan. For example, on 2 December 1995 it was reported that Senator Dole would introduce a resolution in the Senate in support of the troop deployment. The *Washington Post* reported that "Clinton said he was gratified by Dole's move and that it was a first step in making the Bosnia effort a bipartisan one."[82]

The Bosnian Serbs. The framing of the Bosnian Serbs in a negative manner continued during this period. The *New York Times* focused on the wartime brutality of the Serbs; this was usually linked with Serb protests over having to relinquish control of Sarajevo to the Muslim/Croat Federation. One article reported on the UN condemnation of the Bosnian Serbs for war crimes. Stressed was the report's "unequivocal" listing of "atrocities" perpetuated by the Serbs. A generous quote was allowed UN Secretary General Boutros Boutros-Ghali, who was reported as saying that the "Bosnian Serbs had been engaged in 'a consistent pattern of summary executions, rape, mass expulsion, arbitrary detentions, forced labor and large scale disappearances.'"[83] The focus was often on what the Serbs did to other Bosnians. For example, on 1 December 1995, the *New York Times* reported on the Bosnians living in

Tuzla (where U.S. soldiers would soon be based): "For some Bosnians the misery and loss caused by the war is too deep for peace to make much of a difference. Amala Zaimovic, a 30-year-old judge, stood on a hillside overlooking Tuzla in front of the grave of her brother Adnan. He died six months ago, when a Serbian shell struck a cafe, killing 73. The massacre has traumatized the city."[84]

The Serbs were still considered rebels, at least as far as the *Washington Post* was concerned. Throughout this period the Bosnian Serbs were consistently labeled as "separatist Serbs," "separatist Bosnian Serbs," and "Serb Separatists." The emphasis on the Serbs as separatists lends itself to describing the peace plan's proposal to have Bosnia a federation of two semiautonomous states as "one country, albeit split in two . . . one part Serb and the other a Croat-Muslim federation."[85] Rarely is mentioned that the Serbs have their own government; rarely is it mentioned that the government is called the Bosnian Serb Republic. The emphasis on Serb aggression manifested itself in speculation as well. For example, the *Washington Post* reported a lone incident of sniper fire in Sarajevo. The Serbs were given the blame: "Sniper fire hit a Sarajevo streetcar today in the first attack on civilians since a truce took effect Oct. 12. . . . One man was slightly wounded in the arm by the gunfire, which was believed to have come from a Serb position."[86] If there was to be trouble with the implementation of the Dayton Accord, it would undoubtedly arise from the Serbs: "Most of the resistance will probably come from the Serbs," unnamed "United Nations peacekeepers" were reported as stating.[87]

PERIOD THREE: 5 DECEMBER 1995 THROUGH 14 DECEMBER 1995

The White House Push for Congressional Support

As the date for the signing of the Dayton Accord neared, the White House addressed an increasing number of its comments to congressional leaders. The peace plan, the mission, U.S. Leadership and values were still mentioned, but comments addressed to members of Congress soared.

Comments pertaining to the peace plan were still framed the same way as before. The president highlighted the casualties of the Bosnian war, then stated that "because the parties have said they will turn from war to peace, we can now prevent further suffering; we can now shine the light of justice in Bosnia; we can now help its people build a future of hope."[88] Secretary Christopher provided further support for this line of reasoning: "The Dayton agreement has given us our best hope to achieve a lasting peace. We wanted an agreement that addressed all the fundamental issues that divided the parties, with no short cuts or ambiguities, and that is what we obtained."[89] During a State Department briefing, Glyn Davies directly addressed criticism of the plan: "Those who initialed the agreement and who will sign the agreement in Paris have been expressing no misgivings to us. Nobody has been nibbling away at it; none of the signatories has been coming to us and asking us to revisit portions of the agreement."[90] Mike McCurry shed light on the importance of the administration's connection of the three Balkan presidents and President Clinton's attendance at the Paris signing of the formal Accord: "[For President Clinton] signing the document that is the final peace accord and also looking at the Presidents, seeing them eye to eye as they make their commitments to honor the security guarantees that they have given him related to the presence of our U.S. troops in Bosnia [is of considerable importance]."[91] Of negative comments about the Accord, Secretary Christopher stated that it was a comprehensive and complex agreement and that there "would be many occasions in the future for [the United States] to bring to the attention of the parties their obligations under the agreement."[92] As late as 14 December 1995, the day prior to the formal signing of the agreement, the administration was still responding to negative comments about the plan. Mike McCurry, detailing the conversations among President Clinton and the three Bosnian presidents, stated that there was "nothing about any of the conversations the President had with the three Presidents this morning that would indicate anything but a commitment by them to make good on their agreement."[93]

The mission, too, was discussed often in the days following the president's return from Europe. McCurry stated that the military mission was "precisely defined, very carefully structured, and scheduled to last about a year."[94] Shortly after his return, the president retold Americans that the troops were not being sent to "make war, but to wage peace."[95] Just prior to the congressional vote of approval for the mission, President Clinton said that the purpose of the mission was to "take advantage of the remarkable opportunity we have when all of the parties have agreed to make peace."[96]

Upon returning from Europe, the president and his officials again resumed discussion of American leadership and values. On 5 December 1995 Secretary Christopher stated that meeting the responsibilities of leadership "is profoundly in the interest of our nation and the world."[97] President Clinton also made an effort to advance his conception of American leadership when he addressed the Committee for American Leadership in Bosnia: "During my recent trip to Europe, everywhere I went and every person with whom I talked, from people on the street to prime ministers, said that very same thing: American leadership matters; American leadership is welcome; American leadership is necessary. But leadership is not a spectator sport. It demands our participation."[98] It was Secretary Christopher, however, who best reiterated the arguments used by the administration to frame its conception of U.S. leadership in the Bosnian mission. Christopher, stating this to be a "watershed week for American leadership [in Europe]," outlined three important elements to American leadership: One, "NATO is here to stay," and the United States is the only leader of NATO. Two, America's European allies recognize "that American leadership is essential." This is crucial because even the Europeans have said that "without American leadership and participation . . . NATO would not be able to carry out its mission." Furthermore, asserting U.S. "leadership in Bosnia puts us in a stronger position to advance our interests all through Europe." Finally, "the very nature of our coalition in Bosnia has historic implications. Russia will contribute 2,000 troops. Nearly every country from central Europe will participate."[99] Mike McCurry later stressed that the United States had a "moral obligation . . . to live up to its leadership responsibilities in the world."[100]

Throughout the days following the president's return from Europe and up to the congressional vote of support, there was an increasing number of references to congressional support for the mission. These repeatedly stressed the bipartisan nature of the congressional vote. When asked about those who were supporting the troops but not wanting to support the mission, Mike McCurry stated:

[I]t would not be wise of me to cast aspersions on the motives of those who are being supportive of our troops. And even as, for example, former President Bush yesterday indicated some concern about the nature of the mission, he also simultaneously said that our credibility in this world and the integrity of U.S. leadership is at stake. And ultimately, as members of Congress vote to support our troops, they are supporting the decision the Commander in Chief has made to send them there.[101]

On 6 December 1995 President Clinton addressed the Congressional Committee for American Leadership in Bosnia. At this time, he again framed the issue of congressional support in a bipartisan manner:

This is a very, very, very important thing in terms of our relationships with Europe and what we expect in terms of partnership with Europe in the years ahead.

Let me say to those of you who come here from both parties, I understand that bipartisanship in foreign policy has never meant agreement on every detail of every policy. And while we may differ from time to time on the specifics of our policies, we still must agree and we have never fundamentally disagreed on our purpose: to defend our interests, to preserve peace, to protect human rights, to promote prosperity around the world.[102]

Later, on 11 December 1995, the president stressed the importance of a congressional show of support for the mission: "I would welcome a Congressional expression of support. . . . Congressional support is immensely important to the unity of our purpose and the morale of our troops."[103] On 14 December, after the results of the vote had been made public, the president stated the he thought that both Houses of Congress had voted to support the troops and that "the Senate, in what could only be characterized as an overwhelming bipartisan vote, gave its support to the mission subject to conditions to which the administration agrees."[104]

Press Framing Continues: The Troops, the Congress, and the Serbs

Troops, Not the Mission. As the days from the initial announcement of the Dayton Accord passed, there was less press reporting concerning the debate about the mission itself and an increasing amount of reporting concerning the dynamics of the mission. This occurred even though the treaty had yet to be signed and Congress had yet to vote on the issue. In this sense, then, the press was acting as if the mission were a fait accompli instead of the yet-to-be-decided issue that it was at this time. For example, the following headlines clearly demonstrate a focus on mission preparation instead of discussion of the merits of the mission itself: "U.S. Bound for Bosnia by Train, Truck, Air," "President Authorizes Deployment to Bosnia," "Clinton Reassures Bosnia-Bound Forces Mission Is 'Safe as It Can Be,'" "Reservists Called Up for Training," "Military Families Battle the Stress of Separation," "Deployment of U.S. Troops Goes Slowly," "Advice to an Incoming General: Be Firm, Friendly," "U.S. Jets Start Shuttle to Tuzla," "Army Stress Control Unit Mobilizes, Too, to Seek Out Peacekeeping's Hidden Toll," "U.S. Troops in Bosnia Find a 'Shellshocked' People," "Main Peril for G.I.'s in Bosnia Lies Just Beneath the Surface," "Hungarian Town Mobilizes for G.I.'s Bound for Bosnia," and "In U.S. Peacekeeper Arsenal, Weapons Honed for Bosnia."[105] The *New York Times* editorially supported the mission once again, but this time as if the mission were already completed: "NATO gathers a force of 60,000 troops to help secure the peace in Bosnia."[106] Concerns about deployment raised by American sources were marginalized as well: "Officials from European countries say they believe that American fears of casualties in Bosnia are overdrawn."[107] The papers also stressed the importance of U.S. leadership in Europe: "[T]he United States retains a unique military and political credibility in Europe."[108]

Congress. After the congressional vote of approval, the *New York Times* editorially commented. Those Republicans supporting the president were viewed in a positive light: "Bob Dole . . . exercised responsible leadership by co-sponsoring the resolution consenting to the mission and guiding it to passage." Those opposed to the president's mission were severely castigated: "Phil Gramm [Bob Dole's presidential primary contender] looked petty and unconvincing in his opposition to the mission and its funding." Ultimately, the *New York Times* continued its support for President Clinton: "[T]he case for American leadership in this case is clear and compelling."[109] However, it was also stressed at this time that the president did not need the support of Congress; indeed, it was frankly stated by the *New York Times* that the president did not need the support of Congress for the mission: "President Clinton does not need the support of Congress for the mission, but it [*sic*] would prefer to have it." Later in the same article it was emphasized that "Congress was virtually powerless to halt the mission."[110]

Congress was still described as deeply divided, even after the votes came in to support the mission. For example, on 14 December 1995, the day after the congressional vote, the *New York Times* described the vote as a "Flimsy Bosnia Mandate," which ultimately emanated from a "deeply divided" Senate and House of Representatives, whose "Vote Shows Misgivings Are Deep."[111] This last article even went so far as to state that President Clinton had failed to "build a genuine constituency for his Balkan strategy on Capitol Hill."[112] However, the actual vote shows the House voting 287 to 141 in favor of the Buyer-Skelton resolution supporting the troops (or 67percent for and 33 percent against), and the Senate voting 69 to 30 in support for the Dole-McCain resolution supporting the troops (or 70 percent to 30 percent). This practice was also apparent in *Washington Post* coverage. Thus, the press was actually calling a two-thirds majority "deeply divided," thereby keeping alive the partisan nature of its early reportorial strategies.

The Serbs. This frame remained constant up through the congressional vote. The Serbs were still portrayed as rebels and potential troublemakers. For instance, on 5 December 1995 the *New York Times* reported that as "the soldiers [already in Bosnia] prepare for the arrival of the main combat force, tensions have clearly risen among the Bosnian Serbs."[113] This is especially important because the Serbs have "objected vehemently to the [Dayton Accord's] stipulation that all of the city [Sarajevo] be handed over to the Muslim-led government."[114]

The *Washington Post* continued its particular branding of the Serbs as rebels, separatists, and troublemakers. For example, on 6 December 1995 the *Washington Post* published an article that focused exclusively on the Serbs in Sarajevo. In this article the Bosnian Serbs were again described as rebels: "[To the people in the Sarajevo suburbs only] Bosnian Serb rebels—political leader Radovan Karadzic or, better yet, military chief Ratko Mladic—carry authority here."[115] Even the fears that the Bosnian Serbs living in Sarajevo had were belittled:

People want nothing to do with a settlement they say will turn them out of their homes.

Not that the Bosnian peace accord actually does that. Many of the Serbs in the Sarajevo suburbs can remain in the homes that they and their families have lived in for years. What they must do, according to the plan, is to allow their onetime Muslim neighbors—in many cases, former friends—to return home.

That, they say, is an impossible demand.

The Bosnian government's attempts to persuade Serbs [that they will be allowed to stay and be treated fairly] have fallen on deaf ears. No one interviewed in any of the suburbs believes . . . President Alija Izebegovic or any of his followers. They are, in Serb minds, the enemy.[116]

SUMMARY

White House Frames

The Clinton administration framed the question of U.S. involvement in Bosnia essentially as moral obligation. The moral quality of the commitment to involvement was conveyed by administration officials through repeated assertions and not detailed arguments. Claims were repeatedly advanced as completed arguments but with little evidence. It was supposed to be enough that humanitarian reasons underpinned the administration's claims for advancing the mission. From this general moral climate developed three administratively generated frames, and two frames in which the administration was responding almost exclusively to press questions. These frames revolved around issues of the peace plan, the mission, U.S. leadership and values, questions of Congress, and Serbian resistance to provisions of the Dayton Accord.

The Clinton administration characterized the peace plan as "ending the slaughter" and as a "victory for all" parties involved with the peace plan: Bosnians, Muslims, Croats, Americans, and Europeans; it had been a group effort. The Accord was for the good, for it was a principled agreement "not just of goals, but of means." This is to say that it contained detailed descriptions of implementation of the following goals: a single Bosnian state, a unified federal government, free democratic elections, and assurances of basic human rights. The peace plan was marshalled in as an unquestionable good and quickly gave way to discussion concerning the implementation of the mission itself.

The mission was essentially framed as a "clear and limited" undertaking with a definitive timetable for withdrawal. American soldiers would be allowed to aggressively and proactively defend themselves if necessary. In addition, it was stressed that this was to be a NATO—not UN!—mission, that the United States commanded NATO, and that U.S. soldiers would take their orders from American commanders. The troops were not there to fight a war but to keep the peace. The mission was important because peace and stability in Europe are abiding American interests. Moreover, with a stable Europe, Americans will find a helpful Europe, a Europe willing to be our partner in working on those issues of importance to Americans: organized crime, drug trafficking, and controlling nuclear proliferation. Because of this, we have a moral obligation to help because we are in a position to help.

Touching on the prior two frames but strong enough to stand on its own is the frame of U.S leadership and values. The peace plan and mission were seen as the logical extensions of American values and our role as world leader. This made it our responsibility to see the mission through to the end. The administration consistently advanced the claim that NATO was the only force that could enforce this peace plan and that the United States, as NATO's leader, must assume the lead role. Also stressed was that the Balkan states, and Europe in general, desired U.S. leadership. The United States is the sole remaining superpower; to abrogate its responsibility was just not possible for the Clinton administration. As the president stated: "The violence done to those innocent civilians does violence to the principles on which America stands."

The administration rarely spoke of Congress without prompting from the press. However, when it did speak of Congress it was with a tightly unified voice that presented its conception of the issue clearly and concisely. The question of congressional support was presented as a bipartisan issue: Congress was *expected* to ask questions. The president believed that Congress would ask the questions that the American people would want asked; if the case were made clear to the American people, then it would be clear to Congress. The administration was gratified that Congress was keeping an "open mind" about the mission. The administration stated that it would provide Congress with time to review the deployment plans and that there would be no deployment until Congress was heard on this matter.

Comments concerning Serbian resistance to the peace plan composed more of a response than a frame through which to view the crisis. This press-created issue was no issue to the administration. Indeed, administration officials said little about this, and when statements were made, they invariably communicated the same thought: President Milosevic of Serbia was empowered to sign for the Bosnian Serbs. The United

States expects full compliance. Some complaining is to be expected, especially with hostilities so high and with all sides making concessions in order to have the peace.

The Press Framing of Administrative Utterances

The press actively supported President Clinton's Bosnian mission, both editorially and in regular news articles. In this sense, then, the very frame that the president used for the Bosnian mission was employed by the press. However, the press also advanced oppositional frames to those advanced by the administration. These frames consisted of descriptions of Congress, descriptions of Bosnian Serb resistance to the Accord, and multiculturalism as a good.

Both the *New York Times* and the *Washington Post* were supportive of the Bosnian mission. Although some criticism was made, principally having to do with the ethnic division of Bosnia (not enough effort made at preserving a multiethnic state), the mission was generally hailed as "necessary" and "prudent." The press framing of the mission was essentially a reiteration of White House *assertions*. This is to say that the press used what administration officials said as completed and true *arguments*. News articles frequently paraphrased administration assertions, then used quotes from administration officials to demonstrate the truth of what had just been paraphrased. Although criticism was provided, most notably from Republican congressional sources, it was usually planted in between the positive paraphrases of the press and quotes from administration officials. News items detailing mission arguments eventually gave way to articles detailing mission dynamics: the dangers the troops faced; profiles of specific units; and human interest stories.

The press advanced an oppositional frame when making reference to Congress. Whereas the Clinton administration had been exceptionally careful to make the Bosnian mission into a matter for bipartisan support, the press framed it in a partisan manner. Congress was framed early as being divided on the issue and as being hostile to President Clinton. Any congressional questions on the mission were framed in such a manner as to evoke a partisan origin. Republicans were framed as being opposed to the president's plan, not as being concerned with the welfare of U.S. troops. Questions concerning Bosnia were linked to the budget battle going on at the time between the White House and the House of Representatives, even though the White House and members of the House stated otherwise. When Bob Dole announced support for the mission, those Republicans still speaking out against involvement were described as not following Dole's leadership instead of as questioning President Clinton's policy. Two weeks after the president's announcement to send U.S. troops, the press was framing the upcoming congressional vote to support or not support the mission as irrelevant. Those who voted against the measure were cast as petty and mean.

The most telling example of framing by the press involves the Bosnian Serbs. Very few Muslim or Croat reactions to the Dayton Accord were provided; however, the Bosnian Serbs were heavily focused on. The Bosnian Serbs were cast as rebels and separatists, even though they only reacted to the Muslim/Croat withdrawal from Yugoslavia. According to the press, the Bosnian Serbs did not live up to their bargains and could not be trusted; the press created speculation concerning future Serbian reactions as well. The Serbs were depicted as being the destroyers of multiculturalism and ethnic harmony in Bosnia. If brutality were experienced in the former Yugoslavia, it was the Serbs who were to take the lion's share of the credit. Serbian human rights violations were reported to the almost total exclusion of Muslim or Croat violations. When war crimes were mentioned, it was almost always Serbian leaders who were mentioned, even though there were, in November 1995, fifty-four individuals—Bosnian Croats, Muslims, and Serbs—indicted for war crimes. All of this led to a belittling of Serb concern when their fear of living under Muslim rule was mentioned by the press.

Finally, in the week following the announcement of the Dayton Accord, the press, especially the *Washington Post*, framed the entire mission in ethnic terms. The ideal presented involved a multiethnic, multicultural Bosnia. This, according to the press, is what existed before, and it should be so now as well. The fault, or failure, to achieve this once again was initially bestowed on the Dayton Accord, but this blame fell quickly to the Bosnian Serbs to bear.

NOTES

1. U.S. Department of State, "Remarks Announcing the Bosnia-Herzegovina Peace Agreement and an Exchange with Reporters: November 21, 1995," *Weekly Compilation of Presidential Documents* 31.47 (27 November 1995): 2049.

2. U.S. Department of State, "Remarks Announcing the Bosnia-Herzegovina Peace," 2050.

3. U.S. Department of State, "Remarks Announcing the Bosnia-Herzegovina Peace," 2050.

4. U.S. Department of State, "Remarks Announcing the Bosnia-Herzegovina Peace," 2050.

5. U.S. Department of State, "Remarks Announcing the Bosnia-Herzegovina Peace," 2051.

6. White House, Office of the Press Secretary, "Press Briefing by Mike McCurry" (21 November 1995): 8-9.

7. U.S. Department of State, Office of the Spokesman, "Press Conference Following the Initialing of the Balkan Proximity Peace Talks Agreement" (21 November 1995).

8. U.S. Department of State, Office of the Spokesman, "Remarks by U.S. Secretary of State Warren Christopher and President Milosevic of Serbia, President Tudjman of Croatia, President Izetbegovic of Bosnia-Herzegovina and Representatives of the European Union, the Contact Group and Negotiating Team Members at the Initialing of the Balkan Proximity Peace Talks Agreement" (21 November 1995): 3.

9. U.S. Department of State, Office of the Spokesman, "Daily Press Briefing: DPC#170" (22 November 1995): 7.

10. U.S. Department of State, Office of the Spokesman, "Daily Press Briefing: DPC#170."

11. U.S. Department of State, Office of the Spokesman, "Daily Press Briefing: DPC#171" (27 November 1995): 3.

12. U.S. Department of State, Office of the Spokesman, "Interview of Secretary of State Warren Christopher by Jim Lehrer—PBS-TV 'News Hour with Jim Lehrer'" (27 November 1995): 1.

13. U.S. Department of State, Office of the Spokesman, "Daily Press Briefing: DPC#170," 6.

14. U.S. Department of State, "The President's Radio Address: November 25, 1995," *Weekly Compilation of Presidential Documents* 31.48 (4 December 1995): 2060.

15. U.S. Department of State, "Address to the Nation on Implementation of the Peace Agreement in Bosnia-Herzegovina: 27 November 1995," *Weekly Compilation of Presidential Documents* 31.48 (4 December 1995): 2062.

16. U.S. Department of State, "Address to the Nation on Implementation," 2063.

17. U.S. Department of State, Office of the Spokesman, "Press Conference Following the Initialing," 8.

18. U.S. Department of State, Office of the Spokesman, "Daily Press Briefing: DPC#170," 3-6.

19. U.S. Department of State, Office of the Spokesman, "Daily Press Briefing: DPC#170," 3-6.

20. U.S. Department of State, "The President's Radio Address: November 25, 1995," 2057-2058.

21. U.S. Department of State, "Address to the Nation on Implementation," 2060.

22. U.S. Department of State, "Address to the Nation on Implementation," 2060-2064.

23. U.S. Department of State, Office of the Spokesman, "Interview of Secretary of State Warren Christopher by Jim Lehrer, 3.

24. U.S. Department of State, Office of the Spokesman, "Interview of Secretary of State Warren Christopher on National Public Radio—Robert Siegel 'All Things Considered'" (27 November 1995): 1-2.

25. U.S. Department of State, Office of the Spokesman, "Daily Press Briefing:

DPC #170," 5.

26. U.S. Department of State, Office of the Spokesman, "Daily Press Briefing: DPC#170," 5.

27. U.S. Department of State, "Remarks Prior to a Meeting with Congressional Leaders and an Exchange with Reporters: 28 November 1995," *Weekly Compilation of Presidential Documents* 31.48 (4 December 1995): 2064.

28. U.S. Department of State, "Remarks Prior to a Meeting," 2064.

29. "Peace in Bosnia," Editorial, *New York Times* 22 November 1995: A22.

30. "Peace in Bosnia," A22.

31. "Peace in Bosnia," A22.

32. "Making the Case on Bosnia," Editorial, *New York Times* 28 November 1995: A22.

33. "Bosnia Opportunity," Editorial, *Washington Post* 29 November 1995: A24.

34. Ann Devroy and Helen Dewar, "Clinton Challenged on Plan for Troops," *Washington Post* 22 November 1995: A21.

35. Atkinson, Rick, "Perry Declares Troops Bosnia-Ready," *Washington Post* 25 November 1995: A1.

36. Alison Mitchell, "Clinton's Next Task Will Be to Sell Plan to the U.S. Public," *New York Times* 22 November 1995: A1.

37. Alison Mitchell, "Clinton Seeks Public Support on Bosnia Plan," *New York Times* 26 November 1995: A1. An exceptionally positive report concerning the president's assertions about the Bosnia mission by this same reporter can be found in "Clinton Lays Out His Case for U.S. Troops in Balkans; 'We Must Do What We Can,'" *New York Times* 28 November 1995: A1.

38. Katherine Q. Seelye, "Legislators Get Plea by Clinton on Bosnia Force," *New York Times* 29 November 1995: A18.

39. Mitchell, "Clinton Seeks Public Support," A1.

40. Eric Schmitt, "Pentagon Confident, But Some Serbs 'Will Fight,'" *New York Times* 27 November 1995: A1.

41. Adam Clymer, "The Silent Opposition," *New York Times* 28 November 1995: A1.

42. Devroy and Dewar, "Clinton Challenged," A21.

43. Michael Dobbs, "Balkan Leaders Approve Bosnia Pact," *Washington Post* 22 November 1996: A1.

44. Devroy and Dewar, "Clinton Challenged," A21.

45. Ann Devroy and Helen Dewar, "U.S. Troops Vital to Bosnia Peace, Clinton Says," *Washington Post* 28 November 1995: A1.

46. Elaine Sciolino, "Accord Reached to End the War in Bosnia; Clinton Pledges U.S. Troops to Keep the Peace," *New York Times* 22 November 1995: A1, A10.

47. Kit R. Roane, "A Town Feels Betrayed by Milosevic and Talks of Fighting On," *New York Times* 23 November 1995: A12.

48. Raymond Bonner, "Rising Serb Leader Offers Accord Rare Praise," *New York Times* 26 November 1995: A12.

49. Chris Hedges, "In Sarajevo Suburbs, Talk of Resistance," *New York Times* 27 November 1995: A1.

50. Dobbs, "Balkan Leaders Approve," A1.

51. Michael Dobbs, "Three Shaped Pact," *Washington Post* 22 November 1995: A20.

52. John M. Goshko and John F. Harris, "U.N. Votes to Withdraw Sanctions on the Balkans," *Washington Post* 23 November 1995: A1.

53. Goshko and Harris, "U.N. Votes to Withdraw Sanctions," A1.

54. For examples see: William Drozdiak, "European Governments Respond with Relief," *Washington Post* 22 November 1995: A22; Goshko and Harris, "U.N. Votes to Withdraw Sanctions," A1; John Pomfret, "The Dayton Hurrahs vs. Bosnian Reality: Can Serbian Leader Deliver Peace?" *Washington Post* 23 November 1995: A35.

55. John Pomfret, "U.S.-Led NATO Force Faces Risky Mission," *Washington Post* 28 November 1995: A10.

56. Michael Dobbs, "U.S. Gains Assurances on Troops," *Washington Post* 24 November 1995: A1.

57. John Pomfret, "Plan Legitimizes Years of 'Ethnic Cleansing,'" *Washington Post* 22 November 1995: A1.

58. Pomfret, "Plan Legitimizes," A1.

59. Dobbs, "Three Shaped Pact," A20. Importantly, no source for this rather striking accusation was ever provided.

60. Christine Spolar, "In Sarajevo, Peace Can't Defeat Skepticism," *Washington Post* 27 November 1995: A1.

61. Dana Priest, "1,400 U.S. Troops Part of Advance Group," *Washington Post* 28 November 1995: A9. Although subtle, the notion of the importance of diversity was included even in assessments of the military composition of the NATO forces. For example, one article included this statement: "Three predominantly Muslim countries—Egypt, Pakistan and Malaysia—would add diversity to the operation, while Slovakia, Slovenia and especially Hungary have offered critical transit facilities." It is interesting that Muslim countries may add "diversity," while Eastern European countries such as Slovakia may only contribute to easing transportation difficulties. See Atkinson, "Perry Declares Troops Bosnia-Ready," A1.

62. Raymond Bonner, "In Suburbs of Sarajevo, Serbs Firm on Leaving," *New York Times* 30 November 1995: A10.

63. U.S. Department of State, "Remarks at a Dinner Party Hosted by Prime Minister Major in London: November 29, 1995," *Weekly Compilation of Presidential Documents* 31.48 (4 December 1995): 2080.

64. U.S. Department of State, Office of the Spokesman, "Statement by Secretary of State Warren Christopher before the House Committee on International Relations" (30 November 1995): 2.

65. U.S. Department of State, "The President's News Conference with European Union Leaders in Madrid, Spain: December 3, 1995," *Weekly Compilation of Presidential Documents* 31.49 (11 December 1995): 2120-2121.

66. U.S. Department of State, Office of the Spokesman, "Interview of Secretary

of State Warren Christopher on ABC-TV's 'This Week with David Brinkley'" (3 December 1995): 2.

67. U.S. Department of State, "The President's News Conference with Prime Minister John Major of the United Kingdom in London, England: November 29, 1995," *Weekly Compilation of Presidential Documents* 31.48 (4 December 1995): 2070.

68. U.S. Department of State, Office of the Spokesman, "Statement by Secretary of State Warren Christopher before the House Committee on International Relations," 3.

69. U.S. Department of State, "The President's News Conference with Prime Minister John Bruton of Ireland in Dublin: December 1, 1995," *Weekly Compilation of Presidential Documents* 31.49 (11 December 1995): 2107.

70. U.S. Department of State, "Remarks to the Parliament of Ireland in Dublin: December 1, 1995," *Weekly Compilation of Presidential Documents* 31.49 (11 December 1995): 2099.

71. U.S. Department of State, "Remarks to Troops in Baumholder, Germany: December 2, 1995," *Weekly Compilation of Presidential Documents* 31.49 (11 December 1995): 2111-2112. The idea of the quality of American troops was also addressed by the president, not to the troops themselves but rather to the American people during his 2 December 1995 "Radio Address to the Nation": "[O]ur troops are the best trained, best equipped, best prepared fighting force in the world. They are skilled; they are strong; they are determined to succeed." See U.S. Department of State, "The President's Radio Address: December 2, 1995," *Weekly Compilation of Presidential Documents* 31.49 (11 December 1995): 2116.

72. U.S. Department of State, "Remarks to Troops in Baumholder," 2111-2112.

73. U.S. Department of State, "The President's Radio Address: December 2, 1995," 2116.

74. White House, Office of the Press Secretary, "Press Briefing by Mike McCurry" (29 November 1995): 4.

75. White House, Office of the Press Secretary, "Press Briefing by Mike McCurry" (30 November 1995): 2.

76. U.S. Department of State, "Exchange with Reporters Prior to Discussions with Prime Minister John Bruton of Ireland in Dublin: December 1, 1995," *Weekly Compilation of Presidential Documents* 31.49 (11 December 1995): 2104.

77. Todd S. Purdum, "Clinton Rallies Edgy Troops for Bosnia," *New York Times* 3 December 1995: A16.

78. Ann Devroy, "Clinton Reassures Bosnia-Bound Forces Mission Is 'Safe as It Can Be,'" *Washington Post* 3 December 1995: A32.

79. Michael Dobbs, "Congress Raising Questions about Bosnia Exit Strategy," *Washington Post* 30 November 1995: A32.

80. Dobbs, "Congress Raising Questions," A32.

81. John F. Harris and Eric Pianin, "Clinton Accepts Hill's Defense Spending Bill," *Washington Post* 1 December 1995: A1.

82. Ann Devroy, "Clinton Defends Sending Troops to Bosnia," *Washington Post* 2 December 1995: A15.

83. Barbara Crossette, "Talking Tough, U.N. Condemns Bosnian Serbs," *New*

York Times 30 November 1995: A11.

84. Chris Hedges, "Bosnia Town Prepares for G.I.'s and Switch from War to Peace," *New York Times* 1 December 1995: A14.

85. John Pomfret, "Once-Red Carpet Is Out for NATO," *Washington Post* 30 November 1995: A33.

86. William Drozdiak, "NATO Votes to Start Bosnia Deployment," *Washington Post* 2 December 1995: A14.

87. Hedges, "In Sarajevo Suburbs," A1.

88. U.S. Department of State, "Remarks on Signing the Human Rights Proclamation: December 5, 1995," *Weekly Compilation of Presidential Documents* 31.49 (11 December 1995): 2125.

89. U.S. Department of State, Office of the Spokesman, "Intervention by Secretary of State Warren Christopher at the Meeting of NATO Foreign and Defense Ministers on Bosnia" (5 December 1995): 2.

90. U.S. Department of State, Office of the Spokesman, "Daily Press Briefing: DPC#176" (6 December 1995): 2.

91. White House, Office of the Press Secretary, "Press Briefing by Mike McCurry" (8 December 1995): 15.

92. U.S. Department of State, Office of the Spokesman, "Press Availability: Secretary of State Warren Christopher on European Issues" (8 December 1995): 5.

93. White House, Office of the Press Secretary, "Press Briefing by Mike McCurry" (14 December 1995): 3.

94. White House, Office of the Press Secretary, "Press Briefing by Mike McCurry" (6 December 1995): 7.

95. U.S. Department of State, "Remarks on Signing the Human Rights Proclamation," 2124.

96. U.S. Department of State, "Remarks to Citizens Involved in Humanitarian Relief Efforts for Bosnia and an Exchange with Reporters: December 12, 1995," *Weekly Compilation of Presidential Documents* 31.50 (18 December 1995): 2178.

97. U.S. Department of State, Office of the Spokesman, "Intervention by Secretary of State Warren Christopher at the Meeting," 2.

98. U.S. Department of State, "Remarks to the Committee for American Leadership in Bosnia and an Exchange with Reporters: December 6, 1995," *Weekly Compilation of Presidential Documents* 31.49 (11 December 1995): 2131.

99. U.S. Department of State, Office of the Spokesman, "Press Availability: Secretary of State Warren Christopher on European Issues," 1-2.

100. White House, Office of the Press Secretary, "Press Briefing by Mike McCurry" (6 December 1995): 9.

101. White House, Office of the Press Secretary, "Press Briefing by Mike McCurry" (6 December 1995): 11.

102. U.S. Department of State, "Remarks to the Committee for American Leadership," 2132.

103. U.S. Department of State, "Letter to Senate Democratic Leader Thomas Daschle on Implementation of the Balkan Peace Process: December 11, 1995," *Weekly Compilation of Presidential Documents* 31.50 (18 December 1995): 2177.

104. U.S. Department of State, "Remarks Prior to Discussion with Balkan

Leaders and an Exchange with Reporters in Paris, France: December 14, 1995," *Weekly Compilation of Presidential Documents* 31.50 (18 December 1995): 2184.

105. Rick Atkinson, "U.S. Bound for Bosnia by Train, Truck, Air," *Washington Post* 4 December 1995: A21; Ann Devroy, "President Authorizes Deployment to Bosnia," *Washington Post* 4 December 1995: A1; Devroy, "Clinton Reassures Bosnia-Bound Forces," A32; Dana Priest and John E. Young, "Reservists Called Up for Training," *Washington Post* 5 December 1995: A12; Rick Atkinson, "Military Families Battle the Stress of Separation," *Washington Post* 5 December 1995: A16; Bradley Graham, "Deployment of U.S. Troops Goes Slowly," *Washington Post* 7 December 1995: A31; Bradley Graham, "Advice to an Incoming General: Be Firm, Friendly," *Washington Post* 12 December 1995: A28; "U.S. Jets Start Shuttle to Tuzla," *Washington Post* 9 December 1995: A19; James Brooke, "Army Stress Control Unit Mobilizes, Too, to Seek Out Peacekeeping's Hidden Toll," *New York Times* 7 December 1995: A6; Philip Shennon, "U.S. Troops in Bosnia Find a 'Shellshocked' People," *New York Times* 11 December 1995: A10; Philip Shenon, "Main Peril for G.I.'s in Bosnia Lies Just Beneath the Surface," *New York Times* 10 December 1995: A1; Stephen Kinzer, "Hungarian Town Mobilizes for G.I.'s Bound for Bosnia," *New York Times* 4 December 1995: A1; Eric Schmitt, "In U.S. Peacekeeper Arsenal, Weapons Honed for Bosnia," *New York Times* 5 December 1995: A1.

106. "Stirring of a New NATO," Editorial, *New York Times* 7 December 1995: A30.

107. Craig R. Whitney, "Europe Has Few Doubts on Bosnia Force," *New York Times* 5 December 1995: A8.

108. Roger Cohen, "France to Rejoin Military Command for NATO Alliance," *New York Times* 6 December 1995: A1.

109. "The Republican Split on Bosnia," Editorial, *New York Times* 14 December 1995: A30.

110. Katherine Q. Seelye, "Congress and White House Barter over Support for U.S. Mission," *New York Times* 5 December 1995: A7. These same assertions were again repeated the next day. See Katherine Q. Seelye, "G.O.P. Opposition Forces Dole to Delay Vote on Bosnia," *New York Times* 6 December 1995: A14.

111. R. W. Apple, Jr., "Flimsy Bosnia Mandate," *New York Times* 14 December 1995: A1.

112. Apple, "Flimsy Bosnia Mandate," A1.

113. Chris Hedges, "Vanguard Forces Arriving in the Balkans," *New York Times* 5 December 1995: A8.

114. Roger Cohen, "Christopher Suggests 'Sensitivity' to Needs of the Bosnian Serbs," *New York Times* 7 December 1995: A7.

115. Christine Spolar, "Sarajevo Serbs Find No Peace in Dayton Pact," *Washington Post* 6 December 1995: A29.

116. Spolar, "Sarajevo Serbs Find," A1, A29. Also, by this time, the number of Serbs reported living in Sarajevo had dropped considerably. Initial press reports placed the figures at 120,000. This is a Serbian figure, with the *New York Times* reporting that the United Nations believed there to be approximately 50,000 in Sarajevo suburbs. However, the *New York Times* and *Washington Post* consistent-

ly reduced the Serbian figure. The *Washington Post* reported 70,000, and the *New York Times* reported 80,000 Serbs living in the suburbs of Sarajevo. On 13 December 1995 the figure was again reduced, to 60,000, even though the official Serbian number was still 120,000, and no explanation was given for the reduction in the number. See Raymond Bonner, "Bosnian Serb Leader Signals Acceptance of Peace Plan," *New York Times* 25 November 1995: A3. See, too, Devroy and Dewar, "U.S. Troops Vital," A10; Drozdiak, "NATO Votes to Start Bosnia Deployment," A14; Cohen, "Christopher Suggests 'Sensitivity,'" A7; Chris Hedges, "Bosnian Serbs Take Vote, and Pact Takes Battering," *New York Times* 13 December 1995: A16.

Chapter 6

The Haitian Crisis:
From Bush to Clinton

Over time the administration and the press developed interpretive frames that allowed for very different assessments of the events in Haiti. Both the Bush and Clinton administrations framed the Haitian situation essentially as a foreign policy problem. In their eyes the primary goal of any expenditure of resource or military intervention was the stabilization of the democratically elected Haitian government as an independent political entity. The press, on the other hand, ultimately framed the Haitian situation as a domestic problem. It saw the U.S. role in terms of an obligation to idealized norms of freedom of immigration and the legalities of the administration's policy of direct returns. Thus, this chapter will provide a chronological exposition of executive policy, a policy shadowed by the growth of a press critique. This critique ultimately became so clearly divergent as to constitute a fully articulated counterpolicy. This chapter is divided into three sections: First, a short synopsis of the Bush administration's response to the situation in Haiti is presented; second, the various responses of the *New York Times*, the *Washington Post*, and the Clinton administration from 14 January 1993 through 30 June 1993 are detailed; and third, a summary of the framing devices used by the press and the administration is provided.

SYNOPSIS OF PRESIDENT BUSH'S RESPONSE

Early on 4 October 1991, President George Bush began an exchange with reporters concerning the overthrow of President Jean-Bertrand Aristide of Haiti. The president stated that the United States was "interested in the restoration of the democratically elected government of Haiti" but refused to say more until a press conference scheduled for later that day.[1] At this subsequent conference, President Bush was asked if he would be willing to use military force to restore democracy in Haiti. He replied that he was reluctant to do this and that the United States would wait and see how the OAS responded to the coup. The president's response was detached, and there did not seem to be any reason to believe a crisis for the U.S. had developed.

On this same day, President Bush issued Executive Order 12775, which declared a United States trade embargo on Haiti. The wording of the order stands in stark contrast to the president's earlier statements:

I, George Bush, President of the United States of America, find that the grave events that have occurred in the Republic of Haiti to disrupt the legitimate exercise of power by the democratically elected government of the country constitute an unusual threat to the national security, foreign policy, and economy of the United States, and hereby declare a national emergency to deal with the threat.[2]

On 28 October 1991 President Bush issued a second executive order in regard to Haiti. Through Order 12779, the president stated that the events in Haiti continued to constitute a threat to the United States, and he further tightened the economic embargo imposed upon Haiti. This remained the status quo until 13 April 1992, when President Bush sent a message to Congress. This missive provided detailed reasons for the continued economic sanctions against Haiti. Furthermore, the connection between the Bush policy and the OAS efforts to restore democracy were strengthened; and, for the first time, the situation was called a crisis by the administration. President Bush had made it clear that during this declared state of "national emergency" for the United States his policy was to wait and see what the OAS and the United Nations would accomplish.

On 24 May 1992 President Bush issued Executive Order 12324, which authorized U.S. Coast Guard vessels to repatriate Haitians, bound for the United States, who had not been granted asylum through our embassy in Haiti. The president justified this action, citing the large number of Haitians, over 34,000 since 30 September 1991, who had attempted to leave the island nation for the United States; Bush called it "a dangerous and unmanageable situation."[3] This policy of direct return was designed to keep Haitians safe; indeed, according to President Bush, "the safety of the Haitians is best assured by remaining in their country. We urge any Haitians who fear persecution to avail themselves of our service at our Embassy in Port-au-Prince."[4]

During a press conference three days later on 27 May 1992 the president was asked about the recent influx of Haitian immigrants and his policy of repatriation: "[This] policy seems to run contrary to what America has stood for over the past couple hundred years, in that Americans opened their arms to all ethnic groups and different classes who sought to free themselves . . . from oppression in their homelands."[5] President Bush uses this question to set up an important component in his policy: Haitian refugees are primarily economic refugees, not political. Indeed, the president stated, "I am convinced that the people in Haiti are not being physically oppressed."[6] President Bush stated quite clearly that the U.S. government had every legal right to screen people coming into the country and that the country was not bound to "have an open policy where everybody in economic deprivation around the world can come to the United States."[7] The next day, on 28 May 1992, the president issued a statement that denied vessels trading with Haiti the use of U.S. ports. President Bush also clarified his policy, stating that the sanctions were directed at coup leaders, not the Haitian poor; and he announced that the embassy at Port-au-Prince had expanded operations for processing political refugees.

President Bush made no other formal statements concerning Haiti until 30 September 1992, when he sent a message to Congress about the current state of affairs in Haiti.[8] In this communique the president continued the state of emergency sanctions; it is noted as well that these sanctions were made in conjunction with the OAS. Further, President Bush noted, the OAS had "repudiated" and "vigorously condemned" Aristide's overthrow. The president also stated that "the crisis between the United States and Haiti . . . has not been resolved."[9]

During a press conference on 23 October 1992, President Bush was confronted by a reporter who insisted that over 40 percent of those seeking asylum at Port-au-Prince were found by State Department officials to be politically oppressed. The president challenged this reporter and stated that he would "like to see that documentation" because political refugees would not be turned back. President Bush attempted to put an end to future ungrounded speculations of this sort when he drew on his authority as president and stated: "I must have different information than you, but I've got pretty good information as President of the United States that these people are not being persecuted when they go to file their claims for asylum."[10]

The situation with Haiti remained essentially unchanged during the three remaining months of President Bush's term. The Bush administration had initiated a Haitian policy that would act to set the frame through which President Clinton would initially have to address the situation. Clearly, this was a foreign policy issue and one in which the United States was a partner, not the leader. Furthermore, the policy of direct returns was framed as a humanitarian act, thereby foregoing legal definitions for moral ones. As frames, President Bush's utterances about Haiti would act as a constraint on President Clinton's utterances about the same situation. The Bush administration did accomplish several important policy steps. By declaring a national emergency for the United States, President Bush enacted Emergency Presidential Powers that would legally enable him to take extreme measures against the Haitian coup leaders. Bush initiated a policy of direct repatriation on the high seas. This policy was justified in part as a measure to save unwanted loss of human life and by stating that the vast majority of Haitian refugees were economic, not political refugees. This implied that the current in-Haiti processing was adequate. The president also initiated a trade embargo with Haiti; this included a ban on vessels trading with Haiti from using U.S. ports. President Bush also made it quite clear that the sanctions were directed at the coup leaders, not the Haitian poor (e.g., petroleum products, food stuffs, humanitarian aid, and similar items were excluded in the ban). For proactive measures the Bush administration had expanded the Port-au-Prince embassy refugee processing facilities. Finally, President Bush had made an important component of his policy continuing U.S. cooperation with the United Nations and the OAS.

PRESIDENT CLINTON INHERITS A CRISIS

When Bill Clinton assumed the presidency, he inherited Bush's Haitian policy and the emerging press questions about the repatriation of refugees. Candidate Clinton had promised a policy markedly different from that of President Bush, but throughout the many months following his ascension to the presidency, it became increasingly clear that the heart of the Bush policy remained in force.[11] The Clinton administration issued its first statements on the Haitian situation on 14 January 1993. One is directed to the people of Haiti and the other to the people of the United States. In these similar statements, President-elect Clinton made clear how his administration would view the situation in Haiti, and he made his first utterances upon what had become an important ongoing situation for the United States. In short, he was beginning the process of framing the event in the terms that his administration wished it to be seen. The president made clear what his goals in this situation would be: "My major goals are the restoration of democracy in Haiti, the saving of human lives and the establishment of a system for fair treatment of refugees."[12] These goals were to be accomplished through a "political settlement" of the crisis. Moreover, the political means would involve "intensive negotiations," with various parties—United Nations, OAS, President Aristide, and the coup leaders—"working together," engaging in "important negotiations" to bring about the political settlement that would change the "human rights" conditions in Haiti, ultimately leading to President Aristide's return. President-elect Clinton made it clear that his administration would be a team player with the United Nations and the OAS.

Despite these announced changes, President Clinton would remain strongly influenced by the policy he had inherited from the Bush administration. Although candidate Clinton had promised to end the Bush policy of direct repatriations, President-elect Clinton announced that the practice would temporarily continue: "[T]he practice of direct return of those who depart Haiti by boat will be continued. I will end the practice of direct return when I am fully confident I can do so in a way that does not contribute to a humanitarian tragedy."[13] Along with the continuation of direct return, President-elect Clinton announced four concrete actions that he would initiate as an extension to the Bush policy, in effect, making the policy his own: First, the rapidity with which refugee processing within Haiti occurs would be increased; two, processing centers would be created outside of Port-au-Prince; three, more Immigration and Naturalization Service (INS) officers would be posted to Haiti; and four, the United States would encourage expanded UN and OAS human rights monitoring inside of Haiti. Clinton closed his statement by saying that these new actions would "maintain [U.S.] humanitarian obligations to refugees while taking all practical steps necessary to protect against tragic loss of life."[14]

With this statement President-elect Clinton had initiated his administration's frame for viewing the crisis. The president-elect announced the situation as a "crisis" in his announcement's title but then made clear that the action to bring the crisis to closure would be a "process" of "collaborative effort" aimed at restoring democracy. The initial frame that President-elect Clinton tried to set was one of calm, deliberate negotiations being carried out by rational parties on both sides. Although the practice of direct returns would continue, it was linked with humanitarian concerns: prevention of unwarranted loss of life that the dangerous sea voyage could bring about. Further, the humanitarian actions of the administration were highlighted by its efforts to ensure fair and safe refugee processing within Haiti and other "measures" that would be "actively explored."

This view was reiterated by Press Secretary George Stephanopoulos during a 1 February 1993 press briefing. When told by a reporter that the Haiti situation had "hit a new roadblock in negotiated solutions"[15] due to 300 HIV-infected Haitians on Guantánamo Bay going on a hunger strike to gain entry into the United States, Stephanopoulos replied:

"The President's position remains the same. He wants to make sure that we continue to do everything we can to reach a negotiated settlement, to bring democracy back to Haiti."[16]

The Initial Press Response

The press response to administrative utterances did relate the information conveyed by the administration, but it also showed the beginnings of a contending frame. For example, the Clinton administration had highlighted its sense of urgency and quickened pace of negotiations; in short, they seemed to be attempting to instill new energy into the negotiation process. During the week following President-elect Clinton's initial statements, the *New York Times* did reinforce this impression. The paper stated that there had been signs of "energetic work" and that the Clinton administration had "strenuously promoted a plan" to bring in UN/OAS observers.[17] Additionally, the paper related that the "pace of diplomacy to find a political settlement appears to be quickening."[18]

Beginnings of an Oppositional Frame: Direct Returns Questioned

Although the sense of optimism was relayed, both the *New York Times* and the *Washington Post* highlighted Clinton's apparent about-face from his previous stance on ending the Bush administration's policy of direct returns. Although the press did relate the Clinton administration's reasons for continuing the policy, it also offered its own, oppositional assessment. For example, the *New York Times* stated: "His official explanation for reversing himself is to avoid the humanitarian catastrophe of capsized boats and overcrowded camps. But Mr. Clinton's real worry appears to be political fallout in Florida in reaction to a flood of poor, black Haitian refugees."[19] The *Washington Post* reported President Clinton's official explanation for keeping the policy of direct returns in place—to avert a humanitarian tragedy—yet it, too, made it into a political as opposed to humanitarian decision: "A political settlement of the crisis [in Haiti] . . . is viewed as essential by the Clinton administration to halt the threat of a mass exodus of boat people to Florida."[20] This same position, highlighting the imagined concern with South Florida politicians, is again conveyed: "The specter of hordes of Haitian boat people wading ashore in South Florida has driven President Clinton to reverse campaign promises and erect a virtual Coast Guard blockade of Haiti, leading to charges that his approach, like that of his predecessor, is racist and inhumane."[21] This same motive is argued by the editorial writers at the *Washington Post*. Their assessment of the major breakthrough in negotiations that allowed for human rights monitors into Haiti was not generous. At bottom the *Washington Post* saw base political motives: "The aim is to lower the level of general bullying, warm the atmosphere in which negotiations could restore normal politics and, not least, reduce the number of Haitians driven to seek refuge in Florida."[22] This line of reasoning was further apparent in other *Washington Post* reports that stressed that "since the election, Clinton has bowed to 'political pressure' to stop a deluge of Haitians from reaching Florida."[23] Whether true or not, neither the *Washington Post* nor the *New York Times* ever discussed the ramifications of accelerated mass migration into already overburdened South Florida; furthermore, the danger of tens of thousands of Haitians at sea in shoddy boats was virtually ignored. The press was introducing its own frame. The restoration of democracy in Haiti was not the primary issue; instead, the policy of direct returns was focused on. The frame was asserting a domestic-focused interpretation of President Clinton's policy; direct returns was being forced into a legal, as opposed to humanitarian, frame. The continuation of direct returns was framed as a domestic, political campaign promise that had been broken.

The press opposition to direct returns took for granted a right of all departing Haitians to asylum in the United States; thus, President Clinton's decision to continue direct returns was called an "unconscionable about face" and "repellent"; or, in the case of the *Washington Post*, "racist and inhumane." Moreover, the press rarely differentiated between economic and political refugees as both the Bush and Clinton administrations had made a point of doing. For example, the *New York Times* reported that Clinton had announced that "he would return the boat people without giving them a chance to apply for asylum."[24] The press also implied that all Haitians fleeing did so for political reasons. For instance: "an atmosphere of harsh repression that has contributed to an exodus of refugees and posed a potential immigration crisis."[25] Despite Haiti's status as the poorest country in the Western hemisphere, the press consistently advanced political oppression as the primary motive for immigration. For example, "Critics of the plan charged that Clinton is acting exactly as President Bush has in denying Haitians who fear for their lives a way to escape political oppression."[26] This strong editorial implication provides another example: "The outpouring of refugees from Haiti will continue as long as the country remains in the grip of anarchy and violence, with no public authority other than undisciplined soldiers."[27] By framing in this manner, the press undermined President Clinton's claim of humanitarian motives undergirding his policy of direct returns.

When economic conditions are mentioned, they appear less salient than the reported political oppression within the country; for we have already learned the real cause of the fleeing boat people: political oppression. Thus, a contemporary and patriotic view of immigrating to the United States dominates even when economic concerns are included with political oppression: "Haiti, already the poorest nation in the hemisphere, has seen its economy crumble and political repression grow since Aristide's overthrow."[28] The economy is only secondary or perhaps a symptom of political oppression.

The primacy of the frame of political oppression is perhaps most stridently presented in the *Washington Post*, which described conditions of violence and then failed to provide sources or direct quotes; in short, hearsay is provided for establishing the validity of political conditions:

Soldiers and police arrested at least 10 protesters in breaking up Thursday's demonstration [by students in support of Aristide] at the medical school, and troops clubbed students and teachers about the head in dispersing protesters at the high school.

Journalists and newspaper vendors have been threatened, beaten and arrested in the past two weeks, and radio stations were warned that news must be presented in ways that will "not have a harmful effect."[29]

The Administration Restates Its Position

President Clinton received his first formal question about Haiti on 5 February 1993: "[I]s it time to strengthen pressure on Haiti? Do you think we should have stronger action."[30] His response echoes those of George Bush: "I am committed to restoring democracy to Haiti. I am doing my best to work through the U.N. and the OAS."[31] At this same time, President Clinton used such terms as "determination" and "push ahead" to characterize his administration's diplomatic efforts. The president also refined his argument for diplomatic efforts by highlighting the underlying reasoning for his initiatives: "We have to be able to restore democracy in a way that convinces everybody that their human rights will be respected and . . . protected."[32] If this route were to fail, the president promised to embark upon an even "more vigorous course" toward the restoration of democracy.

On 10 February 1993 President Clinton was asked about his "naval blockade" of Haiti and about his criticism of the Bush policy in light of its similarity to his own. The president's response is an instructive one: "My policy is not the same as President Bush's policy because I'm trying to bring democracy back, because I am committed to putting more resources there to process people who want to be political refugees."[33] Although a reporter asserted that the embargo would hurt "the people at the bottom" instead of the coup leaders, the president consistently justified his actions and called them a necessary measure to secure the safety of the Haitian people who attempted the dangerous sea crossing. The president declared the likely inundation a potential "human tragedy of monumental proportions."[34] The president challenged the reporter and asked if the embargo were lifted, "then what incentives does the government have to change?"[35] For the first time, too, the president made mention of broken past promises of the federal government to help South Florida.

Press Opposition to the "Blockade" and Direct Returns

The exchange about a "naval blockade" provides a good example of specific naming of actions used by the press. In actuality, there were only seventeen Coast Guard vessels and five navy boats. They were stationed outside of Haitian waters and only intercepted boats filled with Haitians heading for the United States. This action in no way constituted a blockade, which is internationally considered an act of war restricting all commerce and people from entering or leaving a particular area. Yet the press referred to the presence of the ships as a blockade. For example, the *Washington Post*, reporting on the deployment of U.S. ships to intercept and return fleeing Haitians, began the news story this way: "The United States plans to surround Haiti with Navy and Coast Guard vessels and planes, mounting a virtual blockade to stop a potential surge of refugees fleeing the island, Adm. J. William Kime, commandant of the Coast Guard, said today." After this statement, an administration official, the same Admiral J. William Kime, was quoted as saying that the "interdiction policy is not a blockade." However, after Kime's comments on the interdiction have been briefly relayed, advocates for Haitian refugees are more fully cited: "'People should have the freedom to flee repression. They're putting a barricade around Haiti. . . . Whether it's an encirclement or a white picket fence, a blockade is a blockade. . . . Blockades are acts of war.'"[36] Although the administration's position is reported, clearly other descriptions dominate and have their saliency increased by the placement and consistency of use. This interpretation is consistently advanced, too. The Rev. Antoine Adrien, Aristide's highest ranking in Haiti representative, is reported by the *Washington Post* as having called the interdiction policy "'a floating Berlin wall.'"[37] In a later story the *Washington Post* reported Harold H. Koh, the "Yale Law School professor . . . representing Haitians who claim they are political refugees," as saying the administration had established "'a floating Berlin Wall.'"[38] Although the Clinton administration consistently referred to the policy as one of interdiction and direct returns, the press consistently reported it, except when quoting administration officials, as "forced repatriation," "forced return," and "blockade."

The Clinton administration is also accused by the press of harming the poor in Haiti, and not the "people at the top" of the country, through the continuation of the embargo. For example, the *Washington Post* made what might be considered an indictment against the administration: "The embargo imposed by the OAS in October 1991, a U.S. initiative, added to impoverishment but did little to weaken the resolve of the current rulers to remain in power."[39] The administration contended that if the sanctions are lifted, there would be no incentive for the present rulers to restore democracy. However, this reasoning was virtually ignored by the press. By 16 February 1993, a *Washington Post* editorial called for the lifting of the embargo: "It is also time to start trimming back an economic embargo whose principal impact has been not on the elements of power and privilege in Haiti but on an already-impoverished mass population."[40]

Throughout the first eight weeks after President Clinton assumed office, the press maintained that the policy of direct returns was illegal. This case was still under review with the United States Supreme Court, but the press consistently reported the policy as being illegal. Their reasoning for asserting this rests primarily upon candidate Clinton's statements during the 1992 presidential race that Bush's policy of direct returns was illegal. For instance, on 15 January 1993 the *Washington Post* stated, "The Bush policy is 'no less legal now that it has been endorsed by Clinton than it was when it was announced by Bush.'"[41] An editorial stated: "To discourage Haitian refugees, President-elect Clinton has embraced a Bush administration policy that, among its other defects, appears to be grossly illegal."[42] The *New York Times* presented this general interpretation as well, and characterized "the forcible return of potential refugees as illegal."[43] Candidate Clinton's utterances of calling Bush's policy "illegal" and "immoral" were frequently reported. Indeed, on this same issue, in early March the *Washington Post* highlighted candidate Clinton's campaign pledge to end Bush's policy; it seems that the constant assertion of the illegality of the policy rested on two earlier events. One, candidate Clinton called it illegal during the 1992 presidential race: "After Assailing Interdiction Program as Illegal During Campaign, Clinton Has Adopted It."[44] Two, a U.S. Court of Appeals had said it was illegal. It seemed not to matter that the order to revise the policy was granted a stay by the U.S. Supreme Court until it could be reviewed there. A *New York Times* editorial stated that forcing "desperate refugees back into the face of danger betrays American values and mocks U.S. and international law."[45] Against these assertions, the positive steps taken by the administration to provide asylum hearings in Haiti were seldom detailed. The administration's humanitarian commitment and arguments were seldom discussed, nor was the fact that the U.S. government is not compelled by any law to grant asylum hearings outside of the United States. The latter was mentioned once by the *Washington Post*.[46]

In the span of many months, the press had advanced a legal conception of Clinton's policy of interdiction and direct returns. In a 4 March 1993 editorial, the *New York Times* stated that President Clinton had "asked the Supreme Court to find that [Bush's] policy legal or, better still, to rule that courts can't order the President to obey a treaty and immigration law."[47] The editorial continues, stating that at present "the U.S. is legally bound not to return a fleeing Haitian without deciding eligibility for asylum."[48]

Consolidation of the Press Frame

Despite steady criticism of the administration's policies on Haiti, the sinking of the ferry *Neptune* on 18 February 1993 prompted little criticism from the press. The ship was a regularly scheduled mode of transportation used between Haitian ports and was not carrying a cargo load of America bound immigrants. However, the *New York Times* did publish several full-length feature stories on the sinking, and these stories did contain framing elements that implied ultimate responsibility for the sinking on Clinton and Bush administration policies. For example, on 19 February 1993 it was reported that the *Neptune* had not sailed for several weeks "largely because the owners feared Haitians trying to reach the United States would hijack the vessel."[49] Hijacking was of real concern to the owners, however, because boats "seized on the seas by the Coast Guard are routinely destroyed and their passengers returned to land."[50] The press had also implied that the ferry was overcrowded because road conditions were intolerable and there was no fuel for small aircraft; thus Haitians, of necessity, must use the ferry. The bad conditions and shortages of fuel were, according to the press, a direct result of the U.S.-led embargo. This connection was forcefully argued in a 21 February 1993 *New York Times* report: "The roads connecting Jeremie and Port-au-Prince are in terrible condition, and few busses run because of fuel shortages caused by an embargo imposed after the overthrow of the Rev. Jean-Bertrand Aristide."[51] Contrary to this report, however, no embargo on petroleum products existed at that time.[52] By 21 February 1993 this ferry sinking grew from being reported as "one of the world's worst ferry disasters"[53] to being reported as "one of the world's worst maritime disasters."[54]

By this time, four weeks into the Clinton administration, the press had consolidated its frame. What follows is a characteristic example of this description:

Since a military coup in September of 1991 overthrew the nation's President, the Rev. Jean-Bertrand Aristide, more than 40,000 Haitians have attempted to flee to the United States, almost all of them attempting the 600-mile journey in rickety boats.

In recent weeks, the Coast Guard has maintained a blockade off Haiti to prevent a greater sea-borne exodus that was first inspired by the hope that the Clinton administration might ease limits on claims for political asylum.[55]

The framing elements emphasize the domestic nature of the situation. The internal situation in Haiti is political, not economic; therefore, all Haitians wishing to flee are political refugees that must be granted asylum in the United States. The policy of direct returns is thus illegal; the motives for the policy are not humanitarian but political. The administration reneged on its promise of eliminating the policy and caved in to the political pressure from South Florida officials.

On 2 March 1993 the specter of a continuity with the Bush policy was again raised when a reporter asked President Clinton if he had any "second thoughts about [his] criticism of George Bush's Haiti policy," especially given the Clinton administration's Supreme Court appeal to keep the policy of direct returns operational.[56] The president's reply was standard: "I still think there's a big difference between what we're doing in Haiti and what they [the Bush administration] were doing in Haiti."[57] Of note here, however, is that the president assigned what he believed to be a new dimension to the Haitian situation but that is in fact what we have already seen to be the very justification President Bush used for his policy:

Something that was never brought up before but is now painfully apparent is that if we did what the plaintiffs in the court case want [ending of the repatriation policy], we would be consigning a very large number of Haitians . . . to some sort of death warrant. . . . I mean, if you look at . . . the number of people who did not even try to come to the United States in a much shorter trip recently [the *Neptune* sinking].[58]

On 2 March 1993, the day the administration went to court over the legality of direct returns, the administration also detailed the exact progress made with the Haiti situation. In a formal statement issued to the press, George Stephanopoulos reiterated the administration's belief that the policy of direct returns was directly linked with President Clinton's belief that it will avert a "humanitarian tragedy." This statement also related the forward-moving progress of the negotiations and the administration's "series of initiatives to promote human rights and democratization in Haiti."[59] The quickened pace of negotiations and the improvements made on the Bush policy were again highlighted that same day by Stephanopoulos during a press briefing. Although the press did raise the issue of Clinton's campaign pledge to end the direct return policy of Bush, Stephanopoulos consistently presented items that flow from the administration's earliest utterances on Haiti:

[The] President has significantly changed U.S. policy toward Haiti in the last several months. He has reinvigorated the process toward peace and democracy. He has supported the efforts of the U.N. and the OAS to negotiate, and a U.N. and an OAS civilian monitoring team has been deployed in Haiti. And we hope that this will create an atmosphere that's conducive to respect for human rights and political dialogue.

At the same time, he's moving the negotiating process forward. He's invited President Aristide for a meeting . . . . He's directed U.S. officials to significantly increase the capacity to review asylum cases. He sent a monitoring team to Haiti and he's directed the State Department to send a technical mission. . . . He's made it easier for Haitians outside of Port-au-Prince to apply for refugee status and U.S. resettlement and to enhance the safety of the repatriation process for the returnees. We've made the capacity for asylum cases—we've reduced it from about two months to about a week in Haiti.[60]

As the administration contended, this represented a "significant change in policy." The administration consistently stressed that it was "moving the negotiating process forward." The policy of direct returns was linked with the president's ability to conduct foreign policy and with the averting of a "humanitarian disaster."

By this time the contrasting frames of the press and the administration were fully operational. The *New York Times* was characterizing those being returned without asylum hearings as "political refugees" in the thousands.[61] Moreover, around this time we see the implied rights of boat people to enter this country being strongly asserted. A 2 March 1993 *New York Times* article relays a blatant description: "'What Haiti needs is an underground railroad. For many people that railroad was the boats, and we have shut that off.'"[62] Along these same lines the press once again brought up the issue of the HIV-infected Haitians being detained at Guantánamo Bay. Having brought up the current court case on this issue, the *New York Times* reported a contrast of pictures of the refugee camp. Beginning with Haitian advocates' descriptions, the paper defined the camp as a "pen for pigs," a "prison camp, surrounded by razor wire and guarded by the military." Although the *New York*

Times reported that the administration described the camp as a "humanitarian mission camp with a church, beauty salon, television set and weight-lifting room," it undermined the humanitarian claims with a sarcastic comment: "People with problems cannot exercise."[63] These amenities were made to seem sinister through another gratuitous quote that "likened the Government's emphasis on the camp's perquisites to 'bragging about the orchestra at Buchenwald.'"[64] This human interest aspect to the situation in Haiti was begun by the *Washington Post* as early as 11 February 1993. The camp was then described as "a grim barbed-wire encampment" with "prison-like conditions." Too, the story suggested that those "detained . . . lived in flimsy, leaky barracks, among rodents and scorpions, in part because of a legal battle over their fate that is wending its way through the U.S. courts."[65] The *Washington Post* does not make specific mention about what constitutes the other "part" of the reason for the Haitians' detention. However, the paper does report a quote from an INS official that makes the point for them: "Asked what would keep the Haitians at Guantanamo even after the ban [on HIV-infected immigrants] is lifted, Austin [the INS official] said, 'Maybe because as a policy matter you don't want to bring them here.'"[66]

Although the press had reported the changes that President Clinton had made in the Haiti policy since taking office, it was still President Bush's policy as this headline suggested: "White House Again Defends Bush's Policy on Haitians."[67] Another, "Same Haiti Policy, Still Illegal." Indeed, the focus on only two aspects of the Clinton administration's policy acted to minimize the positive changes that the new administration had made. The press had already developed a standardized version of events. Reporting that President Clinton met with only a limited number of reporters instead of having a large press conference during President Aristide's visit, the *Washington Post* reported: "That had the effect of shielding Clinton from questions about his Haiti policy, in which he has continued the Bush administration policy of forcibly returning refugees on the high seas and kept the HIV-positive Haitians confined at Guantanamo Bay despite a campaign pledge to lift the ban."[68]

Moreover, the press was beginning to assert its own opinion as to the pace with which the Clinton administration was moving. Although the administration had been consistent and up-front in highlighting the changes and rapidity with which it had been engaging in a political settlement, the press was beginning to feature elements that suggested a slowing of the pace. For instance, on 2 March 1993 the *New York Times* ran a story entitled, "Despite Plans, U.S. Refugee Processing in Haiti Is Said to Lag."[69] In March 1993 the Haitian military arrested a man who had been granted political asylum by the United States.

Asked what action he would take, the president replied that he was "upset," that it was a "serious" matter, and that he believed "very strongly" that the Haitian government should release the man. This incident was minor, and the Haitian soldier was released after only three days. But it was used by the press to make a statement against Clinton's policy of direct returns. The *New York Times* reported on 14 March 1993 that critics of President Clinton's policy "see the arrest as a test of President Clinton's willingness to revise a Haitian refugee policy that he attacked as cruel in the Presidential campaign but then continued after taking office. By forcibly returning all fleeing Haitians, critics say, the Clinton administration puts those in real danger at risk."[70] Too, the press belittled the administration's concern of a mass boat departure by including a quote from a press described expert on asylum: "'As it stands now, our policy makers are immobilized by a theoretical fear that any form of generosity will result in a large-scale departure of Haitian boat people.'"[71]

Aristide's Visit and the Continuation of the Press Frame

On 13 March 1993 the president once again reiterated his commitment to restoring Aristide to power. He also reiterated the administration's conception of Haiti's problems: "I am committed to the restoration of democracy in Haiti. It is the only thing that will fully resolve the economic problems and the enormous social dislocation and the enormous numbers of people who are willing to risk their lives to leave the island."[72] The president also touched on the pace with which the negotiations were moving, saying that the administration would take a "more active role," that the United States was committed to working with the United Nations and OAS, and that the United States would not be "dictating policy."

Presidents Clinton and Aristide met at the White House on 16 March 1993. During this visit, the president and State Department officials were united in presenting a platform upon which to view the situation in Haiti and future U.S. action. The president reiterated his personal commitment to the restoration of democracy in Haiti. The president also issued a strong statement to the leaders of Haiti that was designed to "make it clear in the strongest possible terms" that the illegal government would not be tolerated indefinitely. Moreover, President Clinton stressed that he wanted to "push forward" and "step up dramatically the pace of negotiation."[73] These comments were in keeping with prior administrative utterances upon Haiti. The president also restated his concern with a definitive date being set for the return of President Aristide: "It is a very grave thing for the United States alone to be setting a date certain in an endeavor that involves the United Nations and the Organization of the American States."[74] In an exchange with reporters, both presidents were provided the opportunity to answer questions about policy designed to return President Aristide to power. During this time, President Clinton announced that "stronger measures" would be taken by the administration if democracy was not restored. Further, he implied that he would not rule out tougher sanctions but that the diplomatic initiatives being undertaken by the United Nations and OAS should be allowed to take effect first. It is at this time also that President Aristide made a public call for a nonviolent return to power, thereby formally eliminating at this time any opportunity for U.S. military intervention.[75]

During this period the administration reemphasized its concern with the economic, as opposed to political, situation in Haiti. The President linked the restoration of democracy in Haiti with "a program of genuine economic progress."[76] On this same day, during a background briefing with senior administration officials, the concern with pace and the restoration of democracy in Haiti was again stressed by the administration: "[I]t was an excellent meeting in the sense that both presidents saw this as a partnership, that we're beginning a process here of pushing the negotiation much more seriously, much more vigorously within the context of a U.N.-OAS international approach."[77] Definitive statements were also made by the administration concerning the request by the press for a "date-certain" being set for President Aristide's return: "President Clinton indicated to President Aristide that he did not think it was advisable for the United States to be setting any particular date-certain. This is a U.N.-OAS led negotiation, the timing of a new government in Haiti and President Aristide's return will be set by that negotiation."[78] That the administration's plan had President Aristide's public and formal approval was demonstrated when President Aristide was asked if the administration's plan was satisfactory to him. He replied simply: "Totally."[79]

However, news items during this period continued the framing of events in the same manner as before. The arrest of the soldier granted asylum was used to highlight the press-perceived problems with the policy of direct returns. Although both the Clinton administration and President Aristide were in agreement about U.S.-Aristide roles in the restoration of democracy in Haiti, the press advanced a different frame through which to view the various events. On the day of the meeting between Presidents Clinton and Aristide, the *New York Times* ran a story that highlighted an enemic pace of negotiation, as opposed to the "vigorous pace" maintained by the administration: Aristide was reported as being "perhaps" and "maybe" disappointed "with the pace of diplomatic activity intended to return him to the presidency of

Haiti."[80] Along these same lines, the *New York Times* headline and byline read: "Haitian Is Offered Clinton's Support on an End to Exile: But No Deadline Is Cited: In Pledging to Restore Aristide, U.S. Avoids Strong Steps, Fearing New Violence."[81] Yet a thorough search of White House documents and the *Weekly Compilation of Presidential Documents* revealed no administrative utterances suggesting a fear of provoking violence by coup leaders; in fact, senior-level administrative officials were remarkably candid in describing the potential of a "win-win" situation for all parties. Moreover, we see the media obsession with a "date-certain" for Aristide's return: "But Mr. Clinton refused to set a deadline by which Washington would demand Father Aristide's return to power as President."[82] Yet the reason the administration gives for not setting a "date-certain" is not provided. During this period of time the *New York Times* also made it clear that it still viewed all refugees coming from Haiti as political refugees: "The administration angered many Haitians when Mr. Clinton reversed his campaign pledge to allow political refugees asylum."[83]

From the Aristide visit forward, the administration moved through a period of relative calm with respect to the situation in Haiti. Throughout April 1993, the president and his administration continued the framing devices they had used during the previous months. The situation in Haiti was a foreign policy issue; direct returns was a humanitarian policy; the Haitian refugees were primarily economic, not political; and the restoration of democracy was predicated upon President Aristide's return.

On 13 April 1993, George Stephanopoulos was asked about the possibility of sending U.S. troops into Haiti.[84] Stephanopoulos replied that the United States was not considering sending U.S. troops, but as President Clinton had stated earlier, the United States would participate in a limited way in the professionalization of Haiti's military and police force once the United Nations and OAS had worked out an agreement for Aristide's return. Stephanopoulos concludes his remarks on Haiti by reaffirming the administration's commitment to a negotiated settlement and the belief that the negotiations would be successful.[85] Just six days later Stephanopoulos was again asked about the possibility of sending U.S. troops into Haiti. He reiterated the administration's position that U.S. troops would not be sent; however, the administration was still "prepared to help assist the professionalization of the Haitian military after an agreement [had been reached to return Aristide]."[86]

By late April 1993 the press was still questioning the efficacy of the administration's policy. Indeed, during one press conference the president was told that his diplomatic initiative was "on the verge of collapse" and perhaps nothing short of military intervention could help.[87] However, the president disagreed, stating that this was not what he had been told and that the diplomatic process was working. This position was echoed by Dee Dee Myers in an 29 April 1993 press briefing: "On Haiti, I think we're still committed toward restoring democracy in Haiti, to restoring President Aristide. I think that process is ongoing and I think we are making progress there."[88] This articulation of optimism and progress was continued throughout the month of May as well.[89]

Progress is often made by prompting others to move, and on 3 June 1993, President Clinton found it necessary to adjust his policy by issuing Proclamation 6569, which bans from entry into the United States any Haitian national felt to be working actively to impede the progress of the negotiations. Furthermore, on 4 June 1993 the president hinted at the "possibility of creating a worldwide sanctions program against Haiti."[90] This is also the first time that the president had explicitly linked the restoration of democracy to a larger U.S. concern: "One of the cornerstones of our foreign policy is to support the global march toward democracy and to stand by the world's new democracies. The promotion of democracy, which not only reflects our values but also increases our security, is especially important in our own hemisphere."[91]

The president's statement stressed once again the administration's view of the negotiation process. Sanctions did not indicate a setback but were viewed as strong messages in the ongoing political dialogue. For Clinton, while progress was still being made on some fronts, those parties in Haiti who were not willing to negotiate must now suffer specific sanctions. These sanctions were surgical in nature; they were specifically designed to target the top Haitian leaders. As an unnamed senior administration official stated: "[W]e've gone after the top leadership in the de facto regime and in the top of the Army."[92] Moreover, the sanctions were a specific tool used to keep the progress moving in the negotiations to return President Aristide to power: The "sanctions are a tactic. They're a tool to try to accomplish a goal. And our goal here is a negotiated solution."[93] The importance of the perception of a continuation of progress is imparted by the administration later in this background briefing. After stating that the sanctions are just a tactic to keep the pace of negotiations moving, the senior administration official makes it clear what is meant:

I think we feel very, very comfortable that we've moved this thing very rapidly, and when we hit a snag you're seeing the determination not to allow it to stall out. This is a sign that the administration intends to keep this thing moving.

We're talking moving as rapidly as we possibly can. And I don't mean that—I don't want to see some story saying, therefore I was evasive and it's going to be slow.[94]

The press response to these increased sanctions was ambivalent at first. On the one hand, the surgical nature of the new sanctions pleased the press; on the other hand, the possibility of imposing further sanctions, including oil, was not an acceptable option for the administration to pursue. After detailing that U.S. administration officials had made the announcement about increased sanctions and the possibility of a UN/OAS oil embargo, the *Washington Post* reported the following: "But yesterday's announcement was aimed at punishing individuals, not the general Haitian population widely seen as paying the highest price since the OAS imposed sanctions after Aristide's ouster."[95] Indeed, the press seemed bent toward proclaiming the harmful effects of the sanctions upon Haiti's poor and the inconsequential effects on the leaders: "The OAS sanctions were widely criticized as punishing the poorest Haitians—many of whom are supporters of Aristide—while being ineffectual in swaying the military."[96]

The press response to the administration's continuing negotiation is reflected in little but passing coverage. However, on 3 June 1993, the *New York Times* reported that the president in May had acknowledged that his policy in Haiti had failed:

Referring to the Haitian military's rejection last month of an America-backed United Nations plan to deploy an international peace force there, Mr. Clinton acknowledged that his policy had failed. . . .

Mr. Clinton's Haitian policy is still unclear. Mr. Clinton has continued the Bush administration policy of forceable [*sic*] repatriation of Haitians seeking political asylum.[97]

This queer line of reasoning—a *failed policy* evinced only by a *single failure/event*—surfaced again in the *New York Times* on 5 June 1993: "In a tacit acknowledgement that its diplomacy has failed to restore Haiti's democratically elected government, the Clinton administration today imposed sanctions."[98] Yet nowhere in the administrative responses is this viewpoint taken. It was made quite clear by administrative officials, and President Clinton, that the tactic of increased sanctions was only that, a tactic to keep the negotiation process moving forward.

In early June the administration was ordered by a federal court to release the Haitians held in Guantánamo Bay, Cuba. In a 9 June 1993 press briefing, Dee Dee Myers stated that the administration would comply with the judge's order. On 17 June 1993, Clinton publicly commented on the possibility of a multinational peacekeeping force in Haiti; he stressed that "President Aristide rejected it and the de facto government rejected it."[99] The president also stressed that he personally believed it would be necessary due to the amount of distrust between the parties. President Clinton also mentioned the possibility of an oil embargo to help force the pace of negotiations.

On 30 June 1993, the president issued Executive Order 12775, which effectively blocked Haitian nationals from using U.S.-based funds and materials to aid the de facto regime in Haiti; it also prohibited "the sale or supply, by United States persons, or from the United States, or using U.S.-registered vessels or aircraft, of petroleum or petroleum products or arms and related materials of all types."[100] The president stressed that the measures were taken in response to the United Nation's Security Council's call and that they were representative of the commitment by the United States to the restoration of President Aristide and democracy to Haiti. On 3 July 1993, an accord was signed by the military leaders of Haiti and President Aristide setting a date for his return to Haiti.

SUMMARY

Two very different narratives emerged during the first half of 1993. The Clinton administration narrative about Haiti had its genesis in the Bush administration policy. The Bush policy had set the stage in several important respects. First, it stressed cooperation with the United Nations and OAS; the United States would work with, but not lead, the negotiations for President Aristide's return. Second, President Bush began the policy of direct returns. This policy was founded on a humanitarian component. Returns were made to prevent massive loss of Haitian lives through a mass relocation via unseaworthy boats. Third, the Bush administration had maintained that the Haitian refugees were primarily economic, not political, in nature. Finally, the Bush administration began the expansion of asylum screening in Port-au-Prince.

White House Frames

When Bill Clinton took office, he inherited the Bush administration policy on Haiti. The president quickly announced his own policy on the matter; in effect, President Clinton adopted the previous administration's policy, modified it, and made it his own. In his first formal utterance concerning Haiti, made as president-elect, Bill Clinton outlined three broad goals of his Haitian policy. First, he was committed to the restoration of democracy. Throughout the first half of 1993 it became apparent that this was a complex goal. The restoration of democracy was predicated upon a working partnership with the United

Nations and OAS. The administration was committed to a negotiated solution to the problems facing Haiti. The United States was a team player, not the leader here. Negotiations were to be carried out in such a manner that everyone—President Aristide and coup leaders—would be convinced that human rights would be respected. This aspect of policy hinged on the deployment of a UN/OAS human rights monitoring team in Haiti. The Clinton administration relayed the impression that negotiations were "moving forward" and that the "pace" was "quickening" through "heightened negotiations." The impression of movement was important to maintain because negotiated settlements take time.

Second, the Clinton administration relayed a sincere commitment to saving human lives. This reasoning directly underpinned the continuation of the original Bush policy of direct returns. The President made this policy his own. He was committed to avoiding a "humanitarian tragedy" and the "tragic loss of life" that was sure to follow if there were a massive flotilla of refugees leaving Haiti. It was apparent that such a flotilla would leave once Bill Clinton took office; thus, he made Bush's policy his own in an effort to stem the tide.

Third, the Clinton administration was committed to fair treatment for political refugees. In-Haiti refugee processing was accelerated; application processing time went from eight weeks to one. The president opened processing centers outside of Port-au-Prince, thereby making it easier for potential refugees to apply for asylum. The president also increased the number of INS officers in Haiti. The placement of the UN/OAS human rights monitoring team helped to provide an atmosphere in which potential refugees would not fear for their safety when applying for asylum.

The Press Framing of Administrative Utterances

The narrative of the press was quite different from that presented by the administration. The papers combined seven elements that acted to underpin their narrative of the situation. First, they continually highlighted alleged "roadblocks" in the administration's push for a negotiated settlement in Haiti. For example, the Haitians in Guantánamo were continually referred to in such a manner as to imply that all political refugees were denied entry into the United States; in fact, they were only excluded due to the legal restriction barring HIV-infected persons from immigrating into the United States.

Second, the press continually made President Clinton's apparent campaign pledge reversal an icon for refugee mistreatment. This was always used to report on the humanitarian aspect of the situation in

Haiti. Ultimately, the reversal was ascribed to potential political fallout from South Florida. The humanitarian considerations advanced by the administration were not valid options for the press. It was inhumane to keep the Haitians out because they were being politically oppressed and because candidate Clinton had promised to let them in.

Third, the press constantly asserted that Haitian refugees were political. Any consideration given to their economic status was always secondary in importance and prominence. This assumption was in part relayed through the use of the terms "forced reparation" and "forced returns." The administration referred to the returns as "direct returns." Too, the press referred to the deployment of U.S. ships to interdict fleeing Haitians as a "blockade" even when administration officials continually stressed that a blockade was not in effect.

Fourth, the press continually assumed U.S. leadership in the negotiation process. This acted to belittle the role and legitimacy of the United Nations and OAS. It also acted to belittle the role that President Aristide played in the negotiation process. The key players in the drama were President Aristide, the Haitian coup leaders, the Clinton administration, the United Nations, and the OAS. The United States is a member state in the OAS and was only facilitating the negotiations. Yet the press continued to blame delays in action on the lack of resolve of the Clinton administration. This U.S. focus is perhaps best illustrated with the media prompting to use U.S. troops to restore Aristide every time there was a slowdown in the pace of negotiations.

Fifth, the press consistently reported that the OAS-sponsored embargo was only hurting Haiti's poor.

Sixth, the press consistently maintained that the policy of direct returns was illegal. This was predicated on two points. One, candidate Clinton had denounced the policy as illegal while he was running for office. Two, a Federal Appeals Court had ruled the policy as illegal. Minimized was the important fact that the administration had been granted a stay of the lower court's ruling and that the policy was to be reviewed by the Supreme Court.

Seventh, the press maintained a point of view that upheld the right of any immigrant, for any reason, to enter this country. The underlying assumption is that anyone wishing to enter the country must be fleeing from political oppression. In Haiti, however, the descriptions of political oppression are not well documented by the press, and two presidential administrations state plainly that there is a minimal amount of political oppression.

NOTES

1. U. S. Department of State, "Exchange With Reporters on the Situation in Haiti: October 4, 1991," *Weekly Compilation of Presidential Documents* 20 (7 October 1991): 1396.

2. U. S. Department of State, "Executive Order 12775—Prohibiting Certain Transactions with Respect to Haiti: October 4, 1991," *Weekly Compilation of Presidential Documents* 20 (7 October 1991): 1406.

3. U.S. Department of State, "White House Statement on Haitian Migrants: May 24, 1992," Weekly Compilation of Presidential Documents 28.22 (1 June 1992): 924.

4. U.S. Department of State, "White House Statement on Haitian Migrants," 924.

5. U.S. Department of State, "Remarks and Question-and-Answer Session with the Mount Paran Christian School Community in Marietta: May 27, 1993," *Weekly Compilation of Presidential Documents* 28.22 (1 June 1992): 938. This quote represents a contemporary, urban-liberal interpretation of U.S. immigration policy and thus is a misrepresentation of the history of immigration in this country. The U.S. government, since the turn of this century, has imposed various and strict immigration regulations. For example, far from opening our arms to "all ethnic groups and different classes," the U.S. government in 1921 passed the Emergency Quota Act. This act effectively restricted the number of immigrants based solely on nationality. Each country had a specific quota. Catholic countries had small quotas; poor countries had small quotas; Great Britain, France, and Spain had high quotas. In 1924 the National Origins Act was passed, which reduced the total number of immigrants entering this country to 150,000 per year. The Origins Act persevered until the early 1960s, and then we see a change in policy that drastically curtailed immigration from Western European countries while virtually opening the door for Asian and Communist countries. Today, the United States has rampant and easy entry: The United States takes in over 1 million immigrants per year (legal and illegal). Immigration occurs in cycles; it has never been open as the press maintained.

6. U.S. Department of State, "Remarks and Question-and-Answer Session," 939.

7. U.S. Department of State, "Remarks and Question-and-Answer Session," 939. Incidental to this, President Bush also stated that his policy had come under scrutiny by some concerned with alleged racist implications. Bush "vehemently" denied this and cited the right of the United States to screen applicants. The president also reminded the press that his administration had stepped up food relief services to help stop the flow of refugees. This last action bolsters the president's contention that Haitians are primarily economic refugees.

8. There is one recorded utterance, however, on 7 June 1992. Bush is asked whether he is considering using troops in Haiti. The answer is a firm no.

9. U.S. Department of State, "Message to the Congress Reporting on the Continuation of the National Emergency with Respect to Haiti: September 30, 1992," *Weekly Compilation of Presidential Documents* 28.40 (5 October 1992): 1830.

10.   U.S. Department of State, "Question-and-Answer Session in Miami, Florida: October 23, 1992," *Weekly Compilation of Presidential Documents* 28.44 (2 November 1992): 2086.

11.   The following is a verbatim transcript of the official release made by candidate Clinton on 31 July 1995: "Statement by Governor Bill Clinton on Haitian Refugees: I am appalled by the decision of the Bush administration to pick up fleeing Haitians on the high seas and forcibly return them to Haiti before considering their claim to political asylum. It was bad enough when there were failures to offer them due process in making such a claim. Now they are offered no process at all before being returned. This policy must not stand. It is a blow to the principle of first asylum and to America's moral authority in defending the rights of refugees around the world. This most recent policy shift is another sad example of the Administration's callous response to a terrible human tragedy. This problem will not be resolved until Washington addresses more firmly and coherently the question of restoring democracy to Haiti. The military regime must be made to understand that it cannot successfully oppose the restoration of democracy simply by waiting. I urge the Administration to redouble its efforts, with the OAS, to tighten the embargo and to insist that our European allies observe it, particularly with regard to oil. As I have said before, if I were President, I would—in the absence of clear and compelling evidence that they weren't political refugees—give them temporary asylum until we restored the elected government of Haiti." Available from: Newsgroups: nptn.campaign92.dems. From: xx001@nptn.org (NPTN Moderator).

12.   Office of the President-elect, "Statement of President-elect Bill Clinton on the Crisis in Haiti" (14 January 1993): 1. Unless otherwise noted, all White House documents were retrieved from the Clinton@Marist Newsgroup (/.data/politics/pres.clinton) using "Gopher."

13.   Office of the President-elect, "Statement," 2.

14.   Office of the President-elect, "Statement," 2.

15.   White House, Office of the Press Secretary, "Press Briefing by George Stephanopoulos" (1 February 1993): 10.

16.   White House, Office of the Press Secretary, "Press Briefing by George Stephanopoulos" (1 February 1993): 10.

17.   Howard W. French, "Aristide Urges Big U.N. Observer Team for Haiti," *New York Times* 14 January 1993: A2.

18.   Steven A. Holmes, "U.S. Sends Flotilla to Prevent Exodus from Haiti by Sea," *New York Times* 16 January 1993: A5.

19.   "For Haitians, Cruelty and Hope," Editorial, *New York Times* 17 January 1993: E16.

20.   Douglas Farah, "Haiti's Army Accepts Plan for Talks," *Washington Post* 18 January 1993: A14.

21.   William Booth, "Truth or Dare, Haitian Style," *Washington Post* 24 January 1993: A1. The charges of inhumanity and racism were not ascribed to any definitive source in this article.

22.   "Strategy in Haiti," Editorial, *Washington Post* 16 February 1993: A12.

23.   Joan Biskupic, "Administration to Defend Bush Haitian Policy in Court,"

Washington Post 1 March 1993: A9.

24. Howard W. French, "Haitians Express Sense of Betrayal," *New York Times* 17 January 1993: A3.

25. French, "Haitians Express Sense," A5.

26. William Booth, "Navy, Coast Guard to Surround Haiti," *Washington Post* 16 January 1993: A1.

27. "Mr. Clinton and the Haitians," Editorial, *Washington Post* 16 January 1993: A22.

28. Douglas Farah, "Coast Guard Patrols, Clinton's Switch on Repatriation Delay Haitian Exodus," *Washington Post* 21 January 1993: A14.

29. Michael Tarr, "Observers Arrive in Haiti," *Washington Post* 15 February 1993: A35.

30. U.S. Department of State, "The President's News Conference with Prime Minister Brian Mulroney: February 5, 1993," *Weekly Compilation of Presidential Documents* 29.5 (8 February 1993): 149.

31. U.S. Department of State, "The President's News Conference with Prime Minister," 150.

32. U.S. Department of State, "The President's News Conference with Prime Minister," 151.

33. U.S. Department of State, "Remarks at a Town Meeting in Detroit: February 10, 1993," *Weekly Compilation of Presidential Documents* 29.6 (15 February 1993): 184.

34. U.S. Department of State, "Remarks at a Town Meeting," 184.

35. U.S. Department of State, "Remarks at a Town Meeting," 184.

36. Booth, "Navy, Coast Guard," A16.

37. Farah, "Coast Guard Patrols," A16.

38. Joan Biskupic, "Court Hears Administration Defend Bush Haitian Policy," *Washington Post* 3 March 1993: A11.

39. Julia Preston, "Haiti Agrees to Monitoring by U.N., OAS," *Washington Post* 10 February 1993: A28.

40. "Strategy in Haiti," A12.

41. Al Kamen and Ruth Marcus, "Clinton to Continue Forcible Repatriation of Fleeing Haitians," *Washington Post* 15 January 1993: A16.

42. "Mr. Clinton and the Haitians," A22.

43. Elaine Sciolino, "Clinton Says U.S. Will Continue Ban on Haitian Exodus," *New York Times* 15 January 1993: A2.

44. Biskupic, "Administration to Defend," A9.

45. "For Haitians, Cruelty and Hope," E16.

46. Ruth Marcus, "Clinton Backs Aristide Return to Power, But Sets No Date," *Washington Post* 17 March 1993: A28.

47. "Same Haiti Policy, Still Illegal," Editorial, *New York Times* 4 March 1993: A24.

48. "Same Haiti Policy, Still Illegal," A24.

49. Howard W. French, "Hundreds Are Lost as Crowded Ferry Capsizes Off Haiti," *New York Times* 19 February 1993: A8.

50. French, "Hundreds Are Lost," A8.

51. Howard W. French, "Ferry Disaster Underlines Haiti's Everyday Needs," *New York Times* 21 February 1993: A8.

52. The ban on petroleum products began on 30 June 1993 with Executive Order 12853.

53. "Of 800 to 1,200 Aboard Haitian Ferry, 285 Lived," *New York Times* 20 February 1993: A3.

54. French, "Ferry Disaster Underlines," A8.

55. Larry Rohter, "Haitian Hijacks a Missionary Plane to Miami," *New York Times* 19 February 1993: A8.

56. U.S. Department of State, "Exchange with Reporters Prior to a Meeting with Secretary General Manfred Woerner of the North Atlantic Treaty Organization: March 2, 1993," *Weekly Compilation of Presidential Documents* 29.9 (8 March 1993): 347.

57. U.S. Department of State, "Meeting with Secretary General Manfred Woerner," 347.

58. U.S. Department of State, "Meeting with Secretary General Manfred Woerner," 347. Similar reasons are given in the "Statement by the Director of Communications on the Situation in Haiti: March 2, 1993": "The current practice of direct returns is based upon the President's conviction that it is necessary to avert a humanitarian tragedy that could result from a large boat exodus." From *Weekly Compilation of Presidential Documents* 29.9 (8 March 1993): 348. The remainder of this statement reiterated the administration's justifications for its policy: supporting the UN and OAS resolutions and enhancing the safety of the Haitian citizens. It was also announced that the president had, on 20 January 1993, ordered the Department of State to develop proposals for more rapid refugee processing and for enhanced safety for those repatriated.

59. U.S. Department of State, "Statement by the Director of Communications on the Situation in Haiti: March 2, 1993," 348.

60. White House, Office of the Press Secretary, "Press Briefing by George Stephanopoulos" (2 March 1993): 2-3.

61. Howard W. French, "Despite Plans, U.S. Refugee Processing in Haiti Is Said to Lag," *New York Times* 2 March 1993: A13.

62. French, "Despite Plans," A13.

63. Deborah Sontag, "White House Again Defends Bush's Policy on Haitians," *New York Times* 9 March 1993: A16.

64. Sontag, "White House Again," A16.

65. Lynne Duke, "Haitians Hope Strike Will Open Safe Haven," *Washington Post* 11 February 1993: A4.

66. Duke, "Haitians Hope Strike," A4.

67. Sontag, "White House Again," A16.

68. Marcus, "Clinton Backs Aristide," A28.

69. French, "Despite Plans," A13.

70. Deborah Sontag, "Haiti Arrests Man on Way to Asylum in the U.S.," *New York Times* 14 March 1993: A8.

71. Sontag, "Haiti Arrests Man," A8.

72. U.S. Department of State, "Remarks in an Interview with the Southern Florida Media: March 13, 1993," *Weekly Compilation of Presidential Documents* 29.11 (22 March 1993): 417.

73. U.S. Department of State, "Remarks with President Jean-Bertrand Aristide of Haiti and an Exchange with Reporters: March 16, 1993," *Weekly Compilation of Presidential Documents* 29.11 (22 March 1993): 437.

74. U.S. Department of State, "Remarks with President Jean-Bertrand Aristide," 438.

75. It may actually be illegal under Haiti's Constitution for the president to ask for outside military intervention. To do so requires the immediate resignation of the president.

76. U.S. Department of State, "Remarks with President Jean-Bertrand Aristide," 437.

77. White House, Office of the Press Secretary, "Background Briefing by Senior Administration Officials" (16 March 1993): 2.

78. White House, Office of the Press Secretary, "Background Briefing by Senior Administration Officials" (16 March 1993): 2.

79. U.S. Department of State, "Remarks with President Jean-Bertrand Aristide," 438.

80. Steven A. Holmes, "Aristide Holds to Faith," *New York Times* 16 March 1993: A13.

81. Gwen Ifill, "Haitian Is Offered Clinton's Support on an End to Exile," *New York Times* 17 March 1993: A1.

82. Ifill, "Haitian Is Offered," A1.

83. Ifill, "Haitian Is Offered," A13.

84. It is important to note that as early as 10 February 1993, the *Washington Post* had implied that the administration was willing to use force: "U.N. officials said they understood from Clinton administration officials that Washington would react forcefully if the Haitian regime moved to thwart the joint U.N.-U.S. effort [to establish human rights monitors in Haiti]. See Julia Preston, "Haiti Agrees to Monitoring by U.N., OAS," A28. However, I found no administrative utterances to this effect, and the *Washington Post* provided no quotes or sources for this assertion.

85. White House, Office of the Press Secretary, "Press Briefing by George Stephanopoulos" (13 April 1993): 6-7.

86. White House, Office of the Press Secretary, "Press Briefing by George Stephanopoulos" (19 April 1993): 2.

87. U.S. Department of State, "The President's News Conference: April 23, 1993," *Weekly Compilation of Presidential Documents* 29.16 (26 April 1993): 655.

88. White House, Office of the Press Secretary, "Press Briefing by Dee Myers" (29 April 1993): 18.

89. White House, Office of the Press Secretary, "Press Briefing by George Stephanopoulos" (4 May 1993); "Press Briefing By George Stephanopoulos" (13 May 1993); "Press Briefing By George Stephanopoulos" (26 May 1993).

90. U.S. Department of State, "Statement on Sanctions against Haiti: June 4,

1993," *Weekly Compilation of Presidential Documents* 29.22 (7 June 1993): 1030.

91. U.S. Department of State, "Statement on Sanctions against Haiti: June 4, 1993," 1029.

92. White House, Office of the Press Secretary, "Background Briefing by Senior Administration Official" (4 June 1993): 3. This position is also reiterated on page 8.

93. White House, Office of the Press Secretary, "Background Briefing by Senior Administration Official" (4 June 1993): 5.

94. White House, Office of the Press Secretary, "Background Briefing by Senior Administration Official" (4 June 1993): 19.

95. Douglas Farah, "U.S. Tightens Sanctions on Regime in Haiti," *Washington Post* 5 June 1993: A18.

96. Julia Preston, "U.N. Votes to Clamp Oil Embargo on Haiti," *Washington Post* 17 June 1993: A1.

97. Richard L. Berke, "Mulroney Offering Troops to Help Blockade Haiti," *New York Times* 3 June 1993: A10.

98. Steven A. Holmes, "Haitian Rulers Are Target of New Sanctions by U.S.," *New York Times* 5 June 1993: A2.

99. U.S. Department of State, "Exchange with Reporters Prior to a Meeting with White House Fellows: June 17, 1993," *Weekly Compilation of Presidential Documents* 29.24 (21 June 1993): 1105.

100. White House, Office of the Press Secretary, "To the Congress of the United States" (30 June 1993): 1.

Chapter 7

The Haitian Crisis, Part Two: From Initial Success Erupts Crisis

THE GOVERNORS ISLAND AGREEMENT: INITIAL SUCCESS

On 1 July 1993 the White House issued a statement that contained details of a $37.5 million economic aid package for Haiti that would begin once an agreement returning President Aristide to power had been reached. Called the Haiti Reconstruction and Reconciliation Fund, it was developed to support continued negotiations and a "phased political solution" to the restoration of democracy in Haiti.[1] Furthermore, the aid package was designed to "respond to concrete progress toward restoring democracy."[2] The signing of the Governors Island agreement by President Aristide and General Cedras, the military high commander of Haiti who represented the de facto regime, occurred on 3 July 1993. This agreement set the date for restoring President Aristide to power: 30 October 1993. The press lauded this event, and coverage during the early part of July focused on the details of implementation, the unusual problems facing Haiti, and the successful return of Aristide. The Clinton administration was uncharacteristically laconic concerning the signing of the accord.

Throughout the period after the signing, the administration stressed its cooperation with the "international community." On 30 August 1993, a senior administration official reported that the U. S. was working with other Caribbean states to ensure the proper implementation of the Governors Island agreement and once again reiterated the economic rebuilding plan.[3] On 30 September 1993, progress seemed apparent on implementation of the accord, so the United Nations, with the cooperation of the Clinton administration, suspended sanctions—but did not terminate them. On 12 October 1993, President Clinton sent a letter to congressional leaders that detailed the chain of events leading to the signing of the agreement. This letter stressed that the United States was continuing to work in conjunction with the United Nations and OAS and that the U.S. government was continuing the state of national emergency until President Aristide was returned safely to power. In short, the administration announced its continuing role as a partner within the "international community." It did not seek recognition as the driving force behind the successful signing of the accord. The administration did, however, stress its "leadership role with the international community."[4] The state of national emergency for the United States was continued, said the President, until all conditions of the agreement were met.[5]

Press Framing of Economic Aspects

Following the signing of the Governors Island agreement, the *New York Times* coverage focused increasingly on the economic situation within Haiti; these reports contained many specific references to the economic component of the agreement. Of course, the paper also elaborated on the other components of the agreement, but the focus on the economic was in strong contrast to the near absence of coverage of the Haitian economy prior to the signing of the agreement. For example, on the day of the signing, 3 July 1993, Haiti was described by the *New York Times* as the "hemisphere's poorest country."[6] Following the signing of the Governors Island agreement, the *New York Times* described Haiti as a "desperately impoverished country" with an "economy near collapse."[7] Haiti, in short, was now described as a "desperately poor country."[8] Or, in the *Washington Post*'s characteristic description, an "impoverished Caribbean nation."[9]

The *New York Times* offered an interesting explanation for Haiti's economic situation: "The most immediate explanation for Haiti's current suffering is an international oil embargo imposed only last month by the United Nations. Although it forced the army to accept a political accord providing for Father Aristide's return, it has also had a crushing effect on almost everyone."[10] The *Washington Post* also stressed Haiti's impoverished conditions but in a manner that firmly linked the present conditions to the 1991 military coup: "21 months of military-backed rule and economic hardship in the hemisphere's poorest nation."[11] The *Washington Post*'s description contained narrative linkages similar to those in this *New York Times*'s account: "The Haitian economy, poverty-stricken in the best of times, has been devastated by the embargo and the pariah status of de facto governments since the coup. I might add that even as the Haitian economy improves, most

Haitians are still going to aspire to emigrate to the United States and Canada."[12]

Military Training and the Administration's Motives

Following the signing of the accord, the press also reported on those components of the Governors Island agreement that addressed the professionalization of Haiti's military and the establishment of a civilian police force. Reports about the number and type of U.S. military personnel to be involved were misleading, however. For instance, it was initially reported that the United States did not want to "have a large military or police force in Haiti because any American military presence in the region is politically sensitive."[13] Yet as details of the exact numbers and types of American military personnel were reported, the *New York Times* implied a larger presence of military *troops* as opposed to *trainers*. For example, it was reported that the contingent would consist of UN forces composed primarily of "hundreds of experts with expertise in police work and military affairs . . . most of them drawn from French-speaking countries."[14] However, once the exact number of troops were known, the exact composition of the force became ambiguous and even a matter for speculation. For instance, on 22 July 1993, the *New York Times* stated: "The United States has offered to send about 350 *troops* and *military engineers* to Haiti as part of an international force to help retrain Haiti's army and work on military construction projects.[15] However, in the same story, the United States was said to be sending "50 to 60 military trainers" to help professionalize the army. It was also reported that the United States was "also prepared to send a separate contingent of about 300 Army engineers as part of a larger team to work on a number of military construction projects." On 23 July 1993, the *New York Times* stated that the United States had "offered about 350 United States military personnel, including engineers, to assist in 'modernizing the armed forces of Haiti.'"[16] The *Washington Post*, however, more accurately described the American contingent: "Army engineers or Navy Seabees—perhaps as many as 300." Further, it was "understood that the U.S. military team 'won't be combat troops or peace keepers.'"[17]

During this time, too, the *New York Times* ascribed motives to President Clinton for having worked so diligently for the restoration of democracy in Haiti: "Embarrassed by his own inaugural about-face on a campaign promise to change the way Haitian refugees were treated after being intercepted on the high seas, Mr. Clinton set out to press for the restoration of Haitian democracy and return the country's leftist young leader [Aristide] to power."[18] On the question of refugees the

Washington Post asserted, as of the signing of the agreement, that the United States was the guarantor of the Governors Island agreement and thus "implicitly attests to the fact that life under the present regime is unlivable. If that deal collapses, there would be no question about Haitians being genuine candidates for political asylum."[19]

CRISIS ERUPTS

On 11 October 1993, the U.S.S. *Harlan County*, carrying U.S. and Canadian military trainers, was not able to dock in Port-au-Prince due to mob activity. The military personnel carried within the vessel were military trainers and engineers that both President Aristide and the de facto regime had requested through the Governors Island agreement. On 12 October 1993 a senior administration official provided a background briefing to the press on this interruption to the Governors Island agreement. During this briefing, the official reiterated President Clinton's commitment to a negotiated solution and the use of sanctions in conjunction with the United Nations and OAS. Also stressed was the progress made to this point: A new government had begun to be installed, and a new prime minister—Malval—had been sworn into office. Furthermore, President Aristide had granted top coup leaders amnesty for political crimes.

The Nature of the Mission

The administration official also explained the nature of the U.S.S. *Harlan County's* mission. It was a "technical assistance mission" to retrain police and military personnel and to rebuild Haiti's crumbled infrastructure. The United States had planned to send approximately 600 military trainers and Seabees to start the retraining and rebuilding process. The entire affair rested upon the cooperation of the Haitian authorities; as the administration official stressed, this was a "cooperative mission." According to the administration, the nature of the mission was important to consider: "This . . . is not, has never been a peacekeeping, peacemaking mission. It is a technical assistance mission which depends upon an environment in which that can go forward."[20] During this briefing, the press mentioned the possibility of sending in U.S. marines to create a stable environment. The senior administration official responded in a manner that should have stopped further speculation: "That [the sending in of U.S. troops] is not something that is constitutional within the Haitian constitution. It is not something that Aristide has ever wanted to happen. For Aristide to return on the backs of the United States, or any other army, is to undermine his legitimacy as President. It is not something we have discussed."[21]

Immediately following this briefing, Dee Dee Myers held a press briefing about the Haitian situation. During this time, she reiterated the administration's commitment to the Governors Island agreement. She pointed out that five of the ten steps in the agreement had already been implemented and that the United States was concerned about the possibility of another "humanitarian crisis" due to the present situation. During this briefing the press raised several issues. The first of these revolved around the issue of a blockade around Haiti. Myers replied that the United States was looking to reimpose sanctions only. Myers also restated that the president would "not send U.S. forces in there unless they're able to protect themselves in the environment. But he won't send them into an unsecured environment, either."[22] The press asked about national pride: "[D]oesn't it look as though we cut an ran [sic] when a couple of thugs made noise on a pier in Haiti?" Myers replied with the same theme expressed earlier by the senior administration official: "Absolutely not. This was not a peacekeeping mission. This is part of an ongoing process. Our objective now is to get that process . . . back on track."[23]

In a statement issued by the press secretary this same day, a continuation of the administration's previous utterances was given. In this statement the mission of the U.S. troops was stressed:

The American military's part in this effort is to help in the task of professionalizing the Haitian military through non-lethal training in basic military skills and through humanitarian assistance, by means of civic action construction programs. The only U.S. military role is in the military professionalization and humanitarian assistance effort, a non-confrontational role. The mission of U.S. military personnel is not to maintain security in Haiti. This is a technical assistance—not a peace-making or peace-keeping—mission.[24]

On this same day, 12 October 1993, President Clinton made a brief statement as he was leaving the White House. The president reasserted that the troops were not peacekeepers or peacemakers. Moreover, the president stressed that the United States had been invited to play this role by President Aristide and the de facto government. Nevertheless, once the United States tried to fulfil its commitment, it was not allowed to do so; thus the ship left. The press asserted that the Governors Island agreement might now be "dead" or "abrogated." The president responded:

[I] do not think it is dead. I still think it will come back to life. But right now it has been abrogated by people who have decided to cling to power for a little bit longer apparently once the pressure of the sanctions has been off.

I want the Haitians to know that I am dead serious about seeing them honor the agreement that they made.[25]

On 13 October 1993, Dee Dee Myers held another press briefing. At this time she refuted press claims that the administration was unprepared for the mob activity on the dock: "It was our expectation and it's still our expectation that the [Haitian] military will work to secure the environment. Instead they stood by and allowed the demonstrators to demonstrate and kept the embassy personnel from reaching the docks."[26] The point was, the Haitian military was expected to secure the area and provide a safe environment for U.S. and international trainers to work in; that was not the role U.S. troops were expected to play. The Clinton administration contended that whether or not it suspected trouble or knew about the mob, it still had to try to honor the agreement. Myers ended her discussion about Haiti by noting the "direct action" that the administration was taking in response to the breaking of the agreement: Sanctions would be reimposed as soon as possible.

In summary, the administration's position was that the leaders of the de facto government had failed to live up to their part of the Governors Island agreement. The de facto leaders had broken their promise to maintain order and provide a secure environment for U.S. and Canadian military personnel. The administration stressed the nonconfrontational role of the military engineers and trainers; thus, the withdrawal of the ship was not a retreat, or a policy crisis, but a prudent decision. If the agreement was not soon honored, then the Clinton administration would call for the immediate reimposition of sanctions.

Initial Press Responses

By 14 October 1993, the press was beginning to raise the issue of President Clinton's Somalia policy in conjunction with events in Haiti. Demonstrators were reported in Port-au-Prince as chanting, "we will turn this into another Somalia." It is true that the president had inherited the Bush administration's policy on Somalia as well as Haiti; however, President Clinton refused to accept the analogy and thus was quick to point out that Somalia was a very different situation: He argued that Somalia was a peacekeeping mission—Haiti was not. During a brief exchange with reporters the president stated that he "was not about to put 200 American Seabees into a potentially dangerous situation for which they were neither trained nor armed to deal with at that moment."[27] For the president, it did not matter if the mob on the dock was encouraged by events in Somalia, because all they had to do was look at how the United States and United Nations bolstered their forces there; that is, the sanctions would be reimposed and perhaps strengthened.

The day the U.S.S. *Harlan County* was scheduled to reach Port-au-Prince, the *Washington Post* reported upon recent criticism surrounding President Clinton's foreign policy. The criticism, according to the *Washington Post*, was due in large part to the recent (early October) fire-fight in Somalia in which eighteen American soldiers were killed and seventy-five were wounded. These casualties acted as a catalyst for congressional criticism about U.S. military involvement in all UN missions: Somalia, Bosnia, and Haiti. In general, it was asked, "[T]o what extent should U.S. troop deployment be guided by U.N. deci sions?"[28] In addition to raising the issue of national sovereignty, Congress was also concerned that it was not being fully briefed about deployment of U.S. troops in UN missions.

The explanation for the motivation behind the Port-au-Prince demonstration and defiance of the UN mission was ascribed, by the *New York Times*, to remarks made by anonymous diplomats and Haitian analysts: one, the Haitians were emboldened by the knowledge that the UN force was lightly armed and ordered not to intervene; and two, a "flurry of opposition in Washington to international peacekeeping engagements" left them feeling secure that the United States would not intervene.[29] As the *Washington Post* reported: "U.S. officials acknowledge that the opponents of Aristide clearly were encouraged by reaction in this country to the killing of Americans in Somalia."[30] No sources or quotes were given to validate these assertions.

The concern with Somalia was a common theme running through the explanations of the press. As the *Washington Post* stated, "Congress, already wary of U.S. involvement in the U.N. peace-keeping mission in Somalia, [is] raising concerns" about Haiti and future U.S. involvement.[31] The *New York Times* reported that members of Congress were concerned because the administration was not briefing them fully about U.S. troop involvement in Haiti. Indeed, the administration was reported, anonymously, as saying that the "decision to remove the ship was also influenced by the public and Congressional reaction to the death of American soldiers serving . . . in Somalia."[32] Although the administration had been extremely clear in stating that the U.S. and Canadian forces were not peacemakers or peacekeepers, the concern over the safety of the U.S. troops loomed large in the press. The *New York Times* even went so far as to quote an anonymous senior administration official as stating that if it were not for the recent event in Somalia that the demonstration would not have taken on the importance that it did.

The removal of the ship itself caused some concern as well. The *New York Times* reported that "the lack of a prompt response to the defiance of the Haitian military has brought a mood of despondency to many of the diplomats [in Haiti].[33] The dateline read "Haiti, Oct. 12—." Therefore, less than twenty-four hours after the U.S.S. *Harlan County* turned back, the *New York Times* implied that there was not a speedy response from the administration to the demonstration. Moreover, the removal of the ship was characterized as an American retreat by the press. The *New York Times* reported that the "American troopship was forced to retreat in the face of a small mob on a Port-au-Prince dock." Even though the administration was reported as saying that the demonstration had not caused a threat to the safety of U.S. personnel, the image of the "American troopship retreat[ing] over the horizon" was given for readers to ponder.[34] Moreover, it was reported that Western diplomats in Haiti "expressed outrage that the United States had . . . capitulated in the face of opposition by the Haitian military."[35] Too, this "abrupt withdrawal" would hurt efforts at restoring democracy and could imperil foreigners living or sojourning in Haiti. The *Washington Post* conveyed similar views. The removal of the ship was reported as "infuriating U.N. and Haitian officials," but no sources were provided.

The *New York Times* editorial of 13 October 1993 called for a get-tough attitude. The administration was importuned to reimpose immediately the sanctions that had been lifted in August in accordance with the Governors Island agreement. The editorial stated: "It was those sanctions—fully supported by Haiti's poor majority, despite the pain it caused them—that finally forced the recalcitrant military to the bargaining table."[36] Accordingly, the editorial advised the administration to strengthen the sanctions, even to the point of a naval block-ade, "in other words, complete isolation from the international community."[37] In contrast, the *Washington Post* continued its negative comments about sanctions. Indeed, the paper still decried the initial sanctions as a "crippling embargo on Haiti, already the hemisphere's poorest nation."[38] Despite this criticism, the *Washington Post* seemed to acknowledge their effectiveness, for "with oil supplies exhausted and the economy grinding to a halt," the de facto regime had signed the Governors Island agreement. On this same day, however, the *Washington Post* editorially stated that U.S. troops should not fight their way into Port-au-Prince but foreclosed other forms of intervention as well: "Nor are the alternatives very promising. Economic sanctions have already destroyed many of the legitimate businesses in Haiti, and the burden of a renewed blockade would fall most heavily on the poor, who strongly support President Aristide."[39] The theme was dilemmatic. Although the *Washington Post* did credit the sanctions with helping to pressure the de facto regime into signing the accord, it reported horrors that made the sanctions appear a morally Pyrrhic victory for the administration: The "oil embargo caused crippling gasoline shortages and threatened to bring the economy to a halt."[40] Rarely was it mentioned that the Clinton administration fed over 680,000 Haitians a week and provided free basic medical care to alleviate the impact of the embargo. A *Washington Post* "news analysis" story summed up the paper's position well: "[T]he embargo, while having relatively little effect on Haiti's military rulers, wrecked what was left of the island's economy and launched the phenomenon of tens of thousands of boat people trying to reach the United States."[41]

Press Descriptions of the "Haitian Mob"

From the time of the 11 October 1993 dockside demonstrations the press was not consistent in its descriptions of the group of Haitians whose demonstrations prevented the U.S.S. *Harlan County* from docking. The *New York Times* called them "a small gang of toughs," "angry mob," "armed demonstrators," "armed mob," "armed civilians," "demonstrators," "Haitians on shore," "raucous dockside demonstrat[ors]," "several hundred heavily armed demonstrators," "small but unruly crowd," "small mob," and "thugs." The *Washington Post* called them "angry mob," "angry, armed mob," "armed civilians," "chanting, armed civilians," "gang of gun-toting thugs," "gun-waving civilians," "Haitians," "mob of armed demonstrators," "small gang of toughs," and "the crowd."

Nor was the size and composition of the U.S. and Canadian forces consistently reported. The *New York Times* reported several conflicting numbers during the course of the four days: "1,300 member force" and "1,600 member force"; "175 Americans and 25 Canadians," "218 American and Canadians," and "194 Americans and 25 Canadians." However, the *Washington Post* reported consistently on this point: "1,300 member force" and "193 Americans and 25 Canadians."

PRESIDENT CLINTON'S FORMAL ADDRESS AND ITS IMMEDIATE RESPONSE

President Clinton held a press conference on 15 October 1993, during which he made his first formal address on the situation in Haiti. He stressed that the United States had suffered extreme provocation: The United States "witnessed a brutal attempt by Haiti's military and police authorities to thwart the expressed desire of the Haitian people for democracy. [U]nruly elements, unrestrained by the Haitian military, [had] violently prevented American and United Nations personnel from carrying out the steps toward that goal."[42] This formal address accomplished three goals. First, the president stated that U.S. interests were vested in the recent Port-au-Prince incident; two, he outlined action taken in response to the event; and three, he reiterated the purpose of the United States in Haiti. The president explained that U.S. interests were most directly involved due to the presence of approximately 1,000 U.S. citizens in Haiti. There were also the embassy personnel to consider. The hemispheric march toward democracy must be continued. Finally, a secure environment must be achieved in order to prevent Haitians from risking their lives in a dangerous emigration to the U.S. The president stressed that the actions taken by his administration were a continuation of actions initiated by the Bush administration. New actions to be taken included reimposition of sanctions, the deployment of six United States Navy vessels off the coast of Haiti to enforce the sanctions, and the placement of a company of marines stationed at Guantánamo Bay, Cuba, on full alert. The explanation of U.S. interests and new actions combined to form the administration's purpose: "to ensure the safety of the Americans in Haiti and to press for the restoration of democracy there through the strongest possible enforcement of the sanctions."[43]

The press response to the President's statement expressed both continuity and change from its previous positions on the situation in Haiti. The emphasis shifted to the internal situation within Haiti and the growing congressional struggle with the president over U.S. military ventures; moreover, the withdrawal of the U.S.S. *Harlan County* received only minor attention after the president's speech. The issue of the "blockade" around Haiti also received minor attention, although on 16 October 1993, the *New York Times* reported that aides to President Clinton had "encouraged comparisons to the naval blockade imposed by John F. Kennedy during the Cuban Missile crisis in 1962."[44] No quotes or sources were provided to substantiate this stunning comparison. And on 18 October 1993 a *Washington Post* editorial stated: "The ships and the blockade are a necessary response to the wave of political murders that culminated in the shooting of the democratic government's minister of justice, Guy Malary. But economic sanctions alone won't suffice. They are a highly indiscriminate instrument and will put the heaviest burdens on the poorest and least culpable Haitians."[45] The solution to this difficulty is provided editorially by the *Washington Post* as well: "Haiti's soldiers must now be invited—under the duress of these stiff sanctions—to try again."[46]

Although the withdrawal of the U.S.S. *Harlan County* slowly faded from concern, prior to making its disappearance it was highlighted as a symbol of the betrayal of international human rights. The *Washington Post* reported that the "evacuation . . . left the human rights monitors and many Haitians who collaborated with them feeling angry and abandoned."[47] The withdrawal of the ship was thus reported as disappointing the human rights monitors in Haiti, who had "decided that the dangers [were] suddenly too great," so they were leaving as well.[48]

Internal Haitian Affairs and the Effects of the Embargo

Most notable following the president's statement was the rise in the number of reports that stressed the internal situation in Haiti. These reports were linked with the sanctions/embargo. For example, the *Washington Post*, on 16 October, printed a story that reported that Duvalierists were supporting the military in order to keep President Aristide out of Haiti; these actions coincided with the Ton Ton Macoutes joining forces with the political attachés who were promoting political violence to terrorize poor Haitians. Indeed, the *Washington Post* reported that the situation in Haiti was now near anarchy and that the "Haitian rulers" were scrambling to forestall the impending UN embargo that would further rack the country.[49] The *New York Times* reported the new military-backed political organizations had "mounted a campaign of intimidation and terror, exemplified by the shooting of Justice Minister Guy Malary."[50] This deteriorating political situation was described by the *New York Times* when it paraphrased Haiti's newly appointed prime minister, Malval. The prime minister reportedly had "expressed the fear that Haiti would soon fall into total anarchy if there was not a quick and peaceful resolution."[51]

Descriptions of the shaky political situation were bolstered by reports of the effects of the sanctions/embargo. The *New York Times* reported that the "embargo set to take effect on Monday [18 October 1993] will hit a nation so poor that more than 850,000 of Haiti's 6.5 million people already depend on foreign aid to survive."[52] In addition, the restorative effects of the sanctions/embargo were questioned: "People familiar with Haiti's economy say that the international naval blockade that began today may cause severe damage but that it is uncertain whether the hardships will force the military leaders to restore democracy."[53] No sources or quotations were provided for this assessment. Later, in the same story, it was reported that the effects of the sanctions/embargo would be catastrophic, in part because in Haiti's poorest regions women and children were "barely holding on to life."

The *Washington Post* was especially concerned with the effects of the sanctions/embargo. It was reported that the "military rulers said they would rather fight to the death than hand power back to exiled president Jean-Bertrand Aristide."⁵⁴ No quotes or sources were provided for this statement, however. Additionally, it was asserted that during the original sanction period "many of the wealthy were able to afford contraband goods, while the poor found it difficult to afford even basic foods or cooking fuel. Many businesses were forced into bankruptcy, pushing up unemployment, which had been above 50 percent."⁵⁵ On 21 October 1993, the *Washington Post* reported on "growing depression and dashed dreams" and the growing resentment about "sanctions that are going to make an already difficult economic situation impossible for many . . . [Haitians]."⁵⁶ This particular article stated, too, that many Haitians would suffer from growing food prices and lack of money. Indeed, it was reported that workers "said almost no one was building boats now, because they had no money to pay for the passage, and because there was so little hope of getting through the multinational naval blockade."⁵⁷

The President's Restatement and the Press Response

President Clinton reiterated his stated course of action toward Haiti during a radio interview given on 18 October 1993. During this time, too, the president made his first formal remarks about the new defense appropriations bill that would change the way that the military operated when working with NATO and other military allies. Specifically, this was a reaction to the concern voiced by members of Congress, most notably Senate Minority Leader Bob Dole, that the president not send U.S. troops into Bosnia or Haiti without congressional approval. The president stated that there "should be no restrictions that would undermine the ability of the President to protect the Americans on Haiti, that would aggravate the likelihood of another mass exodus of Haitians, or that would send a green light to the people . . . [who] broke their word on the Governors Island Agreement."⁵⁸

The president was again asked about the possible use of American troops to restore Aristide to power. He replied that the navy ships were to be used to reimpose the sanctions only and that the sanctions would be used because they were what produced the original agreement. However, the president left open the option of using troops in the future if the situation warranted it. In short, he would not "rule in or rule out options." The president was concerned, however, about the potential for a bill that would require him or future presidents to obtain the permission of Congress prior to using troops in either Haiti or Bosnia. The president replied: "I want to resist and . . . I urge the Senate not to vote for things which unduly infringe on the President's power, and certainly not things that are of questionable constitutionality."⁵⁹ In terms of the reports of rising criticism about his foreign policy decisions, the president stressed that his administration had focused on the future and was not "trying to spend a lot of time establishing partisan blame for the past."[60] For the president, the "past is past."

On 18 October 1993 the administration issued a statement to the press that basically reiterated the points made earlier by the president and his administration officials. On this same date, Dee Dee Myers held a press briefing during which she, too, reiterated the administration's position. The president's formal address given on 15 October had become the touchstone from which administration officials conducted affairs. Thus, Myers relayed that the president was still concerned and restated American interests and recent American actions. She also restated that the present course was one of reimposition of sanctions but that the administration had not ruled in or out any other measures, including the use of U.S. troops.

The concern over the possible attempt to restrict presidential prerogatives was again raised by the press during a 19 October 1993 press conference. Dee Dee Myers once again stated that any restriction upon the president's power would send the signal that the president could not enforce the sanctions imposed on Haiti. The obvious concern was with the arbitrary sending of troops into battle situations without clear reasons being given to Congress for their deployment. Also, with the increasing need for police actions since the demise of the Cold War, Congress was worried about committing U.S. troops to combat roles without proper congressional consultation. Myers addressed these issues:

I think the President can proactively decide he wants to ask Congress's authorization before he sends troops, as President Bush did before Desert Storm. That is a far cry from restricting the President's ability to make that decision. What the President objects to is an altering of the relationship between the Executive and Legislative branches and an impingement on his constitutional ability to make foreign policy.

[We are] looking for a way to establish a working relationship between Congress and the President in this post-Cold War world that recognizes Congress's concerns but protects the President's prerogative to act.[61]

Perhaps to assuage the growing concern in the press about the possible involvement of U.S. troops, or because of the growing concern in Congress that could lead to a showdown over the president's authority to commit U.S. troops, the president submitted a "Letter to Congressional Leaders" on 20 October 1993. In this letter he detailed the recent actions that his administration had taken in regard to Haiti, and he ended with a promissory note: "Close cooperation between the President and the

Congress is imperative for effective U.S. foreign policy and especially when the United States commits our Armed Forces abroad. I remain committed to consulting closely with Congress on our foreign policy, and I will continue to keep Congress fully informed about significant deployments of our Nation's Armed Forces."[62]

Haiti, Somalia, and Bosnia

One of the major shifts in the framing of the press reports involved the linking of the events in Haiti with those occurring in Somalia and Bosnia. Although the *Washington Post* began writing about this prior to the president's statement, both papers increased their coverage of this aspect after the address. The *New York Times* focused on Somalia and Bosnia as they relate to the struggle between Congress and the president over constitutional authority to use U.S. troops. The *Washington Post* did this as well but took the argument one step further by relating it to U.S. foreign policy in a post-Cold War world. Either way, the issue of the president's Haitian policy was subsumed within a larger narrative.

For example, the *New York Times* on 18 October reported on an initiative led by Senator Bob Dole to restrict the use of U.S. forces in Haiti. The *New York Times* wrote that this move by Senator Dole "underscores the political price that the Clinton administration is beginning to pay for policy stumbles in Somalia and Haiti. They have touched off a flood of efforts by a previously passive Congress to assert itself on foreign policy."[63] The *New York Times* briefly touched on the larger world concern when it reported a quote by an unnamed senior administration official: "'What is at issue . . . is not only the President's powers, but a more fundamental question of how we will remain engaged in the world. The initial Congressional reaction on Somalia would have put us in a position of hastily retreating from the world.'"[64] Reports of the next several days focused on a power struggle between Congress and the president. President Clinton was reported as saying that he would strongly oppose any "efforts by members of Congress to restrict his authority to commit troops."[65] Further, doing so would send a "green light" to the Haitian leaders to defy the UN/OAS-sponsored Governors Island agreement.

Again, some linkage is made with larger concerns than just U.S. interests. The *New York Times* stated that Somalia and Haiti were "nothing like the Communist threat the country grew used to reacting to."[66] The new measuring stick proposed by the *New York Times*: "The easiest way to connect the dots and draw a coherent foreign policy is to say that none of these problems is important enough to risk American lives."[67] However, these few, and vague, references to a larger picture than congressional/presidential battling over foreign policy is neither elaborated nor pursued. Indeed, the *New York Times* virtually ignored this aspect and instead embraced a partisan political interpretation of events. The paper stated editorially that many of the Clinton administration's foreign policy difficulties were "inherited by the new Administration" and that the "so-called experts" (the Republican congressional leaders in the minority) "left him a full plate of problems. The least they can do now is avoid gratuitous partisan sniping while he wrestles with their legacy."[68] After only a few days the furor over committing U.S. troops died when the Senate forwarded to the White House a nonbinding resolution that asked the president to ask Congress to authorize any troops that the president wished to have deployed to Haiti. This resolution did not, however, impinge on the president's "broad foreign policy prerogatives as Commander in Chief to send in American troops if he deems that it justified [*sic*] by national security interests or that the safety of Americans living in Haiti is at stake."[69]

The *Washington Post* reported this schism between Congress and the president in a more cosmic manner. The focus was upon a post-Cold War world and the role of U.S. foreign policy within this brave new world. As early as 14 October 1993, the *Washington Post* wrote that the Governors Island agreement's collapse "dealt a new blow" to President Clinton's attempts to demonstrate that he has "a coherent foreign policy capable of leading the world community toward a post-Cold War era of democracy and stability."[70] Another article on the same day suggested that in the post-Cold War world the United States cannot just send the troops in any more.[71] However, it was maintained that Haiti was not the same situation as Somalia; there were U.S. interests and well-defined policy parameters: to prevention of a new flood of boat people to "Florida" and to prevent a "humiliating defeat for U.S. commitments."[72]

On 16 October 1993, the day after the president's statement on Haiti, the *Washington Post* ran a story entitled "Lawmakers Seek New Methods to Handle Post-Cold War Crises."[73] This article asserted that Congress was battling with the president to "change the tattered Vietnam-era War Powers Resolution in favor of new procedures to deal with post-Cold War foreign policy crises."[74] The key to what was occurring was the growing controversy "over possible or likely military operations in Haiti, Bosnia and other trouble spots. . . . [Thus,] many in Congress are concerned that there are not workable procedures for prompt and orderly exercise of its war-authorizing powers."[75] The original War Powers Resolution required that the president consult with Congress before introducing troops into hostile situations and to set a deadline for withdrawal if Congress authorized the deployment. But with the growing need for multinational deployment of forces for peacekeeping or peacemaking missions, the congressional prerogatives of declaring war have often been overlooked.

These arguments appear repeatedly in the *Washington Post*'s coverage of this issue. A later story reported that the troubles in areas such as Bosnia, Somalia, and Haiti were actually signs of trouble in the administration's "foreign policy ability and the strength of [Clinton's] national security team."[76] This article faithfully reported the administration's contentions that it had been successful in the larger areas of concern—Russia, nuclear arms proliferation, China—but that in Bosnia, Somalia, and Haiti, where discernible U.S. interests were not at stake, there were problems:

Despite the sound of things and a vocabulary of confrontation that unfailingly recalls the intensity of the country's Vietnam agony, we see no great crisis unfolding in Washington. There is simply a noisy tactical disagreement over what is the best mix of economic, political and military levers to deal with the rash of post-Cold War conflicts, mostly inside particular countries, which touch American interests but do not touch what people usually mean by vital national interests.[77]

In short, the *Washington Post* asked, What is America's post-Cold War role in the world? The paper rather cogently suggested that there existed a "nostalgia shared by policy makers for the anti-Soviet framework within which much of the West operated for four decades."[78] The *Washington Post* suggested at one point that the Clinton administration's foreign policy goal was "the 'enlargement' of democracy around the world" and that the problem was a concern with the direction, coherence, and execution of the administration's foreign policy.[79] This concern with the events in Haiti as synecdoche for the post-Cold War world was continued in the *Washington Post* until late October. After the Senate failed to pass a resolution limiting the president's powers to wage war, the *Washington Post* stated: "Democratic leaders . . . were preparing a proposal aimed at coming up with procedures for engaging Congress early and often in major foreign policy decisions to avoid the kind of sudden uproars that arose over Somalia and Haiti. They are looking at overhauling the Vietnam-era 1973 War Powers Resolution to accommodate post-Cold War peace-keeping operations."[80] By 26 October 1993 the *Washington Post* stated that the concern in Congress was President Clinton's failure to "develop a coherent foreign policy, especially for multinational peace-keeping missions."[81]

Aristide's Psychological Profile

Around 22 October 1993 the press began to make public a CIA report given to congressional leaders. In this report President Aristide was said to be mentally unstable. The administration was quick to assert that the reports may be substantiated or not but that it did not really matter. Dee Dee Myers explained the U.S. position unequivocally: "[W]e have had a lot of dealings with President Aristide. He's always appeared in our dealings with him responsible [sic]; he's lived up to the terms of his commitment; he was elected by the people of Haiti. Our interest is in restoring a democratically-elected government to that country. It is not for us to tell the people of Haiti who to elect."[82]

This issue, however, received thorough coverage from 22 October 1993 through 29 October 1993, particularly from the *Washington Post*. Initial reports from the *Washington Post* highlighted the administration's support of President Aristide: "[D]espite allegations the ousted Haitian leader is mentally unstable [the administration said] Aristide's conduct demonstrated he is fit to govern."[83] The administration was also reported as having a stake in the believability of the CIA reports, for it had "expended great effort trying to restore Aristide to power since the democratically elected leader was ousted."[84] However, the issue soon began to be viewed as a partisan concern with the Republicans on one side and the Democratic administration on the other. The *Washington Post* reported Vice President Al Gore as saying that the "charges are 'uncorroborated' and are denied by Aristide. . . . 'We have dealt with [Aristide] for nine months now. He has been reliable, he has been very thoughtful, he has been persistent in his efforts on behalf of the Haitian people.' The charges originated with Aristide's opponents."[85] Later in the same article the *Washington Post* reported that "two prominent Republicans appearing earlier on the same program as Gore [had made his statements on] questioned Aristide's fitness."[86] By 27 October 1993 the *Washington Post* had solidified its editorial interpretation of the accusations: "[Y]ou can dismiss the CIA's foolish psychologizing [sic]."[87]

The *New York Times* reached the same conclusion as the *Washington Post*: "It's heartening that Mr. Clinton is standing behind Mr. Aristide and has not taken seriously that attempt at character assassination by psychobable [sic] initiated by some Republican senators during the past week."[88] The *New York Times* ran fewer but similar items about Aristide's CIA psychological profile. The Clinton administration was described as at war with itself over its Haitian policy, with President Aristide at center stage. Congress was described as working with the CIA against the State Department and the National Security Council. The CIA reports were described as having "spread alarm over Administration policy on Capitol Hill."[89] The aspect of "them versus us" was further conveyed: "Mr Clinton said the views of Administration officials who have worked with Father Aristide to help restore him to power carried more weight than allegations that officials of the agency [CIA] made to members of Congress this week."[90]

Imitating the administration's position that Aristide's condition is irrelevant because the Haitian people elected him, the *New York Times* stated: In Haiti, "the debate in the United States about the mental health of their President seems cruelly sterile. After two years of hardship and violence under military rule, no hope rings more fervently than for the return of the Rev. Jean-Bertrand Aristide."[91] These reports concerning Aristide's condition continued sporadically through early November. On 1 November 1993 the *New York Times* reported that supporters "of Mr. Aristide said that the [CIA] payments [to Haitian military informants] proved that the C.I.A.'s primary sources of information in Haiti were Mr. Aristide's political enemies."[92] Both papers frequently reported the administration's defense that President Aristide was elected by the people of Haiti, so the CIA reports were in essence insignificant. By 3 November 1993 the question was not so much about President Aristide's mental health as it was about the CIA's link with Haitian officials:

House and Senate intelligence committees have begun probing the CIA's past ties to key Haitian political figures, including covert payments to Haitian officials for information on local politics. . . .

The probes arise from allegations by Aristide's congressional supporters that the recent unflattering CIA profile of him may have been tainted by the CIA's past associations with his opponents.[93]

THE INTERNAL SITUATION AND THE EFFECTS OF SANCTIONS: THE CONVERGENCE OF PRESS FRAMING

Following the president's 15 October 1993 statement, the press again claimed that sanctions were hurting poor Haitians and not the de facto government's leaders. The president admitted that these types of sanctions always hurt the people first, but it was what got the Governors Island agreement in the first place; he also asserted that once the "blockade finally hit the regime and the elites . . . they suffered, too." He also reminded the press that the embargo was asked for by the government of Haiti. Yet the press had developed its own frame through which it advanced its view of the embargo/sanctions. On 22 October 1993 the *New York Times* reported that Haitians were building boats again due to "increasing economic hardship and political repression."[94] It was also reported that what "is also driving ordinary Haitians to flee is a sense that the United Nations embargo against Haiti will hurt them the most. In the past, Haitians used to say they were fleeing for fear of their lives; now many readily admit they will be leaving because of economic hardship."[95]

On 28 October 1993 the *New York Times* reported on possible administration backing of a French proposal to enlarge the sanctions to include all commercial goods. These sanctions were to be directed, according to the *New York Times*, at "the poor Caribbean nation." Further, the "French proposal calls for a blockade against Haiti that would prevent virtually all commerce from flowing into and out of what is already the poorest country in the Western Hemisphere."[96] The *New York Times* called these measures "draconian economic measures [that] would further impoverish an already desperately poor country."[97]

On this same issue the *Washington Post* reported that Prime Minister Malval had said that Aristide's government was "'not responsible for the sanctions' . . . in an attempt to shift responsibility for the hardship to the military. 'We have respected all our commitments under the agreement, and even gone beyond them.'"[98] On this same day, the U.S. Navy was reported as having interdicted a shipment of soy milk and baby cribs. The sanctions are no longer credited with having brought the military to the bargaining table. Instead, the *Washington Post* describes sanctions/embargoes as "extremely sensitive affairs, since they disproportionately hurt the poor, who must get to work in order to eat."[99]

The Linking of Internal Situation and Sanctions

Linked closely with the reports on the effects of the embargo/sanctions are stories concerned with the internal situation in Haiti. Indeed, approximately 25 percent of the stories contained in both papers after Clinton's 15 October 1993 statement are concerned with this issue. If those stories that take as their central focus the effects of the embargo/sanctions are included in this count, then a full 50 percent of news items are concerned with the internal situation in Haiti. In general, the papers report on the continuing negotiations between Prime Minister Malval and the army leaders. The fear of increased sanctions is generally credited with prompting the talks: "Two Sides in Haiti Meet on Impasse"; "Fearful Rural Haitians Yearn for Aristide's Return"; "After Talks, Haitian Aides Hope for a Break in the Impasse"; and "Haiti's Premier and General Meet as Drive to Settle Crisis Intensifies."[100] The situation in Haiti was painted as grim: "A proposal by Haitian legislators to settle [Haiti's] political stalemate appeared close to collapse today when gunmen staked out Parliament and many deputies, fearing for their lives, refused to enter the building."[101] Contrariwise, the situation was at times painted as hopeful: [T]he "11-point program put forward by previously anti-Aristide lawmakers in Haiti [is] a 'serious effort' to break the deadlock caused by the refusal of the [coup leaders] to relinquish power."[102] The *New York Times* reported that the Clinton administration's "biggest problem now is that Haiti's military leaders . . . apparently think that they can simply wait the Clinton administration out until it loses interest in Haiti, or until it agrees to renegotiate a new power-sharing accord."[103]

The *Washington Post* described Prime Minister Malval's position in Haiti as "waging war against a de facto regime in a country he is supposed to be governing."[104] The internal situation with regard to the settlement process was also highlighted through stories that stressed the legislative struggle between Aristide's government and the "military rulers." The *Washington Post* concluded that a "political impasse" existed.[105] By 26 October 1993, the *Washington Post* had developed a standardized version of the events leading up to the internal struggle:

Aristide, Haiti's first democratically elected president, was overthrown in a bloody military coup on Sept. 30 1991. Cedras and other military officials, under growing international pressure and a crippling U.N. oil and arms embargo, agreed in July to Aristide's return.

Under an agreement signed July 3 by Aristide and Cedras on Governors Island, N.Y., Cedras was to resign by Oct. 15, and Aristide was to return to Haiti on Oct. 30. . . .

However, Cedras and others refused to resign as promised. When the military balked at key points in the accord, the United Nations reimposed an oil embargo that has virtually paralyzed commercial activity and brought the already depressed economy to its knees. A multinational naval force is enforcing the embargo.[106]

U.S. Military Involvement

Reports concerning the possible use of the military of the United States had undergone an interesting transformation following the Port-au-Prince incident. On 22 October 1993 the *Washington Post* reported Senator Jesse Helms as "urging the Clinton administration to abandon its plan to send U.S. troops [into Haiti]"—thus implying that there were such plans.[107] On 28 October 1993 the *Washington Post* suggested that the Clinton administration had only two options: "choose between destroying the [Haitian] economy to reimpose democracy or abandoning Haiti to its military rulers."[108] In the *New York Times* it was reported that "American officials have made it clear to Father Aristide that there is no possibility of sending United States troops to Haiti to guarantee his safety in the event he should return home before a new deal is reached."[109]

The question of the possibility of using U.S. troops to restore President Aristide to power is rarely raised after the end of October. Furthermore, when force is mentioned, it is dismissed as an option. This is true despite the fact that President Clinton clearly stated that he had not ruled out any option. For example, on 6 November 1993 the *New York Times* mused on the possible options that the United Nations and the Clinton administration possessed to resolve the situation:

[Options] available to the United Nations are also unattractive. It can strengthen the oil and arms embargo imposed on Haiti last month in an effort to force the military leaders to leave power, or it can explore military actions.

But the embargo has caused more hardship for the Haitian people than for its intended victims, the military leaders and their supporters. And the United States and other key United Nations members have shown no inclination to use military force.[110]

On 11 November 1993 the *Washington Post* reported similar administrative inclinations: "The administration, smarting from public and congressional criticism of U.S. military casualties in Somalia, has said several times it has no intention of exposing U.S. soldiers to danger in Haiti. Last month, when armed Haitian thugs supporting the military threatened to attack U.S. military advisors en route to Haiti, Clinton ordered the advisor's ship to turn around."[111]

On 23 October 1993 the president responded to a reporter's question about Bob Dole believing it not worth one American life to restore Aristide to power in Haiti. The president's response is instructive: Our "policy is to attempt to restore democracy in Haiti, that we are doing it in the way that we think is best and that is supported by Aristide and Prime Minister Malval. We have ships there, and you know what we're doing. And they've never asked us to run the country for them."[112] Six days later, on 29 October 1993, the president issued a statement on the situation in Haiti. This statement reiterated the administration's earlier utterances about U.S. interests, actions, and purposes in Haiti. It also stated that President Clinton was firmly committed to restoration of democracy in Haiti. The *New York Times* at this time reported that the administration no longer possessed realistic options:

Administration officials acknowledge that they have no good options. They are not prepared to use American troops to forcibly reinstall Father Aristide. They also have no interest in simply turning their backs on the Governors Island accord. This leaves them with little choice but to step up their rhetorical attacks on the Haitian military, tighten economic sanctions and wait for the military leaders to cave in.[113]

By 7 November 1993 the administration's position regarding the situation in Haiti had crystallized. When asked if the embargo on goods entering Haiti should be strengthened, the president agreed. He even suggested that it could proceed in one of two ways: complete or surgical. Further, he was again quick to point out that nothing had been ruled in or out. Even invasion was not ruled out. A reporter reminded President Clinton that President Bush had invaded Panama to remove Noriega, so why not invade Haiti to restore Aristide? The president replied that he did not want to rule anything in or out but that both Aristide and Malval did not want to have U.S. troops invade Haiti.

Sanctions: The Internal Situation in Detail

The end of October saw a continuation of the same narrative elements that had been used since the president's 15 October 1993 statement. Almost all of the stories contained in the two papers now focused on the internal situation in Haiti and the effects on Haiti caused by the embargo/sanctions; in the vast majority of news items the stories would combine the two elements. For example, on 30 October 1993 the *New York Times*, focusing on a story about UN-proposed talks, stated that "tensions are rising in Haiti, but the military hasn't budged."[114] This same story stated: "The effects of the fuel squeeze can be felt throughout the country, as electricity has begun to be tightly rationed and traffic has fallen off sharply. In addition . . . dead bodies have begun to turn up with frequency each night in the streets of the capital."[115] This mixing of focus was now common practice, and the effect was to portray the Haitian military leaders as villains. Commonly, when negotiations were discussed, the conditions in Haiti brought on by the sanctions/embargo were related as well. The *Washington Post* rarely used this same mixing of genres. For example, on 6 November 1993, the paper drew a dismal conclusion: "In a clear show of defiance, the Haitian military today boycotted high-level talks designed to revive the flagging international effort to get exiled President Jean-Bertrand Aristide back into office."[116] The most that is mentioned about the effects of the sanctions/embargo is this 6 November 1993 example: "The current embargo, enforced by U.S and other foreign warships, has ended all sales of gasoline and diesel fuel from gas stations here [Port-au-Prince, Haiti]. The availability of black-market fuel is limited and traffic has slumped to one-fifth of its normal level."[117] The *New York Times*, however, was mixing genres well into November, and in many instances, the reporting of facts and observations crossed the line into interpretation:

In the three weeks that Haiti has been cut off from foreign oil deliveries, this country's economy has come to a near halt.

In provincial towns and rural areas, the situation is far worse. According to radio reports here, Port de Paix, a small city in Haiti's grindingly poor northwest, has gone without electricity for three weeks.

In the small town of Gantheir . . . suffering is evident everywhere. At the town's small medical clinic, the only health care center within miles, a white ambulance sits idle for lack of gasoline. The clinic's pharmacy is almost bare.

[Broadening] the current embargo, which President Clinton says he is loath to do, would threaten even more Haitians with severe malnutrition and disease.

On the other hand, easing up on sanctions, which now cover oil and arms, would send a signal to Haiti's de facto military rulers that after two years of diplomacy on Father Aristide's behalf, the United Nations and Washington are backing away from the goal of restoring him to power.[118]

On 9 November 1993 the question of the effects of the sanctions on the poor of Haiti was once again raised by the press. The administration responded with its standard response to this subject: "The situation in Haiti is . . . quite serious. The economy there is stalled. But the fault for the situation lies with the people there who have thwarted the will of the majority, who have refused to allow the restoration of democracy, who continue to keep that society locked up and the economy there disintegrating."[119] Furthermore, the administration acknowledged the hardship that sanctions placed upon the people of Haiti. It was clearly stated that "sanctions impose a hardship." But the administration also asserted that it provided "massive humanitarian assistance" in the form of feeding over 680,000 people a day and that it provided medical services. Even with this knowledge, the press still asked, does the end justify the means?[120]

This issue concerning the harm that the sanctions were causing, especially to the children in Haiti was continually raised by the press. During one news conference, the president stated that "the people of Haiti need to know that the reason this embargo occurred is because of the police chief, Mr. Francois; and because of General Cedras; and because they welshed on the Governors Island agreement."[121]

To answer the attack on his foreign policy team, President Clinton asserted that his administration had been "dealing with the central, large, strategic issues of this time, dealing with the former Soviet Union, working on bringing down the nuclear threat, working on stemming nuclear proliferation, working on peace in the Middle East, working on putting economics at the forefront of . . . foreign policy."[122] On 4 November 1993, Secretary of State Warren Christopher announced the

Clinton administration's new six priorities in its foreign policy. Notably absent were Bosnia, Somalia, and Haiti. Instead, the administration chose to focus on the conditions of the post-Cold War world in general: economic security, reform in Russia, new framework for NATO, trade relations with the Far East, Middle Eastern affairs, and nuclear nonproliferation.

The issue of foreign policy was continually stressed by both papers, although it was relegated to a position of secondary importance after the effects of the embargo/sanctions and Haitian internal affairs. The news items continued the trend toward analyzing the Clinton administration's foreign policy approach but also began to examine individual players within the administration's foreign policy team. For example, on 31 October 1993 the *New York Times* printed a story on W. Anthony Lake, Clinton's national security adviser. In this story, Lake was described as having attempted to explain Clinton's foreign policy:

The Clinton administration . . . is the first since the Truman administration era that in foreign policy "has not had a single defining issue against which it could define itself." All every other Administration had to do, and it was not always easy, he said, "was to answer the central question: what form will containment of the Soviet Union and Communism take?"[123]

The same story ends with the *New York Times* speculating on the Clinton administration's role in the world:

The Clintonites do not want to rely on a merciless balance-of-power view of the world because it is too cynical for Mr. Clinton, but they also do not want a foreign policy of rampant moralism because they know it can lead to crusades they cannot win. So often in places like Bosnia or Somalia or Haiti they seem to be searching for some third way—between sending American troops and doing nothing at all. But often there is no third way.[124]

A *New York Times* editorial remarked that "everyone is groping for a new framework" because no one had "yet devised a set of guiding principles to guide American conduct in a radically transformed world."[125] Since early October 1993 the *Washington Post* had made the link with the post-Cold War foreign policy and maintained this connection; however, increasingly their stories focused on key players in the administration's foreign policy team: 5 November 1993, Secretary of State Warren Christopher was reported describing the administration's new foreign policy goals; 9 November 1993, Clifton R. Wharton was profiled after he resigned his post as deputy secretary of state; 10 November 1993, another story that highlighted Wharton's reason for resigning his post; 10 November 1993, an editorial focused on Wharton's resignation; 14 November 1993, a story highlighted Secretary of Defense Les Aspin's style as "hesitant by design." By the middle of November the situation in Haiti was not a major foreign policy concern but part of a larger foreign policy picture painted by the administration: "Taking Haiti off the policy front burner is consistent with the administration's recent efforts to back off from the troublesome high-visibility issues that have brought so much grief and to emphasize instead the long-term objectives on which senior officials believe their record is stronger, such as strengthening democracy in Russia."[126]

Official fault for the failure of the Governors Island agreement was assigned in a 13 November 1993 "Letter to Congressional Leaders on Haiti." In this letter, President Clinton presented a brief history of U.S. involvement in Haiti since the 1991 coup and then detailed U.S. involvement since the U.S.S. *Harlan County* was turned back on 11 October 1993. Fault was laid at the feet of the de facto regime: "[T]he Haitian military and police failed to maintain order necessary for the deployment of U.S. and other forces participating."[127]

As the crisis entered its seventh week in early December, the administration was once again echoing its statements of support for Aristide's return. In press conferences administration officials were relating that the president was optimistic about possible outcomes to the situation and was dedicated to the continuation of work to restore Aristide. Further, it was stated that those most hurt by the sanctions—Haitian poor—were receiving the most help. By the middle of December 1993 the crisis situation with Haiti was almost a nonissue and prompted an almost jocular tone from the president: "So we're going to take another run at it and see if we can do something on it. And it's going to require some flexibility on all sides. It just is. And we'll just have to see if we can get there. We're going to try, hard."[128]

SUMMARY

The period after the signing of the Governors Island agreement was a successful one for the Clinton administration. The press lauded the agreement, and the international community awaited its implementation. On 11 October 1993, however, the de facto government failed to provide a safe environment for the military trainers and engineers to disembark, ultimately forcing the U.S.S. *Harlan County* to withdraw. The mob activity that forced the ship back was a serious blow to the integrity and credibility of the Clinton administration. A foreign policy crisis had erupted, and the administration acted quickly to manage the situation.

White House Frames

The initial utterances of the administration were of an explanatory nature. The cooperative nature of the U.S.-led UN/OAS mission was stressed. It was stated clearly and repeatedly by administration officials that the Haitian authorities did not do what they had said they would do; that is, provide a secure environment for the deployment of U.S. and Canadian military engineers and trainers. At this early stage the administration stressed the "nonconfrontational" role of the mission; these troops were not on a peacekeeping or peacemaking mission. Thus, it was within the mission's parameters to leave due to the lack of a secure environment. At this time as well the administration reiterated its commitment to the Governors Island agreement; it stated that it expected the de facto government to honor the agreement. Furthermore, the administration would seek to reimpose sanctions on the de facto government as soon as possible.

On 15 October 1993 President Clinton read a short statement concerning the situation in Haiti. This statement and subsequent press question-and-answer session served as his first and only public and formal reply to the incident. Through this address the president sought to accomplish three broad goals: one, convey to the American public the U.S. interests in Haiti; two, explain the new actions the administration had ordered as a response to the incident; and three, explain American's purpose for being in Haiti. The primary U.S. interest in Haiti was approximately 1,000 U.S. citizens. Their protection and safety were paramount in the president's mind. Too, there was the hemispheric march toward democracy and the humanitarian considerations inside of Haiti to consider. The president had taken certain actions in response to the incident, and these were explained as well. New actions to be taken included reimposition of sanctions, the deployment of six U.S. naval vessels off the coast of Haiti to enforce the sanctions, and the placement of a company of marines stationed at Guantánamo Bay, Cuba, on full alert. The explanation of U.S. interests and new actions combined to form the administration's purpose: "to ensure the safety of the Americans in Haiti and to press for the restoration of democracy there through the strongest possible enforcement of the sanctions."[129]

Shortly after this statement, the Clinton administration found itself embroiled in a battle with Congress over management of foreign policy. At stake was the manner in which the president could command U.S. troops. President Clinton stressed that his administration was looking for ways to work more closely with Congress in the new post-Cold War world. The new relationship must recognize Congress's concerns but also protect the president's prerogative to act. The president further stressed that better cooperation between the executive branch and

Congress was critical for effective U.S. Foreign policy. The president reiterated his commitment to consulting with Congress on foreign policy and pledged to continue to keep Congress fully informed about significant deployments of the nation's armed forces. The president had stressed as well that any restrictions placed on him could send the wrong signal to the de facto government in Haiti and could also hinder his effectiveness in enforcing sanctions and protecting American lives.

The question of sanctions was also continually stressed throughout the aftermath of the incident. The Clinton administration emphasized that it only planned to use sanctions to begin with; however, publicly it never ruled out the use of U.S. troops. As the president stated, he was not going to rule any option in or out; on this point, he and his officials were consistent throughout the incident.

Another issue that received considerable attention from the press and Congress during this period concerned President Aristide's CIA-generated psychological profile. Again, the Clinton administration spoke with a unified voice: President Aristide's competence is not at issue; he was the legally elected president of Haiti. It was not for the United States to judge who the Haitian people could or could not have as their president.

On the questions of sanctions the administration was consistent as well. The president and his officials continually stressed that the sanctions achieved the initial Governors Island agreement; thus, they were an effective tool to employ to force the de facto government to the bargaining table. The administration frankly admitted that they did hurt the poor but that eventually they force the leaders to talk. Stressed during these types of comments were the administration's humanitarian assistance to the Haitian poor: food and medical supplies to over 680,000 Haitians a day.

The Press Framing of Administrative Utterances

The response of the press may be broadly divided into two framing devices: one, sanctions and internal Haitian affairs; and two, the battle between Congress and the president over foreign affairs. With regard to sanctions, the press generally framed its coverage in such a manner as to suggest that they hurt only the Haitian poor; were an ineffective weapon against the county's rich leaders; and in conjunction with the political impasse and the effects of sanctions, had thrown the country into near anarchy.

After the initial success of the Governors Island agreement, the press maintained that the abysmal Haitian economy was a direct result of the sanctions imposed in 1991 but especially a result of the additional sanctions imposed by President Clinton in June 1993. Once the crisis erupted in Haiti, both the *New York Times* and the *Washington Post* called for the return of sanctions. Even though calling for the reimposition of sanctions, the *Washington Post* stressed that they would only hurt the poor while having negligible effects on the country's leaders. The answer was to invite the leaders to negotiate once again. After the president's 15 October 1993 address, the press still supported the reimposition but stressed even more strongly the effects such sanctions have on the poor. The internal situation was described as near anarchy, with the sanctions having a crippling effect. Both papers reported that the sanctions might not return the de facto government to the bargaining table. Both papers reported that the wealthy could afford to wait out the sanctions and that the poor were the real sufferers. As the weeks passed, both papers increased coverage on the effects of the sanctions. The Haitian people were reported as resenting the sanctions, and the internal situation was depicted as grim. The press stated that both sides were talking but that the army leaders were stalling as the economy crumbled. The situation was, in short, economic collapse and political stalemate.

The broad framing device I call Congress versus the president contains three general elements: one, use of U.S. troops; two, the president's foreign policy in general; and three, Aristide's CIA psychological profile. Although the press reported that President Clinton had not ruled in or ruled out any options for responding to the incident, they continuously reported that the administration did not intend to use U.S. troops to restore order and President Aristide to power. Moreover, the *New York Times* reported misleading numbers concerning the initial deployment of military engineers and trainers; these misrepresentations continued, with the paper reporting varied numbers and composition of U.S. troops initially sailing to Port-au-Prince. The withdrawal of the U.S.S. *Harlan County* was described as a retreat and was later used to symbolize the administration's broken promise to the Haitian people.

The president's foreign policy received mixed emphasis. At one point the *New York Times* described President Clinton's motivation for being in Haiti as embarrassment over his broken campaign promise to stop direct returns. Once the crisis erupted, the foreign policy focus evolved differently for each paper. The *New York Times* described foreign policy as a partisan battle between Congress and the president. At issue was U.S. troop involvement in foreign trouble spots: Somalia, Bosnia, and Haiti. A partisan interpretation was given to this issue. The *New York Times* described the discussions as "gratuitous partisan sniping" and suggested that the Republicans left the president with all of the problems. The *Washington Post* also described the battle between the president and Congress, but although it, too, described this battle as partisan "sniping," it also raised it to a question of U.S. policy in a post-Cold War world. The paper was actively exploring America's role in the post-cold War world, and the running presidential/congressional deliberations were reported in a manner that attempted to explore this role.

The conflict between Congress and the president died when the Senate passed a nonbinding resolution that requested the president to keep Congress informed about the use of U.S. troops in UN missions. The concern with foreign policy did not die out, however. Instead, there was a shift in emphasis from the presidential/congressional partisan struggle to the composition of the president's foreign policy team. In short, the issue of the administration's foreign policy evolved into personality sketches. This was particularly true of the *New York Times*, which reported on this issue at a two-to-one ratio over the *Washington Post* after the compromise resolution was forwarded to the president.

Although not of major importance in terms of space provided, the issue of Aristide's competence does merit mention as a framing device due to the consistency of press coverage. Both papers described the question of the CIA's psychological profile as partisan bickering and an attempt at character assassination. Both papers advanced the Clinton administration's claim that it did not matter what the CIA said, that the people of Haiti had elected Aristide and he was their best hope for the restoration of democracy.

NOTES

1. White House, Office of the Press Secretary, "Statement by the Press Secretary" (1 July 1993).

2. White House, Office of the Press Secretary, "Statement by the Press Secretary" (1 July 1993).

3. White House, Office of the Press Secretary, "Background Briefing by Senior Administration Official" (30 August 1993).

4. U.S. Department of State, "Statement by the Press Secretary on the President's Meeting with President Jean-Bertrand Aristide of Haiti: July 22, 1993," *Weekly Compilation of Presidential Documents* 29.29 (26 July 1993): 1432.

5. U.S. Department of State, "Notice on the Continuation of Haitian Emergency," *Weekly Compilation of Presidential Documents* 29.39 (4 October 1993).

6. Howard W. French, "Haitian Military Is Said to Accept Plan to End Crisis," *New York Times* 3 July 1993: A1.

7. Howard W. French, "Haitian Military Leaders and Aristide Sign Pact to End Crisis," *New York Times* 4 July 1993: A1.

8. Howard W. French, "Restoring Stability to Haiti Is Seen as the Next Big

Test," *New York Times* 5 July 1993: A4.

9. Thomas W. Lippman, "U.S. Willing to Send Military, Police Trainers to Haiti," *Washington Post* 23 July 1993: A24.

10. Howard W. French, "Prostrate Haiti Looking to Foreign Aid for a Lift," *New York Times* 11 July 1993: A3.

11. Julia Preston, "Gen. Cedras Accepts U.N. Pact on Haiti," *Washington Post* 3 July 1993: A13.

12. Lawrence E. Harrison, "Haiti's Overseas Resources," *Washington Post* 9 July 1993: A21.

13. French, "Haitian Military Is Said," A2.

14. French, "Restoring Stability," A4.

15. Elaine Sciolino, "U.S. Offers 350 Troops to U.N. Force for Haiti," *New York Times* 22 July 1993: A5. (Italics mine.)

16. David Binder, "Clinton Urges Haitian Leader to Appoint a New Premier," *New York Times* 23 July 1993: A8.

17. Lippman, "U.S. Willing to Send," A24.

18. French, "Restoring Stability," A4.

19. Mary McGrory, "Haiti Scrambles Clinton Options," *Washington Post* 14 October 1993: A2.

20. White House, Office of the Press Secretary, "Background Briefing By Senior Administration Official" (12 October 1993): 5.

21. White House, Office of the Press Secretary, "Background Briefing By Senior Administration Official" (12 October 1993): 6.

22. White House, Office of the Press Secretary, "Press Briefing By Dee Dee Myers" (12 October 1993): 5.

23. White House, Office of the Press Secretary, "Press Briefing By Dee Dee Myers" (12 October 1993): 6.

24. White House, Office of the Press Secretary, "Statement By the Press Secretary" (12 October 1993): 1.

25. White House, Office of the Press Secretary, "Remarks By the President Upon Departure" (12 October 1993): 3.

26. White House, Office of the Press Secretary, "Press Briefing By Dee Dee Myers" (13 October 1993): 10.

27. U.S. Department of State, "The President's News Conference: October 14, 1993," *Weekly Compilation of Presidential Documents* 29.41 (18 October 1993): 2070.

28. Dana Priest, "Administration Aides Defensive on Foreign Policy Strategies," *Washington Post* 11 October 1993: A1.

29. Howard W. French, "Envoys Flee Port as Their Cars Are Struck," *New York Times* 12 October 1993: A12.

30. John M. Goshko, "Pullback Is New Setback for Clinton: Effort to Demonstrate Coherent Policy Hurt," *Washington Post* 14 October 1993: A24.

31. Douglas Farah and Michael Tarr, "Haitians Block U.S. Troop Arrival," *Washington Post* 12 October 1993: A1.

32. Steven A. Holmes, "Bid to Restore Haiti's Leader Is Derailed: U.S. With-

draws Ship and Asks Sanctions," *New York Times* 13 October 1993: A1.

33. Howard W. French, "Haiti Army Celebrates U.S. Withdrawal," *New York Times* 13 October 1993: A12.

34. Steven A. Holmes, "Clinton and Aristide Move to Affirm Policy on Haiti," *New York Times* 14 October 1993: A8.

35. Howard W. French, "U.S. Move Angers Diplomats in Haiti," *New York Times* 14 October 1993: A8.

36. "How to Get Tough with Haiti," Editorial, *New York Times* 13 October 1993: A24.

37. "How to Get Tough with Haiti," A24.

38. Farah and Tarr, "Haitians Block," A1.

39. "On the Dock in Haiti," Editorial, *Washington Post* 12 October 1993: A18.

40. Julia Preston, "Haiti Embargo Revived," *Washington Post* 14 October 1993: A1.

41. Goshko, "Pullback Is New Setback," A24.

42. White House, Office of the Press Secretary, "Press Conference by the President" (15 October 1993): 1.

43. White House, Office of the Press Secretary, "Press Conference by the President" (15 October 1993): 2.

44. R. W. Apple, Jr., "President Orders Six U.S. Warships for Haiti Patrol," *New York Times* 16 October 1993: A1.

45. "Next Steps in Haiti," Editorial, *Washington Post* 18 October 1993: A18.

46. "Next Steps in Haiti," A18.

47. Ann Devroy and R. Jeffrey Smith, "Clinton Reexamines a Foreign Policy under Siege," *Washington Post* 17 October 1993: A27.

48. Garry Pierre-Pierre, "Rights Monitors Are Pulled Out of Haiti," *New York Times* 16 October 1993: A4.

49. Douglas Farah, "Haitian Rulers Scramble to Forestall U.N. Embargo," *Washington Post* 18 October 1993: A12.

50. Garry Pierre-Pierre, "Terror of Duvalier Years Is Haunting Haiti Again," *New York Times* 18 October 1993: A6.

51. Howard W. French, "As U.S. Ships Arrive, Haiti General Refuses to Budge," *New York Times* 18 October 1993: A6.

52. "Embargo Adds to Old Woes," *New York Times* 18 October 1993: A6.

53. Howard W. French, "In Haiti, There Is No Shortage of Fear," *New York Times* 20 October 1993: A5.

54. Douglas Farah and Ruth Marcus, "Haiti's Army Rulers Remain Defiant," *Washington Post* 19 October 1993: A18.

55. Farah and Marcus, "Haiti's Army Rulers," A18.

56. Douglas Farah, "Aristide's Supporters Faltering: Haiti Embargo Adds to Despair," *Washington Post* 21 October 1993: A1.

57. Farah, "Aristide's Supporters," A1.

58. U.S. Department of State, "Interview with Radio Reporters: October 18, 1993," *Weekly Compilation of Presidential Documents* 29.42 (25 October 1993): 2097.

59. U.S. Department of State, "Interview with Radio Reporters: October 18, 1993," 2101.

60. U.S. Department of State, "Interview with Radio Reporters: October 18, 1993," 2102.

61. White House, Office of the Press Secretary, "Press Briefing by Dee Dee Myers" (19 October 1993): 11-12.

62. U.S. Department of State, "Letter to Congressional Leaders on Haiti: October 20, 1993," *Weekly Compilation of Presidential Documents* 29.42 (25 October 1993): 2126.

63. Thomas L. Friedman, "Dole to Offer Bill to Limit President on G.I. Role in Haiti," *New York Times* 18 October 1993: A1.

64. Friedman, "Dole to Offer Bill," A7.

65. Thomas L. Friedman, "Clinton Vows to Fight Congress on His Power to Use the Military," *New York Times* 19 October 1993: A1.

66. Adam Clymer, "Foreign Policy Tug-of-War: Latest in a Long String of Battles," *New York Times* 19 October 1993: A18.

67. Clymer, "Foreign Policy Tug-of-War," A18.

68. "Mr. Dole's Bad Idea," Editorial, *New York Times* 19 October 1993: A28.

69. Clifford Krauss, "Dole Concedes to Clinton in Fight over Right to Send Troops to Haiti," *New York Times* 21 October 1993: A6.

70. Goshko, "Pullback Is New Setback," A24.

71. McGrory, "Haiti Scrambles," A2.

72. Goshko, "Pullback Is New Setback," A24.

73. Helen Dewar, "Lawmakers Seek New Methods to Handle Post-Cold War Crises," *Washington Post* 16 October 1993: A18.

74. Dewar, "Lawmakers Seek," A18.

75. Dewar, "Lawmakers Seek," A18.

76. Devroy and Smith, "Clinton Reexamines," A1.

77. "Congress vs. President," Editorial, *Washington Post* 20 October 1993: A28.

78. Devroy and Smith, "Clinton Reexamines," A28.

79. Devroy and Smith, "Clinton Reexamines," A28. See, too, Helen Dewar, "Senators Approve Troop Compromise: Clinton Authority Is Left Unrestricted," *Washington Post* 21 October 1993: A24.

80. Helen Dewar, "Clinton and Congress Cease Fire," *Washington Post* 22 October 1993: A26. Similar statements are found by the same author the next day: "Senators Act to Rewrite Resolution on Troop Deployment Policy," *Washington Post* 23 October 1993: A5.

81. Helen Dewar, "Now It's the GOP Asserting Role for Congress on Foreign Policy," *Washington Post* 26 October 1993: A20.

82. White House, Office of the Press Secretary, "Press Briefing by Dee Dee Myers" (22 October 1993): 5.

83. "Support of Aristide Defended," *Washington Post* 24 October 1993: A28.

84. "Support of Aristide Defended," A28.

85. Kathy Sawyer, "Gore Defends Aristide, Whose Prospects for Return Seem

Brighter," *Washington Post* 25 October 1993: A14.

86. Sawyer, "Gore Defends Aristide," A14.

87. "Mr. Aristide's Opportunity," Editorial, *Washington Post* 27 October 1993: A24.

88. "Tighten the Sanctions on Haiti," Editorial, *New York Times* 29 October 1993: A28.

89. Steven A. Holmes, "Administration Is Fighting Itself on Haiti Policy," *New York Times* 23 October 1993: A3.

90. Steven Greenhouse, "Clinton Defends Aristide," *New York Times* 24 October 1993: A7.

91. Howard W. French, "Fearful Rural Haitians Yearn for Aristide's Return," *New York Times* 25 October 1993: A3.

92. Tim Weiner, "Key Haiti Leaders Said to Have Been in the C.I.A.'s Pay," *New York Times* 1 November 1993: A1.

93. John M. Goshko and R. Jeffrey Smith, "U.N. Envoy to Go Ahead on Haiti Talks Despite Military's Silence," *Washington Post* 3 November 1993: A16.

94. Garry Pierre-Pierre, "Anxious Haitians Start Building Boats Again," *New York Times* 22 October 1993: A1.

95. Pierre-Pierre, "Anxious Haitians," A10.

96. Steven A. Holmes, "U.S. May Tighten Embargo on Haiti," *New York Times* 28 October 1993: A17.

97. Holmes, "U.S. May Tighten," A17.

98. John M. Goshko, "Aristide Denies CIA Report of Treatment for Mental Illness," *Washington Post* 23 October 1993: A19.

99. William Booth, "Despite Embargo, Wealthy Haitians Can Obtain Gasoline Easily," *Washington Post* 26 October 1993: A21.

100. Howard W. French, "Two Sides in Haiti Meet on Impasse," *New York Times* 24 October 1993: A7; French, "Fearful Rural Haitians Yearn," A3; Garry Pierre-Pierre, "After Talks, Haitian Aides Hope for a Break in the Impasse," *New York Times* 25 October 1993: A3; Howard W. French, "Haiti's Premier and General Meet as Drive to Settle Crisis Intensifies," *New York Times* 26 October 1993: A13.

101. Howard W. French, "Alliance by Anti-Aristide Forces and Flight by Fearful Lawmakers May Doom Pact," *New York Times* 27 October 1993: A10.

102. R. W. Apple, Jr., "U.S. Concludes Aristide Can't Return by Deadline," *New York Times* 27 October 1993: A1.

103. Thomas L. Friedman, "Leaders in Haiti Wrong to Think They Can Tell U.S., Clinton Says," *New York Times* 29 October 1993: A6.

104. Douglas Farah, "Premier of Haiti Steers 'Opposition Government': From Resident, Malval Struggles for Aristide," *Washington Post* 22 October 1993: A25.

105. Douglas Farah, "Haitians Weigh New Plan to End Political Impasse," *Washington Post* 25 October 1993: A12.

106. Douglas Farah and William Booth, "U.N. Envoy Invites Carter to Haiti; Former President, Other World Leaders Would Act as Protectors," *Washington Post* 26 October 1993: A19.

107. R. Jeffrey Smith, "CIA's Aristide Profile Spurs Hill Concern," *Washington*

Post 22 October 1993: A26.

108. Douglas Farah and William Booth, "Efforts to Restore Aristide Tottering: Haiti's Army Fends Off Pressure," *Washington Post* 28 October 1993: A31.

109. Apple, "U.S. Concludes Aristide," A10. There were no sources or quotes to substantiate this assertion.

110. Garry Pierre-Pierre, "Effort to Save Haitian Talks Fails as Military Leaders Shun Meeting," *New York Times* 6 November 1993: A4.

111. John M. Goshko, "Blacks Criticize Clinton on Haiti: Multilateral Military Action to Return Aristide Suggested," *Washington Post* 11 November 1993: A46.

112. U.S. Department of State, "Remarks and an Exchange with Reporters on Haiti: October 23, 1993," *Weekly Compilation of Presidential Documents* 29.43 (1 November 1993): 2166.

113. Friedman, "Leaders in Haiti Wrong," A6.

114. Howard W. French, "U.N. Envoy Proposes Talks to End the Impasse in Haiti," *New York Times* 30 October 1993: A5.

115. French, "U.N. Envoy Proposes," A5.

116. Michael Tarr, "Attempt to Resume Haiti Talks Collapses: Army Leader Boycotts International Session, Leaving U.S. and U.N. Generals in Lurch," *Washington Post* 6 November 1993: A14.

117. Tarr, "Attempt to Resume Haiti," A14.

118. Howard W. French, "Study Says Haiti Sanctions Kill Up to 1,000 Children a Month," *New York Times* 9 November 1993: A8. Other examples of this type of genre mixing can be found in the following news stories: Howard W. French, "As Aristide Fails to Return, His Foes Celebrate in Haiti," *New York Times* 31 October 1993: A12; Garry Pierre-Pierre, "Haiti Is Suffering Under Oil Embargo," *New York Times* 3 November 1993: A7; Pierre-Pierre, "Effort to Save Haitian Talks," A1; Howard W. French, "As Sanctions Bite, Haiti's Poor Feel the Pinch," *New York Times* 15 November 1993: A7.

119. White House, Office of the Press Secretary, "Press Briefing by Dee Dee Myers" (9 November 1993): 7.

120. White House, Office of the Press Secretary, "Press Briefing by Dee Dee Myers" (9 November 1993): 8.

121. White House, Office of the Press Secretary, "Remarks by the President in Press Roundtable" (12 November 1993).

122. U.S. Department of State, "The President's News Conference: November 10, 1993," *Weekly Compilation of Presidential Documents* 29.45 (15 November 1993): 2314.

123. Thomas L. Friedman, "Clinton's Foreign Policy: Top Advisor Speaks Up," *New York Times* 31 October 1993: A8.

124. Friedman, "Clinton's Foreign Policy," A8.

125. "A Defensible Foreign Policy," Editorial, *New York Times* 1 November 1993: A18.

126. Thomas W. Lippman, "U.S. Relaxes Its Drive for Haitian Democracy: No Humanitarian Problems Seen Imminent," *Washington Post* 17 November 1993: A36.

127. U.S. Department of State, "Letter to Congressional Leaders on Haiti:

November 13, 1993," *Weekly Compilation of Presidential Documents* 29.46 (22 November 1993): 2368.

128. U.S. Department of State, "Teleconference Remarks on Community Policing Grants and an Exchange with Reporters: December 20, 1993," *Weekly Compilation of Presidential Documents* 29.51 (20 December 1993): 2616.

129. White House, Office of the Press Secretary, "Press Conference by the President" (15 October 1993): 2.

Chapter 8

Conclusion

This study was conceived as a beginning in previously unexamined territory. The task of analyzing presidential crisis rhetoric within a post-Cold War world has begun. Specifically, I examined the Clinton administration's discursive response to three crisis situations: North Korea in 1993, Bosnia in 1995, and Haiti throughout 1993. In addition, the administration's discourse was examined as part of a larger discourse presented by the national press to the American people. The central concern has been with presidential and press framing of the situations in North Korea, Bosnia, and Haiti. Accordingly, this study sought to answer three specific questions: One, how did the Clinton administration frame the three situations? Two, how did the press, responding to President Clinton, frame the situations? And three, at what time, if at all, did these frames converge to present a unified contextual whole for a particular situation? In this chapter, I provide an overview of the framing analysis performed in this study; in addition, I answer the three specific research questions asked by this study. Finally, I provide an overview of the implications and theoretical contributions of this study.

The formal statements made by President Clinton and his officials have been called the administrative text in this study. This text was subjected to a frame analysis. Moreover, the news items printed in the *Washington Post* and the *New York Times* concerning North Korea, Bosnia, and Haiti were also subjected to a frame analysis. The administrative frames and the press frames were then compared. Framing acts to make some elements of a situation or text more salient than others. Frames (1) define problems, (2) diagnose causes, (3) make moral judgments, and (4) suggest remedies. Pan and Kosicki suggested that news stories have a unifying frame and that this frame determines how a given news story will be interpreted. The work by Entman corroborates this assertion and has demonstrated that frames reside within news narratives and encourage certain ways of thinking about them. Key words, metaphors, concepts, and symbols take on special importance as components of a frame.

Entman called the elements that comprise a frame "event-specific schema." Once established, event-specific schemata make it difficult to modify or replace a particular frame. As Entman stated: "[F]or those stories in which a single frame thoroughly pervades the text, stray contrary opinions . . . are likely to possess such low salience as to be of little practical use to most audience members."[1] When developing new event-specific schemata, however, political elites and the president have great influence in establishing the frames used. During a crisis situation, then, the president should have enormous potential influence over how the event is to be framed. This study examined three crisis situations of various durations: North Korea (three months), Bosnia (three weeks), and Haiti (one year). During these crisis periods the Clinton administration worked within already established frames (event-specific schemata) and worked within a crisis atmosphere (new event-specific schemata). Thus, this study analyzed both the president's ability to affect already established frames and his ability to enact frames in order to structure action and belief in a post-Cold War setting.

THE THREE GUIDING QUESTIONS

One: How Did the Clinton Administration Frame the Situations?

North Korea. North Korea was a persistent crisis situation for the Clinton administration. Although it lurked in the background of international news, it failed to burst forth into a fully developed crisis. The situation was such that the moment for a "fitting utterance" to modify the situation never emerged. Instead, this situation lingered throughout the three-month period following North Korea's decision to withdraw from the nuclear nonproliferation treaty. Because of the abrupt nature of the North Korean decision, the Clinton administration's first utterances enacted new event-specific schemata through which the event could be understood. The initial administrative utterances evolved into three frames that structured future administrative discourse on this subject.

Perhaps the most subtle frame involved the creation of an atmosphere of calm through the very lack of information imparted. Consistently the administration described to members of the press how little information there was to share and that administration officials were busy working on returning North Korea to the treaty. Progress was being made, officials asserted, but no new information was forthcoming. The second frame involved the projection of a determination to have North Korea eventually allow inspections. This attitude never faltered. Indeed, administration officials were usually quick to point out that diplomacy would be used to gain compliance. Because of this, most announcements included some variation on the theme of continued negotiation. Finally, the issue of China composed the third frame used by the administration. This was almost exclusively in response to press questions, but the administration's conception of Chinese involvement was consistently and distinctly advanced. China was considered as an important part of the negotiations with North Korea, but nothing more was attached to Chinese participation in the negotiations. In this way, too, the administration insisted on the separation of China's help and renewal of its MFN status.

Bosnia. Although the Clinton administration had been working on the Bosnia situation for years prior to the initialing of the Dayton Accord, it was not until the Accord's announcement that a true crisis for the Clinton administration materialized. With the announced participation of 20,000 U.S. troops, the administration changed the substance of the debate from speculation to reality. In this sense, then, the administration had to develop new event-specific schemata while attempting to break away from already established schemata that had dominated the perception of the Bosnian situation for years (most notably, that it was unresolvable and that any military participation would mean war with heavy casualties). U.S. troops had now been committed, and the president had to justify both their use and the potential loss of American lives. The administration essentially advanced its justification for American involvement as a moral obligation. The United States could help; therefore, Americans must help. Through repeated assertions, the administration attempted to create a moral climate through which the issues could be viewed. It was within this climate that the administration framed five key issues. These issues involved the peace plan, the mission, and U.S. leadership and values; two other issues, congressional approval and the Bosnian Serbs, were generated as responses to press questions.

The Clinton administration touted the peace plan as a "victory for all" parties involved in the Bosnian affair. Americans, Russians, Europeans, and especially the Croats, Muslims, and Serbs of Bosnia were all considered a part of this plan. Praise was generous and well distributed among the parties. The plan was described as principled but also as solidly consisting of means to achieve the lofty goals it contained; it was substantive. All involved parties had agreed to the provisions, and all had compromised and made sacrifices to achieve the peace.

The mission was framed, through repeated assertions, as "clear, limited, and achievable" within a one-year period. The responsibility for the mission would rest with U.S. commanders. Especially stressed was that this would be a NATO mission, not a UN operation. The United States commanded NATO, and American troops would take their orders from an American general. This mission would be especially important because it would create stability in Europe; a stable and peaceful Europe was extremely important for the United States because Europe could help Americans with those things that mattered most: stopping organized crime, drug trafficking, and the proliferation of nuclear weapons.

Much of the discussion concerning the peace plan and the mission was linked with professing the importance of U.S leadership and values. President Clinton repeatedly stressed that the Dayton Accord derived from American leadership and values; therefore, the United States must take the lead in fulfilling the mandates of the peace plan. The mission was the logical extension of U.S. Values: Americans have the responsibility to see the peace plan through in order to give "peace a chance."

The press frequently asked the administration about congressional approval for troop deployment. Unfailingly, the administrative response given framed the issue in a bipartisan manner. Furthermore, the administration believed that the American people had questions about the mission, so Congress would have questions as well; moreover, these questions should be asked. If the administration made its case to the American people, then Congress would support the mission. The White House consistently reported Congress was keeping an open mind about the mission. Too, congressional support given was graciously accepted.

Questions about Bosnian Serb resistance to the Dayton Accord intermittently surfaced throughout the three-week period covered in this study. Whenever the issue arose, the standard administrative reply was that it was not an issue at all. The administration consistently asserted that Serbian President Milosevic had been empowered by the Bosnian Serbs to negotiate on their behalf and that they had agreed to be bound by his decision. Furthermore, the Bosnian Serb leaders had initialed the plan as well. Some "grumbling" was expected, but the plan was in no danger of being rejected.

Haiti. The Clinton administration inherited a situation that had already developed a well-articulated frame. That is to say, event-specific schemata were already entrenched. The Bush administration had framed the situation in several important ways. First, it had stressed the United States as a cooperative partner, with the United Nations/OAS as the leaders, in restoring democracy to Haiti. Second, the Bush administration had stressed that the policy of direct returns was a humanitarian policy aimed at preventing the deaths of thousands of Haitian boat people. Finally, the Bush administration had repeatedly stressed that the Haitian refugees were primarily economic, not political, refugees.

Just before taking office, President-elect Clinton announced his policy toward Haiti. This policy remained consistent throughout 1993. The policy was constrained by the prior Bush administration frames but also announced new changes aimed at making the policy Clinton's own. In this respect, the Clinton administration was constrained by the initial event-specific schemata. The situation—Haiti—was itself not new, even though Clinton was a new president. Although candidate Clinton had promised sweeping changes in the Bush administration policy, once elected, he found himself constrained by both material conditions (the possibility of 100,000 or more Haitian refugees) and the Bush administration's prior frame. Thus, President-elect Clinton's early announcement is a combination of prior Bush policy and Clinton's own attempt at change.

In his first formal statement on Haiti as president-elect, Clinton announced three broad goals. First, his administration was committed to restoring democracy to Haiti, including the return of President Aristide. The restoration of democracy was to be accomplished through cooperation with the United Nations/OAS. Furthermore, it was to be accomplished through negotiation and the early deployment of human rights monitors to ensure some semblance of political stability within Haiti. Second, the president was committed to saving human lives. In this case, the policy of direct returns was to be continued. This action was clearly announced as humanitarian in motive. Finally, the president announced his own policy changes. He was committed to fair treatment for asylum seekers in Haiti. The president ordered accelerated refugee processing and expanded facilities in Haiti. This was especially important for maintaining the humanitarian aspect of the administration's policy.[2]

The problem defined by the administration was simple. President Aristide was Haiti's first democratically elected president. A coup d'état in September of 1991 forced him to flee the country. Since that time the de facto regime had exploited the country, and severe economic depression had ensued, causing tens of thousands to seek better conditions in the United States. The "international community" could not sit idly by, because this would send a message to other leaders in the Western Hemisphere that such thwarting of democratic will would go unpunished. Therefore, the solution to these problems was the return of

President Aristide and the restoration of democracy. For the president this was a foreign policy issue, one in which his authority as president should not be questioned or debated.

After the signing of the Governors Island agreement on 3 July 1993, the Clinton administration commented relatively little on the situation in Haiti. On 11 October 1993, however, the U.S.S. *Harlan County* was prevented from docking in Port-au-Prince by demonstrators. On 12 October 1993 the administration began to respond to this crisis. Administration officials explained that the leaders of the de facto government had failed to live up to their part of the Governors Island agreement; in short, they had broken their promise to maintain order and provide a secure environment for U.S. and Canadian military personnel. The administration stressed the nonconfrontational role of the military engineers and trainers; thus, the withdrawal of the ship was not a retreat, or a policy crisis, but a prudent decision.

President Clinton formally responded to the situation on 15 October 1993. His statement obtained three goals. First, he announced U.S. interests: the safety of 1,000 American citizens living in Haiti; the maintenance of the hemispheric march toward democracy; and the continuing humanitarian concerns. Second, he explained new U.S. actions: the reimposition of sanctions; the deployment of Coast Guard and Navy vessels to enforce sanctions; and the placement of a marine company at Guantánamo Bay naval base on full alert. Finally, he explained the U.S. purpose of these actions: to ensure the safety of American lives and to press for the restoration of President Aristide and democracy.

Following the Port-au-Prince incident, a battle between the president and Congress erupted over the possible use of U.S. troops in several UN missions: Haiti, Bosnia, and Somalia. During this time the administration focused on its major foreign policy accomplishments—Russia and nuclear containment—and stressed the difference between vital U.S. interests and those areas where U.S. interests were less obvious: Haiti, Bosnia, and Somalia. The Clinton administration stressed that there should be more cooperation between Congress and the president in this new era of post-Cold War relations.

Two other policy considerations were part of the administration's overall frame for this period: the questions of sanctions and Aristide's CIA psychological profile. On the question of sanctions the administration maintained the same framing elements as it had before the Port-au-Prince incident. Sanctions were what forced the de facto government to the bargaining table in the first place. The administration was committed, however, to maintaining humanitarian assistance programs in the form of food and medical supplies to over 680,000 Haitians a day. On the question of President Aristide's mental stability the administration presented a simple argument. The people of Haiti elected him, and the United States had no business telling the people of Haiti who they may have as president.

Throughout 1993 the administration framed its announcements and responses to questions in such a manner as to define the Haitian problem as one of foreign policy. This held true after the Port-au-Prince incident as well, with the blame for the situation in Haiti laid squarely at the feet of the leaders of the de facto government. Further, the problem was one of perception. Haiti was only a small event that would not have risen to such importance if there had not recently been the firefight in Somalia that resulted in eighteen American dead. The larger foreign policy issues were being managed well; notwithstanding, those issues where U.S. interests were less well defined, but more dramatic, were receiving the largest share of the attention. The remedies suggested by the administration were simple and a continuation of the earliest administrative utterances on the Haitian situation. The United Nations/OAS should continue sanctions until the leaders of the de facto government restore President Aristide and democracy.

Two: How Did the Press, Responding to the Clinton Administration, Frame the Situations?

North Korea. Coverage of this situation was sporadic, and a portion of almost every news article was devoted to reexplaining what the situation was and how it had developed. Both the *New York Times* and the *Washington Post* focused on China and similarly framed the issue as well. China was viewed as a help since it wanted to resolve the situation through diplomacy. However, China was also painted as intentionally frustrating U.S. efforts aimed at convincing North Korea to accept inspections because it would not allow UN sanctions to be imposed. Furthermore, both papers claimed that the administration was linking the renewal of MFN status to China's willingness to help pressure North Korea to abide by the nonproliferation treaty. However, neither paper directly cited administration sources when making this claim.

Although both papers framed China in the same manner, they did not share similar frames of other issues. For example, the *Washington Post* often reported the situation as a confrontation between North Korea and the IAEA. Coverage was typically balanced since the focus was on the verbal confrontation between the two parties. The *New York Times* did not focus on a North Korea versus the IAEA scenario. Early in the crisis it attempted to create an element of drama by focusing on what might happen and upon the emotional state of the various countries. For example, immediately following the North Korean pullout, the situation was described as a "surprise," as "unnerving," and as "alarming."[3] The *New York Times* also relied heavily on a South Korean focus and on South Korean sources.

Finally, both papers relied extensively on anonymous sources. Although the general area from which the quoted material was to have been obtained was usually mentioned—"Senior administration officials" or "White House sources"—there were few direct quotes of the president or his officials. Furthermore, the imputed quotations of the anonymous sources did not correspond to the public administrative documents analyzed for this study, suggesting that the "sources" were low ranking or nonexistent. In addition to the heavy reliance on anonymous sources, both papers engaged routinely in speculation, hearsay, and analysis in regular news articles.

Bosnia. The press immediately expressed support for President Clinton and the Bosnian mission. This was essentially accomplished by adopting the very frame through which the administration advanced its assertions about the mission. Any article that detailed the peace plan or mission invariably would paraphrase the utterances of the administration and then provide quotes from administration officials. This practice facilitated the overwhelming perception of support one may glean from reading news articles during the period examined in this study. However, there was oppositional framing of several key issues: Congress, the Bosnian Serb opposition to the Dayton Accord, and ethnic considerations.

In direct contrast to Clinton administration assertions, the press framed Congress as extremely divided on the question of the mission; this division was described as partisan in origin. Those not supporting the president's plan were eventually described as mean-spirited and trite. Moreover, when Republicans questioned the president's policies, they were depicted as fighting the president instead of as supporting the troops or—as the administration maintained—asking the questions that were on the minds of Americans across the country.

The most explicit example of press framing involves the Bosnian Serbs, who were consistently described as rebels and separatists, even though they had only responded to the initial Croat/Muslim separation from Yugoslavia. Why the Serbs were rebels and the Croats/Muslims were not was never explained. The extreme and hostile focus on the Bosnian Serbs facilitated only minimal coverage of Croats and Muslims. Moreover, the frame so thoroughly pervaded press accounts of events that whenever ethnic cleansing or human rights violations were mentioned the Serbs received the blame.

Finally, immediately following the announcement of the Dayton Accord, the press, especially the *Washington Post*, framed the peace plan and Bosnia in general in ethnic terms. According to the press, Bosnia was once a showpiece of multiculturalism and multiethnic unity. The Serbs destroyed what once existed, and now the peace plan legitimated the years of ethnic warfare by dividing the country along ethnic lines. This framing device all but disappeared after one week, corresponding to increased reporting of mission dynamics.

Haiti. The press did report what the Clinton administration said about Haiti. However, as this study progressed, it became increasingly clear that what was being reported was framed in such a manner as to indicate the presence of a fully articulated counterpolicy. The press frame had seven distinct components. One, difficulties in reaching a settlement were continually stressed. Two, President Clinton's campaign pledge reversal was highlighted as an icon for the callous denial of refugee rights. Three, refugees were assumed to be political, not economic. Four, it was assumed that the United States was the leader in the international negotiations. Five, the embargo/sanctions were reported as only hurting Haiti's poor. Six, the policy of direct returns was stressed as illegal. Seven, it was assumed by the press that any emigrant had a right to enter this country.

The press frame was essentially a domestic one, with all seven elements rooted in a domestic focus. The problems highlighted by this domestic frame were different than those highlighted by the administration's frame. The root causes of the problems can be ascribed to one major issue: the continuation of the Bush policy toward Haiti. The policy of direct returns was touted by the press as being illegal and immoral. The inherent immorality is linked to three general ethical violations. One, Clinton broke his word about abolishing the policy of direct returns. Two, the policy of direct returns violates Haitians' rights to enter this country to settle. Three, the embargo/sanctions only hurt the poor in Haiti. Although the press did not openly suggest any remedies to the problems associated with Haiti, the frame itself suggests that all would be well if President Clinton followed through with his campaign pledge. The frame also suggested that the embargo/sanctions were responsible for the continuation of abysmal economic conditions in Haiti; therefore, if they were removed, the conditions would improve. The press focus is clearly on those aspects of administrative policy that are of a domestic nature: the legality of the policy and the president's character as it pertains to a reversal of a campaign pledge.

After the signing of the Governors Island agreement, the press, like the Clinton administration, reported little about Haiti. All was assumed to be going according to plan. Once the Port-au-Prince incident occurred, however, reporting on the situation resumed in earnest. The press frame during this time evolved into two distinct frames. The first focused on the internal workings of Haiti; it was a foreign affairs frame. In this frame were details of the effects of the newly imposed sanctions and the near-anarchic state of the country. It was reported that the Clinton administration's imposition of sanctions was the primary culprit for this. Although the press urged the administration to reimpose sanctions, it was strongly assertive that they would only hurt the poor. The issue of direct returns was almost ignored during the aftermath of the demonstration in Port-au-Prince.

The second frame focused on the domestic affairs of America. The Port-au-Prince incident prompted a congressional battle with the Clinton administration over the use of U.S. troops in UN missions. Although this issue had to do with foreign policy, it was eventually reduced to a partisan political battle. Even after the congressional concern abated, the press continued to report issues of Clinton's foreign policy and America's post-Cold War role as domestic concerns revolving around the composition of Clinton's foreign policy team.

The CIA psychological profile of President Aristide was also a major concern in the press. However, this issue was also filtered through a domestic lens, ultimately being interpreted as part of a larger partisan political battle between Republicans and the president.

Three: Did These Frames Converge to Present a Unified Contextual Whole?

North Korea. The press framed the situation in a manner differently than the Clinton administration. The press advanced a conception of the crisis that highlighted the potential drama of the North Korean's withdrawal from the treaty. The Clinton administration had stressed calm negotiation and North and South Korea's budding reconciliation. The press engaged in rampant speculation and analysis, even to the point of relying primarily on unnamed sources. The Clinton administration consistently reiterated the lack of information available. The press seemed unable to accept this. Even though the administration was exceptionally careful to keep China's MFN renewal and China's help with North Korea separate issues, the press linked the two, without regard to administrative protests to the contrary.

This situation never matured to the point where a fitting utterance might have ameliorated the crisis. Instead, the very dearth of information stifled any sense of an immediate crisis atmosphere. Even though the press attempted early to create an air of crisis, the very lack of information on this situation forced the press to devote article space to reiterate the sequence of events and to rely heavily on hearsay. With the lack of oppositional press framing, the administration was able to handle this matter with comparative ease, and before a deep sense of crisis emerged, the crisis was over.

Bosnia. The press was predisposed to accept President Clinton's decision to send troops to Bosnia.[4] Because of this, perhaps the most important frame the administration advanced—the mission—was actually adopted in whole by both papers examined. The press would often begin an article with a paraphrase of an administrative source, then later provide quotes from an administrative source but not always the quote from which the paraphrase was derived. This practice increased the amount of coverage the Clinton administration was allotted to relate its assertions about the mission. When criticisms of the mission were included, they were usually placed in between the reporter's positive paraphrase and the quote from an administration source, thereby minimizing the argumentative impact of the criticism. Thus, the very event-specific schemata used by the administration to explain the mission were also employed by the press.

Such was not the case in other areas. When the issue of congressional support was discussed, the press advanced a frame inordinately different than that used by the Clinton administration. Indeed, the press generated a frame through which Congress was depicted as being openly hostile and partisan in its deliberations. This was so strong as to render contrary opinions, such as the president's, irrelevant. Thus, at a time when calm deliberation and consensus were extremely important for the U.S. government to project, the press was advancing a contradictory impression of the continuing discussion between Congress and the White House over U.S. involvement in Bosnia. Although the press cited Republicans as projecting an international image of disharmony within the federal government, it was actually the press that generated and disseminated this impression to the world. In this manner, then, the press was miscommunicating the direct assertions of the president of the United States.[5]

If the White House believed the Bosnian Serbs to be rebels and separatists, it did not publicly acknowledge this. International statesmanship was maintained throughout the period examined in this study. Neutrality was essential for the peace plan to work, and the administration publicly conveyed this impression. However, the press framing of the Bosnian Serbs was an extreme digression from the frame generated by the Clinton administration. One of the functions of frames is to make moral judgments, and the press frame did that well with the Bosnian Serbs; they were framed as rebels, liars, and murderers who could not be trusted. Indeed, one could well wonder after reading the press reports how the Clinton administration could even enter into negotiations with people such as the Bosnian Serbs. Key words took on special importance with this frame: *rebels* and *separatists*. Neither word carries a positive connotation in American parlance, especially in the Northeast where these papers find the bulk of their daily readership.

The defamation of the Bosnian Serbs also fitted in well with the press focus on the multiethnic and multicultural aspects of the Bosnian situation. The Bosnian Serbs were held primarily responsible for the destruction of what the press believed to be a formally vital multiethnic country. Responsibility for mass executions, mass relocations, and any other reported horrors were assigned to the Bosnian Serbs to bare. This particular framing element provides a good example of how frames may reduce the salience of opinions that run contrary to an established frame. When the press did report on Muslim or Croat human rights violations, they possessed such low salience that they could easily be overlooked by readers. Thus, another frame ran in opposition to the carefully orchestrated administration utterances on Bosnia. On those rare occasions Muslim or Croat violations were reported, they assumed such low salience as to be inconsequential. Even a lone quotation from a Bosnian Serb, no doubt included in the guise of "objective" reporting, finds its protest enervated by the formidable weight of the press frame: "'The world doesn't know the bad things the Muslims did to the Serbs. . . . You in the press only wrote about what the Serbs did to the Muslims.'"[6]

Haiti. During the period of January through June the press operated with a very different frame than that of the Clinton administration. Simply put, the press presented the situation as a domestic issue, and the administration presented it as a foreign policy issue. Although the press did report what the administration said, the substance of the administrative text was challenged by the presence of the press frame. This is to say, the context surrounding the administrative text was modified by the frame of the press. This changed the meaning of the administration's comments; the administration was seen as responding to press challenges of its own policies.

As time progressed, the disparities between the press frame and the administration's frame grew. By the end of June 1993, each was a fully articulated policy. The Clinton administration stressed a foreign policy that had as its focus the return of democracy and the aversion of a massive humanitarian tragedy. The press frame stressed a domestic focus that highlighted its perception of an inhumane administrative policy of direct returns. Restoration of democracy was not the focus, but the domestic, legal issue of the administration's policy. In such a setting the administration was presented, not as a source of news but as one side of a partisan battle. When the Clinton administration would make a statement on the situation in Haiti, the press would bring in critics of the administration's position. These so-called critics invariably articulated the very counterpolicy that the press was advancing.

After the Port-au-Prince incident the frames of the Clinton administration and the press still did not converge. Only on two issues did the two touch—the question of Aristide's CIA psychological profile and the reimposition of sanctions. However, reimposing sanctions was still presented as hurting only the Haitian poor. Yet the press did back the president in several ways. First, they virtually stopped reporting on the policy of direct returns, even though the policy was continually enforced by U.S. Coast Guard and Navy vessels. Second, the effect of the sanctions was now framed as a foreign policy issue. The stories on this issue were linked with the internal political discussion in Haiti. However, the effects of the sanctions were ascribed to the original sanctions and especially the oil embargo President Clinton enacted in June 1993. Thus, while the press supported the administration's reimposition of sanctions, it also reported that the effects of sanctions were horrible. The press consistently maintained that sanctions would do little good, even though the same sanctions initially compelled the de facto government to sign the Governors Island agreement.

IMPLICATIONS AND THEORETICAL DISCUSSION

This section is composed of three parts: First, I discuss the theoretical assumptions that underpin agenda-setting and agenda-extension research as they relate to the results of this study; second, I discuss the theoretical assumptions that underpin research into crisis rhetoric as they relate to the results of this study; finally, I discuss implications for future studies in the area of presidential crisis rhetoric.

Agenda-Setting and Agenda-Extension

Agenda-setting theory in essence postulates that the press tells us what to think about but not what to think. Furthermore, we learn about an issue in direct proportion to press coverage of that issue. The research reviewed in this study has concluded that the relationship between press and president is a reciprocal one. The president affects press content, and the press affects presidential message content as well. This study did not find press coverage of particular issues pertaining to North Korea, Bosnia, and Haiti reflected in subsequent administrative utterances. However, this study did find that while the content of presidential messages was being reported, the context in which the message was originally uttered often was not conveyed.

Agenda-extension moves beyond agenda-setting theory by postulating an evaluative component to media coverage of issues and events. In short, the press not only tells us what to think about (agenda-setting), but it also tells us how to think about it (agenda-extension). This evaluative component has been called *priming* and *framing* by various communication and political science researchers. Priming, however, refers specifically to the contextual cues embedded within a news story that would be used by the public to evaluate the subject matter at hand. For presidential studies this would imply that the public would be primed to evaluate that president by how well he handled certain issues in relation to the evaluative cues provided by the media. This study focused on the different frames used by the administration and the press, not on the public's evaluation of the president based on media coverage. Thus, this study makes no attempt at ascertaining the effects of priming on the public.

This study did, however, focus on contending frames used to describe three crisis situations: North Korea, Bosnia, and Haiti. Frames are central organizing ideas within a narrative account of an issue or event. Frames provide the interpretive cues for neutral facts. This study has demonstrated that the press constructed frames in opposition to that which the administration used in describing all three crisis situations. This acted to enervate the Clinton administration's attempt at explaining the situations to the American public. Unless the reader had firsthand access to transcripts of the Clinton administration's utterances, all information was filtered through the frame of the press. Thus, the context through which the administration's utterances were understood changed, thereby changing the meaning of the messages. In this manner the administration was not treated as a news source, providing informative utterances about the situation, but rather it was forced into an oppositional role to that of the press. The notable exception to this was the favorable response of the press to the Bosnian mission; here the press actually adopted one of the administration's frames. In general, however, the president and his officials were presented as one side, articulating one definition of the situation, while the press advanced another. With Haiti, the oppositional framing was so extreme that the press introduced so-called critics of the administration who took an oppositional view that almost always duplicated that of the press. Thus, this study found evidence that supports recent research into the effects of framing.

One further observation is in order. Recall that Nacos found a strong relationship between editorial positions and the content of political news coverage. The present study finds this holds true in a post-Cold War crisis orientation. However, the press tendency to support the president during times of crisis was not apparent in the three crises reviewed here. What was apparent was a willingness of the press to advance its own ideals concerning appropriate policy. Furthermore, what was advanced were typically idealized norms of liberalism. This observation is commensurate with recent studies demonstrating a liberal bias in national media. For example, a Roper Center survey "discovered that only 2 percent of all major-media bureau chiefs and political reporters based in Washington identify themselves as conservative, and that 89 percent voted for Bill Clinton in 1992, compared to just 7 percent for George Bush."[7] The liberal bias is demonstrable in language choice as well. A content analysis of political terms used by the *New York Times* in 1994 found that "radical right," "far right," or "extreme right" were used 211 times. The terms "radical left," "far left," or "extreme left" were used only 50 times. This is a 4.2-to-1 ratio.[8]

One might well expect, given the liberal idealism and voting records of the national media, that President Clinton would have received overwhelming support during times of crises. Such was clearly not the case. Whenever the president moved away from an idealistic liberal stance, the press advanced a countercritique.[9] This apparent contradiction is explained by Michael Barone: "Mainline journalism is by no means reliably pro-Democratic, as Clinton White House staffers will attest, but it is reliably anti-Republican. [For example, the] Center for Media and Public Affairs documented that in the fall of 1994 campaigns the three major networks gave Newt Gingrich 100 percent negative coverage."[10] The same obtains for major print media. Lynne Cheney, reporting on the *Washington Post*, made this observation: "When the *Washington Post*'s ombudsman examined the pictures, headlines, and news stories that ran in her newspaper during the concluding 73 days of the 1992 campaign, she calculated that nearly five times as many were negative for Bush as for Clinton."[11]

What is of concern here is the press advancement of its own agenda and beliefs. Although pernicious enough in everyday reporting, during times of crises this practice is especially dangerous, for the public needs as an objective account of facts as possible. The general level of hearsay, speculation, and analysis—underpinned with an idealized liberalism—in news articles makes it exceedingly difficult for a president—Democrat, Republican, or any other—to impart his conception of the crisis accurately. The press did not live up to the standards of reporting contained within the Social Responsibility guidelines. In so doing, the press not only does a disservice to Americans; it acts to undermine the authority and interpretive precision of the president of the United States.

Crisis Rhetoric

With the loss of the Cold War meta-narrative, President Clinton was unable to draw on the inventional resources used by presidents since 1947 to define crises situations. The Cold War was, in a very significant sense, a contest of words in which a prevailing image of the enemy was conveyed to Americans. These common images were an inventional resource that a president might use when advancing a particular foreign policy action. The enemy was often characterized as a "moral threat to freedom," "a barbarian," or part of "an evil empire." Precedent and tradition strongly constrained a president's utterances about foreign affairs. Formally, descriptions of the enemy often called upon Americans' public knowledge about the enemy, thereby justifying action. However, President Clinton was unable to call on such knowledge to justify action in Bosnia and Haiti.[12] In Haiti, for example, the names used by both the administration and the press to describe the de facto Haitian government suggested no prevailing image of the enemy. Those thwarting the restoration of President Aristide and democracy are vague, mostly neutral entities. Tables 1 through 6 illustrate the use of descriptive terms employed by the administration and the press.

Table 1

White House Descriptive Terms Used to Describe the De Facto Government, January-June 1993

9 junta
7 de facto regime
4 all sides
4 de facto government
4 Haitian parties
2 coup leaders
2 government
1 appropriate people
1 gentlemen who are in the command of the military
1 the Haitians
1 illegal government
1 illegal regime
1 military leaders
1 people who have power
1 rump government
1 unelected officials

Table 2

New York Times **Descriptive Terms Used to Describe the De Facto Government, January-June 1993**

8 officials
6 authorities
5 military backed Haitian government
5 military government
3 the military
3 military leaders
2 coup leaders
2 government of Haiti
2 military rulers
1 Haitian leadership
1 Haitian rulers
1 military regime
1 people at the top

Table 3

Washington Post **Descriptive Terms Used to Describe the De Facto Government, January-June 1993**

7 the military
5 de facto government
4 Haitian authorities
4 military backed government
2 army leaders
2 Haitian military leaders
2 military leaders
2 military regime
1 coup leaders
1 current rulers
1 de facto army backed government
1 de facto authorities
1 de facto civilian government
1 de facto rulers
1 the government
1 Haiti's military backed leaders
1 Haiti's political leaders
1 Haiti's present rulers
1 Haitian military
1 military and civilian leaders
1 military authorities
1 military-backed, de facto government
1 military-installed regime
1 military rulers
1 new regime
1 political and military leaders
1 regime
1 those in power

Table 4

**White House Descriptive Terms Used to Describe the
De Facto Government, July-December 1993**

21 de facto regime
8 government of Haiti
7 military and police authorities
5 Haitian military
4 Haitian government
2 Haitian authorities
2 Haitian leaders
2 Haitian military authorities
2 leaders in Haiti
1 elites
1 Haitian officials
1 illegal regime
1 military and police leaders
1 military rulers
1 old regime

Table 5

New York Times **Descriptive Terms Used to Describe the
De Facto Government, July-21 October 1993**

16 Haitian military
11 military leaders
5 military leadership
4 Haitian army
4 Haitian political parties
4 military rulers
3 the army
3 army leaders
3 junta
3 military government
2 authorities
1 army and police leaders
1 army officials
1 economic elite
1 Haitian high command
1 military and police commanders
1 military authorities
1 military-backed government
1 military coup leaders
1 military elite
1 ruling elite

Table 6

Washington Post **Descriptive Terms Used to Describe the De Facto Government, July-21 October 1993**

12 military leaders
8 the military
8 military rulers
4 Haitian military
1 de facto government
1 de facto leaders
1 de facto military rulers
1 Haitian commanders
1 Haiti's rulers
1 military commanders
1 military government

As these tables indicate, there were no "barbaric" or "irrational" descriptions employed. Indeed, even after the 11 October 1993 Port-au-Prince incident, no significant change in terminology was undertaken. The results indicate that the only centralized descriptive label used involved the term *military*. The Clinton administration most often employed the following three descriptions: "de facto regime" (twenty-eight times), "junta" (nine times), and "government of Haiti" (eight times). These terms are, at worst, neutral and may even imply legitimacy. Given the Clinton administration's notable attempts at diplomacy, it seems reasonable not to negatively name those with whom you are negotiating. The *New York Times* most often used the following three descriptions: "Haitian military" (sixteen times), "military leaders" (fourteen times), and "authorities" (eight times). The *Washington Post* most often employed the following three descriptions: "the military" (fifteen times), "military leaders" (fourteen times), and "military rulers" (nine times). As with the administration's descriptions, there is a notable lack of negative labels used. Considering that the United States maintains relations with many military-ruled countries across the world, these labels do not necessarily represent a villainization of the "enemy."

Theodore Windt advanced a conception of crisis rhetoric that contends that a president making a crisis speech will ask support for, and not discussion about, a particular plan of action.[13] As mentioned earlier, Windt has convincingly argued that a presidential crisis speech will consist of an obligatory statement of facts and an establishment of a melodrama between good and evil; moreover, the policy enacted will be framed as a moral act. This study initially suggested that this model for presidential crisis speeches would not hold true for President

Clinton due to the loss of the Cold War meta-narrative. This assumption proved to be correct.

President Clinton spoke many times on the situation in Haiti throughout 1993, but only one brief speech, that given on 15 October 1993, may be considered a speech responding to a perception of crisis. In this speech, the president did make a statement of the facts surrounding the new situation for the United States. This included a discussion of the action taken by the president in response to the new situation. However, there was no establishment of a melodrama between good and evil. No attempt to establish the actions in Haiti to a larger world picture was made. The possible exception came when President Clinton asserted that part of the U.S. interest in the area was to maintain the hemispheric march toward democracy. Furthermore, the president did not frame his newly announced actions as a moral act. Instead, it was simply announced as a continuation of the same policy that had been in place prior to the Port-au-Prince incident. Although this policy did contain specific humanitarian underpinnings, the overall focus was on the breaking of the Governors Island agreement itself. This is to say, the United Nations/OAS and the United States were partners in a signed agreement that had been abrogated. The United States was simply calling for the honoring of the contract.

Such was the case in Bosnia as well. Here the first and last stages of Windt's definition hold true but not the second. President Clinton did provide—repeatedly—statements of fact about the situation in Bosnia. Furthermore, the impending deployment of U.S. troops was framed as a moral act. Indeed, the president placed American values on the line by clearly stating that to not intervene would be to ignore American leadership and responsibility. The United States was acting for peace and to prevent the horrors of war with its attendant abuse of human rights. However, throughout this explanation, there was no grand melodrama to call on, and thus the establishment of a moral frame through which to view the situation was highly contested by both the Congress and the American people.

I would suggest that the lack of a melodrama, and perhaps the president's own style, had the effect of minimizing inflammatory language use on the part of the administration. Although the administration had called the incident at Port-au-Prince "a brutal attempt by Haiti's military and police authorities to thwart the expressed desire of the Haitian people for democracy," it was the only such exhortative statement.[14] Moreover, the overall frame of the administration vitiated the potential injurious effect such a comment could have. In short, the frame used by the administration to describe the situation in Haiti reduced the saliency of the comment; for almost a year the administration had been stressing diplomacy and a negotiated solution. Terms used to describe the de facto government were generally neutral. Even in the crisis atmosphere of October 1993, the one demonizing comment by the administration seemed oddly out of place, almost a flair of temper instead of a consistent manner of conduct. The administration had no previous negative characterizations to draw on. The Cold War meta-narrative was inoperative; the administration's own utterances in the past acted to impair any effective use of inflammatory discourse. This held true in both North Korea and Bosnia as well. The administration publicly responded to the situations in a calm manner. Furthermore, each country—North Korea, Bosnia-Herzegovina, Serbia, and Haiti—was treated as an independent entity and not as a synecdoche for a collective force that during the Cold War would have been called the enemy.

Crisis rhetoric is about the creation of stable contextual frames through which to view the event and justify any action taken in response to the event. As an interanimation of text and context occur, the situational elements combine either to effect a stable frame or to modify a frame in some way. As a frame stabilizes, the president will find increased freedom to pursue his present course of action and increased limits on choices for new action. For instance, President Clinton had a stable frame through which to view the event in Haiti; this was his initial foreign policy frame. Indeed, when President Clinton took office in January 1993, he initially responded to what many perceived to be a preexisting crisis. In this manner, he acted in the role of manager of that crisis. He had a well-developed and articulated frame through which to understand the situation in Haiti. Unfortunately for the President, the press frame did not match his own. Instead, the press developed a fully articulated counterpolicy. In my opinion, the mixing of frames acts to exacerbate or minimize the perception of crisis because there is no stable frame through which to view the event. In North Korea the president had no stable frame, and thus his administration's initial utterances should have had considerable influence in establishing a stable context through which to view the event. This study concludes, however, that such was not the case. Although the administration advanced a consistent, yet weak, frame of the event, the press adopted its own oppositional frame to the event. Thus, with a dearth of information, and contending weak frames, the situation in North Korea never erupted into a full-scale crisis; however, the potential seriousness of the situation never seemed to come to fore either.

Bosnia presents an extremely complex case. The frames of the president and press converged on one issue: the mission. With all other issues the press advanced oppositional frames (except when U.S. values and leadership were brought up to discuss the mission). In my opinion, the mixing of frames acted to exacerbate the perception of potential danger

associated with the mission the president advanced. This was especially true when considering the press framing of the Bosnian Serbs. In
Bosnia, then, only a partially stable context emerged in which the
situation could be viewed. The mission was a metaphysical "good,"
whereas all else was left unsettled. Thus, even while the press was
advancing support for the mission, it was also undermining that support
through the advancement of alternate frames.

The president's 15 October 1993 Haitian speech has provided us with
the opportunity to examine the effects of a presidential crisis speech on
already established frames. Blair and Houck have suggested that
many crisis rhetoric scholars differentiate between a president constructing the perception of a crisis and a president's response to an event
already perceived as a crisis. Blair and Houck stated that such a
distinction is unprovable and unimportant. President Clinton's reply to
the Port-au-Prince situation provides an example that belies these
scholars' assertions, however. First, President Clinton responded several days after continuous news reports, and the news articles reflected a
wide array of coverage. The only consistent response to the incident was
that of the administration. When President Clinton spoke, he was
speaking within a situation possessing an unstable context. His comments might have precipitated the situation into a full-blown crisis
situation; however, drawing on his administration's already established frame, the president maintained a course of action commensurate
with his prior utterances. The administrative text had now interacted
with the context.

Bonnie Dow argued that if the president is responding to an event
already perceived as a crisis situation, then he will enact an epideictic
response that will function to prevent disparate interpretations of the
situation and to "promote continuity, restore communal feeling, and . . .
reconcile the audience to a new situation."[15] In short, the president's
response is designed to manage and stabilize the already existing
perception of crisis. However, President Clinton's 15 October 1993
speech did act to modify the perception of crisis. While the press was
initially raising the question of U.S. troop involvement, the president
spoke so as to retain a sense of control over the situation. He recast the
terms of the debate to stress a negotiated solution. In this manner the
president was arguing that his policy was reasonable and that there
was no immediate danger to U.S. interests. In short, to use Dow's
phraseology, he was using a deliberative approach. Deliberative
strategies are those used to demonstrate that the policy being enacted
in response to a crisis is "expedient, reasoned and prudent."[16] Thus we
have a crisis speech that is an example of the blurring of, according to
Dow, two distinct presidential crisis speeches.

Although this study has been a comparative framing analysis, it has also contributed in the area of post-Cold War crisis rhetoric theory. Specifically, this study allows us to begin to answer what inventional resources a president has today to use when framing a crisis. The Cold War meta-narrative was a part of this country's collective consciousness; it was public knowledge. The public and its knowledge serve to authorize discourse emanating from rhetors speaking and acting on behalf of the public—in our case, the president. Presidents must build certain images of the enemy when speaking about crises, and these images must make links to values and images embedded in American culture. However, it is now difficult for presidents to do this. Public knowledge for the past forty-five years has privileged those images drawing on the Cold War meta-narrative. National values and interests were relatively easy to determine.

However, today it is difficult to know what national interests are at any given time; this weakens the parameters of the rhetorical situation because the context is more dubious and there exists conflicting public perception over what should be done. This leaves a president with few inventional resources from which to draw on when creating or responding to crises. For President Clinton this problem was particularly acute since any utterances he or his officials made were cast into a counterframe advanced by the press. However, this study demonstrated that the president may draw on his own frame, as President Clinton did in responding to the crisis situation in Haiti. Moreover, a president might draw on other values embedded in American culture: patriotism, fair play, honor, and the like. Other options were available but were not used by President Clinton. However, even had President Clinton taken a more active role in advancing his perception of events, this action very likely would have been dogged by an active and adversarial press frame.

Both Martin Medhurst and James Pratt have argued that a president's personal style may have a significant impact on how he handles a crisis situation. This study supports this assertion. By examining the Clinton administration's responses over time, this study was able to note the consistent aspects of the proffered discourse. Most studies of crisis rhetoric focus on one speech or on several different presidents giving one speech on similar crises. This study found that the style employed by the Clinton administration was remarkably consistent over time. The style stressed cooperation, negotiation, and public dignity for all parties. The strength of this frame established by the Clinton administration was so strong that it pervaded President Clinton's formal utterances in all three crises, even his formal reply to the Port-au-Prince incident. Thus, the president's strategy for dealing with a crisis appears to be remarkably similar to his day-to-day style of operation: slow deliberation stressing a negotiated, compromised, and nonconfrontational solution.

In Haiti, President Clinton used those resources that were available from his administration's initial (January) framing of the Haitian situation. Thus, his crisis speech in October 1993 was constrained by this frame. He could not villainize the coup leaders, at least not immediately. To do so would be to undermine ten months of his own framing. He could not immediately justify extreme action in the form of military intervention, for to do so would also counteract ten months of his own framing. He was constrained by his previous utterances: cooperation and a negotiated solution. President Clinton could not even draw on the inventional resources that the press frame offered, for it was oppositional to his own and had stressed a counterpolicy. I feel this would have held true in the situation in Bosnia, had the press not adopted the president's framing of the mission as its own. Although with other issues—Congress, the Bosnian Serbs—the president's frame was contended by those of the press, it was in the administration's best interest to remain silent concerning misrepresentation by the press. After all, the most important aspect—the mission—had been endorsed. In my opinion, a president today must fund his own inventional resources. Until America finds a new role for itself in the post-Cold War world, there will be conflicting frames presented for any international crisis situation.

In the past, it seems that contending frames were suppressed by the enacting of the Cold War meta-narrative. In this study the "rally-'round-the-president" phenomenon found by Nacos did not materialize for Clinton.[17] In both North Korea and Haiti the situation never evolved to closure. With Haiti the press did stop criticizing the policy of direct returns, however, and this lends some support to previous studies that suggest that during times of crises the benefit of the doubt is given to the president. But the press also focused increasingly on the effects sanctions had on the Haitian poor. Consequently, the one policy option available to the president besides direct military intervention was openly deplored by the press. Furthermore, as the situation progressed, the press began to assert that military action was not an option; this was in direct conflict with the president's comments. Moreover, while the president was attempting to articulate his administration's post-Cold War foreign policy, including Haiti, the press reported administrative policy as part of an ongoing partisan political battle. In short, even during a time of crisis the press continued to advance its own oppositional frame. In Bosnia, however, there was some degree of "rally-'round-the-president," but it is not certain whether this was a continuation of past press practices or a partisan endorsement on the part of the press.

As of this writing, public knowledge about America's foreign policy role in the world remains in flux, and no single frame has come to dominate public consciousness. In the past the press may not have agreed with what the president was doing, but executive actions could be consistently framed drawing on public knowledge held in common, the Cold War meta-narrative, for example. No such common knowledge exists today, so it is very likely that other crisis situations will exhibit contending president/press frames.

Future Studies

This study suggests several possible areas for future studies. In the area of priming, researchers might explore the relationship between public opinion polls and frame content. For example, one might compare public opinion polls on a specific crisis issue with the frames used by the president and the press. It would be important to consider which criteria emerge to evaluate the president's performance. One might also explore the bibliographic thesis put forth by James W. Pratt and also by Martin J. Medhurst. For instance, a future study might employ a comparative frame analysis between the president and the press that focused on one of several foreign policy crises experienced by the Clinton administration. In so doing, researchers might provide further insights into post-Cold War crisis rhetoric and, by this means, better explore Clinton's particular rhetorical signature. Such studies would further help future researchers to discriminate better between situational dynamics and the particular style of a particular president.

This study has shed light on the development of crises in the post-Cold War world. Future studies may benefit from employing a comparative frame analysis on classic examples of foreign policy crises; for example, the downing of KAL 007, the invasion of Grenada, the *Mayaquez* affair, or the Cuban missile crisis. With such comparative studies, researchers might begin to better understand the similarities and differences in the nature of president/press interaction during Cold War and post-Cold War crisis situations.

NOTES

1. Robert M. Entman, "Framing U.S. Coverage of International News: Contrasts in Narratives of the KAL and Iran Air Incidents," *Journal of Communication* 41.4 (1991): 21.

2. In my opinion, however, the president failed to capitalize upon the voluntary nature of this aspect of his policy. The United States is not forced under law

to provide asylum processing outside of the United States. Even though a U.S. embassy may be considered U.S. soil, it was certainly a move well beyond international expectations for the United States to open processing facilities outside of the Port-au-Prince embassy.

3. David E. Sanger, "North Korea, Fighting Inspection, Renounces Nuclear Arms Treaty," *New York Times* 12 March 1993: A1; Douglas Jehl, "U.S. Seeking U.N. Pressure to Compel North Korea to Honor Treaty," *New York Times* 13 March 1993: A3; David E. Sanger, "The Nonproliferation Treaty Bares Its Toothlessness," *New York Times* 14 March 1993: E18.

4. For instance, the *New York Times* stated the following editorially: "If all sides conclude that the United States and its allies are prepared to apply military force to support a serious diplomatic initiative, the prospects for peace may improve. No one pretends that the latest American plan is a triumph of principle. But it is a workable compromise" ("Force and Diplomacy in Bosnia," 31 August 1995: A24). "Having come this far in brokering a Balkan peace, the United States is obliged to take on a significant share of the peacekeeping operation" (Peace and Peacekeeping in Bosnia," 6 October 1995: A30). "America's leading diplomatic role in bringing about a Bosnian peace agreement, as well as its claims to NATO leadership, create a strong obligation to contribute significant forces to peace-keeping" ("Congress Must Vote on Bosnia," 20 October 1995: A34). The *Washington Post* also supported the use of troops for keeping the peace in Bosnia: "FINALLY, AFTER 3 [and] 1/2 years of war, NATO planes and U.N. ground troops have replied with heavy and suitable force to a deadly attack seen as coming from the Bosnian Serbs. [I]t sets a standard for allied performance anew" ("Answering the Bosnian Serbs," 31 August 1995: A22). "It would be grotesque, having so far left ground duty to its allies for fear of American casualties, if the United States still did not join the allies after a peace agreement had cut the risk way back" ("A Bosnia Peace Force," 24 September 1995: C6). Press approval is not always forthcoming in instances of war, however. Although the *Washington Post* supported the congressional decision to declare war on Saddam Hussein, the *New York Times* did not: America's vital interests "would not be served by the offensive use of force to expel Iraq from Kuwait" ("The Larger Patriotism," 10 January 1992: A24).

5. The framing of Congress as partisan and hostile to the president's plan to commit U.S. troops into a dangerous situation is hypocritical given the editorial positions advanced by papers just prior to the Gulf War. For instance, the *New York Times* stated editorially that the "President must have some war-making powers; but it is astonishing to claim that all Congress can do is go along. Congress has more authority than that, if only it will reclaim it" ("Who Can Declare War?" 15 December 1991: I26). "The rush to force is all the more dismaying because debate over a declaration of war would serve everyone's interest, the Administration's included" ("War by Default," 16 December 1991: A14). The *New York Times* even went so far as to criticize Congress for delaying discussion because "a debate could be divisive, easing the pressure on Saddam Hussein." However, the editorial continued, asserting that debate "is not divisive unless the policy being debated is" ("Where Is Congress on the Gulf?" 3 January 1991: A20). Clearly, this statement runs contrary to what the *New York Times* argued was the

case with President Clinton's Bosnia mission. Whereas a Democratic Congress would be shirking its duty by not debating a Republican president's policy, a Republican Congress is openly hostile and divided when debating a Democratic president's policy. The *Washington Post* felt it more than appropriate for Congress to debate President Bush's decision to send U.S. troops to the Gulf: "[T]he fact is that the Democratic Congress is in a position to check his [President Bush's] policy if it so desires" ("Resolution 678, 1990," 30 November 1991: A28). Moreover, the *Washington Post* even praised oppositional points of view while approving President Bush's ability to wage war: "Iraq is an issue of judgment. Conscientious legislators have different views about it" ("Congress and War," 11 January 1992: A20).

6. Raymond Bonner, "In Suburbs of Sarajevo, Serbs Firm on Leaving," *New York Times* 30 November 1995: A10.

7. "Our Delicately Balanced Media," *The American Enterprise* 7.4 (July-August 1996): 13.

8. This held true for other papers as well: The *San Francisco Chronicle*, for example, used the terms "radical right," far right," or "extreme right" 147 times, whereas the terms "radical left," far left," or "extreme left" were used only 49 times. This is a three-to-one ratio. See "Media and Communication Clips," *The American Enterprise* 7.2 (March-April 1996): 17.

9. See, too, Irving Kristol, "America's 'Exceptional Conservatism,'" *Neoconservatism: The Autobiography of an Idea* (New York: Free Press, 1995). Kristol wrote: "There is a comfortable symbiosis between our national newsmagazines, our half-dozen or so newspapers that claim national attention, and our national television networks. They are all liberal, more or less, and feel that they share the journalistic mission of 'enlightening' . . . the American public" (383).

10. Michael Barone, "The Return of Partisan Journalism," *The American Enterprise* 7.2 (March-April 1996): 30. Indeed, David Gergen, writing in *U.S. News & World Reports* (22 April 1996), reported on a recent Center for Media and Public Affairs study that found that the ABC, CBS, and NBC evening news programs evaluated Republican candidates negatively 61 percent of the time during the first two months of the presidential campaign.

11. Lynn Cheney, "Press Bias in the '92 Election," *The American Enterprise* 7.2 (March-April 1996): 37. A recent report by *U.S. News & World Reports* (18 November 1996) told of a postelection Center for Media and Public Affairs study of ABC, CBS, and NBC news shows. All three networks favored President Clinton with 50 percent positive statements. Bob Dole received only 33 percent positive statements. This is almost identical to the Center's 1992 study of the Bush and Clinton campaign coverage.

12. Although North Korea might well have been described as the last vestige of Cold War fronts, the administration did not attempt to use this to its advantage.

13. Theodore O. Windt, Jr., "The Presidency and Speeches on International Crises: Repeating the Rhetorical Past," *Essays in Presidential Rhetoric*, ed. Theodore O. Windt, Jr., and Beth Ingold; 2nd ed. (Dubuque, IA: Kendall/Hunt Publishing Company, 1987), 125-134.

14. White House, Office of the Press Secretary, "Press Conference by the

President" (15 October 1993): 1.

15. Bonnie J. Dow, "The Function of Epideictic and Deliberative Strategies in Presidential Crisis Rhetoric," *Western Journal of Speech Communication* 53 (1989): 301.

16. Dow, 303.

17. Brigitte Lebens Nacos, *The Press, Presidents, and Crises* (New York: Columbia University Press, 1990).

Bibliography

SCHOLARLY

Bagdikian, Ben H. *The Effete Conspiracy*. New York: Harper & Row, 1972.

Barone, Michael. "The Return of Partisan Journalism." *The American Enterprise* 7.2 (March-April 1996): 30

Bass, Jeff D. "The Rhetorical Opposition to Controversial Wars: Rhetorical Timing as a Generic Constraint." *Western Journal of Speech Communication* 43 (1979): 180-191.

Bateson, Gregory. *Steps to an Ecology of Mind: Collected Essays in Anthropology, Psychiatry, Evolution, and Epistemology*. San Francisco: Chandler Publishing Company, 1972.

Behr, Roy L., and Shanto Iyengar. "Television News, Real-World Cues, and Changes in the Public Agenda." *Public Opinion Quarterly* 49 (1985): 38-57.

Benoit, William L. "Genesis of Rhetorical Action." *Southern Communication Journal* 59.4 (1994): 342-355.

Bitzer, Lloyd F. "Functional Communication: A Situational Perspective." *Rhetoric in Transition: Studies in the Nature and Uses of Rhetoric*. Ed. Eugene E. White. University Park: Pennsylvania State University Press, 1980. 21-38.

——. "Political Rhetoric." *Handbook of Political Communication*. Ed. Dan D. Nimmo and Keith R. Sanders. Beverly Hills, CA: Sage Publications, 1981. 225-248.

——. "Rhetoric and Public Knowledge," *Rhetoric, Philosophy, and Literature: An Exploration*, Ed. D. M. Burks. West Lafayette, IN: Purdue University Press, 1978. 67-93.

——. "The Rhetorical Situation." *Rhetoric: A Tradition in Transition*. Ed. Walter Fisher. East Lansing: Michigan State University Press, 1974. 247-260.

Black, Edwin. "A Note on Theory and Practice in Rhetorical Criticism." *Western Journal of Speech Communication* 44 (1980): 331-336.

Bormann, Ernest G. "Fetching Good Out of Evil: A Rhetorical Use of Calamity." *Quarterly Journal of Speech* 63 (1977): 130-139.

Bostdorff, Denise M. *The Presidency and the Rhetoric of Foreign Crisis*. Columbia: University of South Carolina Press, 1994.

Branham, Robert J., and W. Barnett Pearce. "Between Text and Context: Toward a Rhetoric of Contextual Reconstruction." *Quarterly Journal of Speech* 71 (1985): 19-36.

Brock, Bernard L., Robert L. Scott, and James W. Chesebro. *Methods of Rhetorical Criticism: A Twentieth-Century Perspective*. 3rd ed. Detroit: Wayne State University Press, 1989.

Campbell, Karlyn Kohrs, and Kathleen Hall Jamieson. *Deeds Done in Words: Presidential Rhetoric and the Genres of Governance*. Chicago: University of Chicago Press, 1990.

Cheney, Lynn. "Press Bias in the '92 Election." *The American Enterprise* 7.2 (March-April 1996): 37.

Cherwitz, Richard A. "Masking Inconsistency: The Tonkin Gulf Crisis." *Communication Quarterly* 28 (1980): 27-37.

Cherwitz, Richard A., and Kenneth S. Zagacki. "Consummatory versus Justificatory Crisis Rhetoric." *Western Journal of Speech Communication* 50 (1986): 307-324.

Cobb, Roger W. and Charles D. Elder. *Participation in American Politics: The Dynamics of Agenda-Building*. Baltimore: Johns Hopkins University Press, 1983.

Cohen, Bernard C. *The Press and Foreign Policy*. Princeton: Princeton University Press, 1963.

Comstock, George, ed. *Public Communication Behavior*. Vol. 1. Orlando, FL: Academic Press, 1986.

Cornwell, Elmer E., Jr. "Presidential News: The Expanding Public Image." *Journalism Quarterly* 36 (1959): 275-283.

Corwin, Edward S. *The President: Office and Powers*, 3rd ed. New York: New York University Press, 1948.

Day, Louis A. *Ethics in Media Communication*. Belmont, CA: Wadsworth Publishing Company, 1991.

Denton, Robert E., Jr., and Gary C. Woodward. *Political Communication in America*. 2nd ed. New York: Praeger, 1990.

Dow, Bonnie J. "The Function of Epideictic and Deliberative Strategies in Presidential Crisis Rhetoric." *Western Journal of Speech Communication* 53 (1989): 294-310.

Edelman, Murray. *Politics as Symbolic Action*. Chicago: Markham, 1971.

———. *The Symbolic Uses of Politics*. Urbana: University of Illinois Press, 1964.

Entman, Robert M. "Framing: Toward Clarification of a Fractured Paradigm." *Journal of Communication* 43 (1993): 51-58.

———. "Framing U.S. Coverage of International News: Contrasts in Narratives of the KAL and Iran Air Incidents." *Journal of Communication* 41.4 (1991): 6-27.

———. *Democracy without Citizens: Media and the Decay of American Politics* New York: Oxford University Press, 1989.

Entman, Robert M. and B. I. Page. "The News before the Storm: The Iraq War Debate and the Limits to Media Independence." *Just Deserts: The News Media, U.S. Foreign Policy, and the Gulf War*, Ed. W. Lance Bennet and D. L. Palentz. Chicago: University of Chicago Press, 1994.

Entman, Robert M., and Andrew Rojecki. "Freezing Out the Public: Elite and Media Framing of the U.S. Anti-Nuclear Movement." *Political Communication* 10.2 (1993): 155-173.

Fedler, Fred, Mike Meeske, and Joe Hall. "*Time* Magazine Revisited: Presidential Stereotypes Persist." *Journalism Quarterly* 62 (1985): 66-73.

Gamson, William A. "News as Framing: Comments on Graber." *American Behavioral Scientist* 33 (1989): 157-161.

German, Kathleen M. "Invoking the Glorious War: Framing the Persian Gulf Conflict through Directive Language." *Southern Communication Journal* 60.4 (1995): 292-302.

Gilberg, Sheldon, Chaim Eyal, Maxwell E. McCombs, and D. Nichols. "The State of the Union Address and the Press Agenda." *Journalism Quarterly* 57 (1980): 584-588.

Goffman, Erving. *Frame Analysis: An Essay on the Organization of Experience.* Cambridge, MA: Harvard University Press, 1974.

Graber, Doris A. "Framing Election News Broadcasts: News Context and its Impact on the 1984 Presidential Election." *Social Science Quarterly* 68 (1987): 552-568.

———. *Mass Media and American Politics*. 3rd ed. Washington, D.C.: Congressional Quarterly Press, 1989.

———. *Media Power and Politics*. Washington, D.C.: Congressional Quarterly Press, 1984.

Green, Barbara, and Leon Hurwitz. "Press Views of Executive vs. Senatorial Powers." *Journalism Quarterly* 55 (1978): 775-778.

Grossman, Michael Baruch, and Martha Joynt Kumar. *Portraying the President.* Baltimore: Johns Hopkins University Press, 1981.

Halper, Thomas. *Foreign Policy Crises: Appearance and Reality in Decision Making.* Columbus, OH: Charles E. Merrill, 1971.

Heisey, D. Ray. "Reagan and Mitterrand Respond to International Crisis: Creating versus Transcending Appearances." *Western Journal of Speech Communication* 50 (1986): 325-335.

Hollihan, Thomas A. "The Public Controversy over the Panama Canal Treaties: An Analysis of American Foreign Policy Rhetoric." *Western Journal of Speech Communication* 50 (1986): 368-387.

Infante, Dominic A., Andrew S. Rancer, and Deanna F. Womack. *Building Communication Theory.* 2nd ed. Prospect Heights, IL: Waveland Press, 1993.

Ivie, Robert L. "Images of Savagery in America's Justification for War." *Communication Monographs* 47 (1980): 279-294.

———. "Metaphor and the Rhetorical Invention of Cold War 'Idealists.'" *Communication Monographs* 54 (1987): 165-182.

———. "Presidential Motives for War." *Quarterly Journal of Speech* 60 (1974): 337-345.

Iyengar, Shanto. *Is Anyone Responsible?: How Television Frames Political Issues.* Chicago: University of Chicago Press, 1991.

Iyengar, Shanto, and Donald R. Kinder. "More than Meets the Eye: TV News, Priming, and Public Evaluations of the President," *Public Communication Behavior*, Ed. George Comstock, Vol. 1. Orlando: Academic Press, 1986, 136.

Iyengar, Shanto, and Adam Simon. "News Coverage of the Gulf Crisis and Public Opinion: A Study of Agenda-Setting, Priming, and Framing." *Communication Research* 20.3 (1993): 365-383.

Johnston, Anne. "Trends in Political Communication: *A Selective Review of Research in the 1980s.*" *New Directions in Political Communication: A Resource Book.* Ed. David L. Swanson and Dan Nimmo. Newbury Park: Sage Publications, 1990. 329-362.

Kane, Thomas. "Rhetorical Histories and Arms Negotiations." *Journal of the American Forensic Association* 24 (1988): 143-154.

Kegley, Charles W., Jr., and Eugene R. Wittkopf. *American Foreign Policy: Pattern and Process.* 4Th ed. New York: St. Martin's Press, 1991.

Kern, Montague, Patricia Levering, and Ralph Levering. *The Kennedy Crises.* Chapel Hill: University of North Carolina Press, 1983.

Kiewe, Amos, ed. *The Modern Presidency and Crisis Rhetoric.* Westport, CT: Praeger, 1994.

King, Andrew A. *Power and Communication.* Prospect Heights, IL: Waveland Press, 1987.

Klope, David C. "Defusing a Foreign Policy Crisis: Myth and Victimage in Reagan's 1983 Lebanon/Grenada Address." *Western Journal of Speech Communication* 50 (1986): 336-349.

Kristol, Irving. *Neoconservatism: The Autobiography of an Idea.* New York: Free Press, 1995.

Kuypers, Jim A., Marilyn J. Young, and Michael K. Launer. "Of Mighty Mice and Meek Men: Contextual Reconstruction of the Shootdown of Iran Air 655." *Southern Communication Journal* 59.4 (1994): 294-306.

Lang, Gladys Engel, and Kurt Lang. "The Media and Watergate." *Media Power in Politics.* Ed. Doris A. Graber. Washington, D.C.: Congressional Quarterly Press, 1984. 202-209.

Liebler, Carol M., and Jacob Bendix. "Old-Growth Forests on Network News: News Sources and the Framing of an Environmental Controversy." *Journalism and Mass Communication Quarterly* 73 (1996): 53-65.

McAdams, Katherine C. "Power Prose: The Syntax of Presidential News." *Journalism Quarterly* 67 (1990): 313-322.

McCombs, Maxwell E., and Sheldon Gilberg. "News Influence on Our Pictures of the World." *Perspectives on Media Effects.* Ed. Jennings Bryant and Dolf Zillman. Hillsdale, NJ: Lawrence Erlbaum Associates, Publishers, 1986.

McCombs, Maxwell E., and Donald L. Shaw. "The Agenda-Setting Function of Mass Media." *Public Opinion Quarterly* 36 (1972): 176-187.

————, eds. *The Emergence of American Political Issues: The Agenda-Setting Function of the Press.* St. Paul, MN: West Publishing Co., 1977

Medhurst, Martin J., Robert L. Ivie, Philip Wander, and Robert L. Scott, eds. *Cold War Rhetoric: Strategy, Metaphor, and Ideology*. Westport, CT: Greenwood Press, 1990.

"Media and Communication Clips." *The American Enterprise* 7.2 (March-April 1996): 17.

Miller, Carolyn R. "Genre as Social Action." *Quarterly Journal of Speech* 70 (1984): 151-167.

Nacos, Brigitte Lebens. *The Press, Presidents, and Crises*. New York: Columbia University Press, 1990.

Nimmo, Dan, and James E. Combs. *Nightly Horrors*. Knoxville: University of Tennessee Press, 1985.

"Our Delicately Balanced Media." *The American Enterprise* 7.4 (July-August 1996): 13.

Pan, Zhongdang, and Gerald M. Kosicki. "Framing Analysis: An Approach to News Discourse." *Political Communication* 10.1 (1993): 55-75.

Pratt, James W. "An Analysis of Three Crisis Speeches." *Western Speech* 34 (1970): 194-203.

Rasmussen, Karen, and Sharon D. Downey. "The Rhetoric of the Persian Gulf War: Imperialism and American Mythology of War." Paper presented at the annual meeting of the Speech Communication Association, New Orleans, 1994.

Rogers, E. M., and J. W. Dearing. "Agenda-Setting Research: Where Has it Been and Where Is It Going?" *Communication Yearbook 11*. Ed. J. A. Anderson. Beverly Hills: Sage, 1988.

Rosemarin, Adena. *The Power of Genre*. Minneapolis: University of Minnesota Press, 1985.

Rossiter, Clinton. *The American Presidency*. New York: Mentor Books, 1962.

Rowland, Robert C. "The Passive Style of Rhetorical Crisis Management: A Case Study of the Superfund Controversy." *Communication Studies* 41 (1990): 342-360.

Salwen, Michael B. "Effect of Accumulation of Coverage on Issue Salience in Agenda Setting." *Journalism Quarterly* 65 (1988): 100+.

———. "Four Theories, Three Decades Later." *Florida Communication Journal* 15 (1987): 12-24.

———. "News Media and Public Opinion: Benign Agenda-Setters? Opinion Molders? Or Simply Irrelevant?" *Florida Communication Journal* 18.2 (1990): 16-23.

Severin, W. J., and J. W. Tankard. *Communication Theories*. 2nd ed. New York: Longman, 1988.

Siebert, Fred S., Theodore Peterson, and Wilbur Schramm. *Four Theories of the Press*. Urbana: University of Illinois Press, 1956.

Smith, Carolyn. *Presidential Press Conferences*. New York: Praeger, 1990.

Smith, Craig Allen. *Political Communication*. San Diego: Harcourt Brace Jovanovich, Publishers, 1990.

Smith, Craig R., and Scott Lybarger. "Bitzer's Model Reconsidered." *Communication Quarterly* 44.2 (1996): 197-213.

Sniderman, Paul M., Richard A. Brody, and Philip E. Tetlock. *Reasoning and Choice: Explorations in Political Psychology*. Cambridge, England: Cambridge University Press, 1991.

Stephens, Mitchell. *A History of News: From the Drum to the Satellite*. New York: Viking Penguin, 1988.

Straitmatter, Roger. "The Impact of Presidential Personality on News Coverage in Major Newspapers." *Journalism Quarterly* 62 (1985): 66-73.

Trent, Judith S., and Robert V. Friedenberg. *Political Campaign Communication: Principles and Practices*. 2nd ed. New York: Praeger, 1991.

Tulis, Jeffrey K. *The Rhetorical Presidency*. Princeton, NJ: Princeton University Press, 1987.

U.S. Department of State. *KAL Flight #007: Compilation of Statements and Documents, September 1-16, 1983* (Washington, D.C.: Bureau of Public Affairs, 1983).

Vatz, Richard E. "The Myth of the Rhetorical Situation." *Philosophy and Rhetoric* 6 (1973): 154-161.

Wanta, Wayne, Mary Ann Stephenson, Judy VanSlyke Turk, and Maxwell E. McCombs. "How President's State of the Union Talk Influenced News Media Agendas." *Journalism Quarterly* 66 (1989): 537-541.

Weaver, David H., Doris A. Graber, Maxwell E. McCombs, and Chiam H. Eyal. *Media Agenda-Setting in a Presidential Election: Issues, Images, and Interest*. New York: Praeger Publishers, 1981.

Wimmer, R. D., and J. R. Dominick. *Mass Media Research*. 2nd ed. Belmont, CA: Wadsworth, 1987.

Windt, Theodore O., Jr. "The Presidency and Speeches on International Crises: Repeating the Rhetorical Past." *Speaker and Gavel* 2.1 (1973): 6-14.

———. *Presidents and Protesters: Political Rhetoric in the 1960s*. Tuscaloosa: University of Alabama Press, 1990.

Windt, Theodore O., Jr., and Beth Ingold, eds. *Essays in Presidential Rhetoric*. Dubuque, IA: Kendall/Hunt Publishing Company, 1983.

Yagada, Aileen, and David M. Dozier. "The Media Agenda-Setting Effect of Concrete versus Abstract Issues." *Journalism Quarterly* 67 (1990): 3-10.

Young, Marilyn J. "When the Shoe is on the Other Foot: The Reagan Administration's Treatment of the Shootdown of Iran Air 655." *Reagan and Public Discourse in America*. Ed. Michael Weiler and W. Barnett Pearce. Tuscaloosa: University of Alabama Press, 1992. 203-224.

Young, Marilyn J., and Michael K. Launer. *Flights of Fancy, Flight of Doom: KAL 007 and Soviet-American Rhetoric*. Lanham, MD: University Press of America, 1988.

———. "KAL 007 and the Superpowers: An International Argument." *Quarterly Journal of Speech* 74 (1988): 271-295.

———. "Superpower Role Reversals: Political Rhetoric Following the Destruction of KAL 007 and the Iranian Airbus." Paper presented at the annual meeting of the World Communication Association. Singapore, 1989.

NORTH KOREA

Presidential Sources

Clinton, Bill. "Statement on China." 3 June 1992 (Press Release: Clinton for President). Available from Internet [Gopher] north america/ politics/ clinton/china

U.S. Department of State. "Interview with Dan Rather of CBS News." *Weekly Compilation of Presidential Documents* 29 (29 March 1993).

———. "The President's News Conference with Prime Minister Kiichi Miyazawa of Japan." *Weekly Compilation of Presidential Documents* 29 (19 April 1993).

———. "The President's News Conference with Prime Minister Yitzhack Rabin of Israel (March 15, 1993)." *Weekly Compilation of Presidential Documents* 29 (22 March 1993).

———. "Statement by the Director of Communications on the Situation in Haiti: March 2, 1993." *Weekly Compilation of Presidential Documents* 29.9 (8 March 1993).

U.S. Department of State, Office of the Spokesman. "Daily Press Briefing: DPC #42." (19 March 1993). Available from the U.S. Department of State: http://www.state.gov.

———. "Daily Press Briefing: DPC#43." (26 March 1993). Available from the U.S. Department of State: http://www.state.gov

———. "Daily Press Briefing: DPC#50." (8 April 1993). Available from the U.S. Department of State: http://www.state.gov

———. "Daily Press Briefing: DPC#58." (22 April 1993). Available from the U.S. Department of State: http://www.state.gov

———. "Daily Press Briefing: DPC#62." (29 April 1993). Available from theU.S. Department of State: http://www.state.gov

———. "Daily Press Briefing: DPC#64." (3 May 1993). Available from the U.S. Department of State: http://www.state.gov

———. "Daily Press Briefing: DPC#68." (10 May 1993). Available from the U.S. Department of State: http://www.state.gov

———. "Daily Press Briefing: DPC#78." (1 June 1993). Available from the U.S. Department of State: http://www.state.gov

White House, Office of the Press Secretary. "Background Briefing by Senior Administration Official." (16 April 1993). Available from the White House: http://www.whitehouse.gov.

———. "Executive Order #12850." (28 May 1993). Available from the White House: http://www.whitehouse.gov

———. "Memorandum for the Secretary of State: Presidential Determination #93-23." (28 May 1993). Available from the White House: http:// www. whitehouse.gov

———. "Press Briefing by Assistant Secretary Winston Lord." (28 May 1993). Available from the White House: http://www.whitehouse.gov

———. "Press Briefing by Dee Dee Myers." (15 March 1993). Available from the White House: http://www.whitehouse.gov

———. "Press Briefing by Dee Dee Myers." (16 March 1993). Available from the White House: http://www.whitehouse.gov

———. "Press Briefing by Dee Dee Myers." (17 March 1993). Available from the White House: http://www.whitehouse.gov

———. "Press Briefing by George Stephanopoulos." (26 February 1993). Available from the White House: http://www.whitehouse.gov

———. "Press Briefing by George Stephanopoulos." (4 March 1993). Available from the White House: http://www.whitehouse.gov

———. "Press Briefing by George Stephanopoulos." (15 March 1993). Available from the White House: http://www.whitehouse.gov

———. "Press Briefing by George Stephanopoulos." (24 March 1993). Available from the White House: http://www.whitehouse.gov

———. "Press Briefing by George Stephanopoulos." (26 March 1993). Available from the White House: http://www.whitehouse.gov

———. "Press Briefing by George Stephanopoulos." (22 April 1993). Available from the White House: http://www.whitehouse.gov

———. "Press Briefing by George Stephanopoulos." (27 April 1993). Available from the White House: http://www.whitehouse.gov

———. "Pres Briefing by George Stephanopoulos," (5 May 1993). Available from the White House:http://www.whitehouse.gov

———. "Press Briefing by George Stephanopoulos." (26 May 1993). Available from the White House: http://www.whitehouse.gov

———. "Remarks by the President Upon Departure." (28 May 1993). Available from the White House: http://www.whitehouse.gov

———. "Report to Congress Concerning Extension of Waiver Authority for the People's Republic of China." (28 May 1993). Available from the White House: http://www.whitehouse.gov

———. "Statement by the President on Most Favored Nation Status for China." (28 May 1993). Available from the White House: http:// www. white-house.gov

———. "Statement by the President." (11 June 1993). Available from the White House: http://www.whitehouse.gov

———. "Text of a Letter from the President to the Speaker of the House of Representatives and the President of the Senate." (28 May 1993). Available from the White House: http://www.whitehouse.gov

New York Times

Holmes, Steven A. "U.S Rebukes North Koreans for Scrapping Nuclear Pact." *New York Times* (18 March 1993): A3.

"In North Korea, Try Diplomacy First." Editorial. *New York Times* 8 April 1993: A20.

Jehl, Douglas. "China and North Korea: Not-So-Best of Friends." *New York Times* 11 April 1993: E4.

———. "China Opposes U.N. over North Korea." *New York Times* 24 March 1993: A10.

——. "North Korea Isn't Convinced It Should Stay in Nuclear Pact." *New York Times* 5 June 1993: A3.

——. "North Korea Says It Won't Pull Out of Arms Pact Now." *New York Times* 12 June 1993: A1.

——. "Seoul Eases Stand on Nuclear Inspections of North." *New York Times* 30 March 1993: A13.

——. "U.S. Agrees to Discuss Arms Directly with North Korea." *New York Times* 23 April 1993: A10.

——. "U.S. and North Koreans Discuss Nuclear Dispute." *New York Times* 3 June 1993: A9.

——. "U.S. and North Koreans Press Nuclear Talks." *New York Times* 11 June 1993: A9.

——. "U.S. Korean Talks Sought on A-Pact." *New York Times* 18 May 1993: A8.

——. "U.S. May Bargain with Korea on Atom Issue." *New York Times* 27 May 1993: A6.

——. "U.S. Outlines Concerns over North Korean A-Arms." *New York Times* 25 February 1993: A7.

——. "U.S. Seeking U.N. Pressure to Compel North Korea to Honor Treaty." *New York Times* 13 March 1993: A3.

——. "U.S. Sees Conciliatory Atom Steps by North Korea." *New York Times* 13 May 1993: A11.

"The Korean Peninsula Heats Up." Editorial. *New York Times* 12 March 1993: A28.

Kristof, Nicholas D. "A North Korean Warning." *New York Times* 13 March 1993: A3.

"North Korea Gets U.N. Deadline." *New York Times* 19 March 1993: A28.

"North Korea Rejects Atomic Inspections." *New York Times* 27 February 1993: A2.

"North Korea Trifles with Doomsday." Editorial. *New York Times* 16 March 1993: A20.

"Nuclear Peace for Pyongyang?" Editorial. *New York Times* 1 June 1993: A16.

"Old Alliances, New Asia." Editorial. *New York Times* 19 March 1993: A28.

Prial, Frank J. "U.N. Weighs Plea to North Korea." *New York Times* 9 May 1993: A12.

Rosenthal, A. M. "Facing the Risks." *New York Times* 16 March 1993: A21.

"Sanctions on North Korea May Get Tighter." *New York Times* 26 March 1993: A13.

Sanger, David E. "Atomic Energy Agency Asks U.N. to Move Against North Koreans." *New York Times* (2 April 1993): A2.

——. "Citing Caution, South Korea Puts Troops on Alert." *New York Times* 14 March 1993: A6.

——. "Neighbors Differ on How to Chasten North Korea." *New York Times* 31 March 1993: A9.

——. "The Nonproliferation Treaty Bares Its Toothlessness." *New York Times* 14 March 1993: E18.

———. "North Korea, Fighting Inspection, Renounces Nuclear Arms Treaty." *New York Times* 12 March 1993: A1.

———. "North Korea Hit by First Sanctions." *New York Times* 16 March 1993: A3.

———. "North Korea Stirs New A-Arms Fears." *New York Times* 6 May 1993: A16.

———. "North Korean Chief's Son Gains Military Post." *New York Times* 10 April 1993: A4.

———. "Son of North Korean Leader May Be Succeeding to Power." *New York Times* 25 March 1993: A10.

———. "South Korea, Wary of North, Debates Building a Nuclear Bomb." *New York Times* 19 March 1993: A3.

———. "West Knew of North Korea Nuclear Development." *New York Times* 13 March 1993: A3.

Taylor, William J. "Cool Off Korean Tension." *New York Times* 27 March 1993: A21.

Washington Post

Hoagland, Jim. "China Policy: Back to Bush?" *Washington Post* 1 April 1993: A23.

Lippman, Thomas W. "U.S. Gives China Renewal of Favored Status in Trade." *Washington Post* 29 May 1993: A21.

"N. Korea Rebuffs IAEA." *Washington Post* (27 February 1993): A24.

Oberdorfer, Don. "Nuclear Inspectors to Demand Access to N. Korea Sites." *Washington Post* 11 February 1993: A31.

———. "South Korean: U.S. Agrees to Plan to Pressure North." *Washington Post* 30 March 1993: A14.

———. "U.S. Steps Up Pressure on N. Korea." *Washington Post* 18 March 1993: A33.

Oberdorfer, Don and R. Jeffrey Smith. "U.S., Asian Allies Discuss N. Korea Arms Inspections." *Washington Post* 24 March 1993: A30.

Reid, T. R. "North Korea's New Nuclear Deadline Nears." *Washington Post* 30 March 1993: A14.

———. "Overtures Made to N. Korea," *Washington Post* 17 March 1993: A25.

Smith, R. Jeffrey. "N. Korea and the Bomb: High-Tech Hide-and-Seek." *Washington Post* 27 April 1993: A11.

———. "N. Korea Censure Seen as Turning Point in Arms Control." *Washington Post* 7 April 1993: A23.

———. "N. Korea Won't Quit Nuclear Ban Treaty." *Washington Post* 12 June 1993: A1.

———. "N. Korea Quitting Arms Pact." *Washington Post* 12 March 1993: A16.

———. "North Korea's Strongman: Canny or 'Crazy'?" *Washington Post National Weekly Edition* October 4-10 1993: 18.

———. "Nuclear Agency Says N. Korea Violates Rule." *Washington Post* 1 April 1993: A17.

———. "Overtures Made to N. Korea." *Washington Post* 17 March 1993: A25.

———. "U.N. Members Agree to Urge N. Korean Adherence to Treaty." *Washington Post* 9 May 1993: A28.

———. "U.S. Denounces N. Korea for Quitting Nuclear Pact." *Washington Post* 13 March 1993: A1.

———. "U.S., North Korea Set High-Level Meeting on Nuclear Program." *Washington Post* 25 May 1993: A14.

———. "U.S. Outlines Compromise in Korea Talks." *Washington Post* 27 May 1993: A43.

Smith, R. Jeffrey, and Barton Gellman. "U.S., North Korea Report Progress in Nuclear Ban Treaty Talks." *Washington Post* 11 June 1993: A33.

Sun, Lena. "U.S. Holding Talks with North Koreans." *Washington Post* 6 May 1993: A34.

Sun, Lena, and Jackson Diehl. "N. Korea Reportedly Snubs China." *Washington Post* 28 April 1993: A13.

Williams, Daniel, and R. Jeffrey Smith. "Clinton to Extend China Trade Status." *Washington Post* 28 May 1993: A34.

BOSNIA

Presidential Sources

U.S. Department of State. "Address to the Nation on Implementation of the Peace Agreement in Bosnia-Herzegovina: 27 November 1995." *Weekly Compilation of Presidential Documents* 31.48 (4 December 1995).

———. "Exchange with Reporters Prior to Discussions with President Mary Robinson of Ireland in Dublin: December 1, 1995." *Weekly Compilation of Presidential Documents* 31.49 (11 December 1995).

———. "Exchange with Reporters Prior to Discussions with Prime Minister John Bruton of Ireland in Dublin: December 1, 1995." *Weekly Compilation of Presidential Documents* 31.49 (11 December 1995).

———. "Executive Order 12982—Ordering the Selected Reserve of the Armed Forces to Active Duty: December 8, 1995." *Weekly Compilation of Presidential Documents* 31.50 (18 December 1995).

———. "Letter to Congressional Leaders on Bosnia: December 6, 1995." *Weekly Compilation of Presidential Documents* 31.49 (11 December 1995).

———. "Letter to Senate Democratic Leader Thomas Daschle on Implementation of the Balkan Peace Process: December 11, 1995." *Weekly Compilation of Presidential Documents* 31.50 (18 December 1995).

———. "Letter to Senators Robert Dole and John McCain on the Balkan Peace Process: December 12, 1995." *Weekly Compilation of Presidential Documents* 31.50 (18 December 1995).

———. "Message to the Congress on the Federal Republic of Yugoslavia (Serbia and Montenegro): December 8, 1995." *Weekly Compilation of Presidential Documents* 31.50 (18 December 1995).

———. "The President's News Conference with European Union Leaders in Madrid, Spain: December 3, 1995." *Weekly Compilation of Presidential Documents* 31.49 (11 December 1995).

———. "The President's News Conference with Prime Minister John Bruton of Ireland in Dublin: December 1, 1995." *Weekly Compilation of Presidential Documents* 31.49 (11 December 1995).

———. "The President's News Conference with Prime Minister John Major of the United Kingdom in London, England: November 29, 1995." *Weekly Compilation of Presidential Documents* 31.48 (4 December 1995).

———. "The President's Radio Address: December 2, 1995." *Weekly Compilation of Presidential Documents* 31.49 (11 December 1995).

———. "The President's Radio Address: November 25, 1995." *Weekly Compilation of Presidential Documents* 31.48 (4 December 1995).

———. "Remarks Announcing the Bosnia-Herzegovina Peace Agreement and an Exchange with Reporters: November 21, 1995." *Weekly Compilation of Presidential Documents* 31.47 (27 November 1995).

———. "Remarks Announcing the Child Survival Initiative for Bosnia-Herzegovina and an Exchange with Reporters: 27 November 1995." *Weekly Compilation of Presidential Documents* 31.48 (4 December 1995).

———. "Remarks at a Dinner Party Hosted by Prime Minister Major in London: November 29, 1995." *Weekly Compilation of Presidential Documents* 31.48 (4 December 1995).

———. "Remarks at the Signing Ceremony for the Balkan Peace Agreement in Paris: December 14, 1995." *Weekly Compilation of Presidential Documents* 31.50 (18 December 1995).

———. "Remarks Following a Meeting with Elie Wiesel and an Exchange with Reporters: December 13, 1995." *Weekly Compilation of Presidential Documents* 31.50 (18 December 1995).

———. "Remarks Following Discussions with Chancellor Helmut Kohl of Germany and an Exchange with Reporters in Baumholder: December 2, 1995." *Weekly Compilation of Presidential Documents* 31.49 (11 December 1995).

———. "Remarks on Departure for the United Kingdom: November 28, 1995." *Weekly Compilation of Presidential Documents* 31.48 (4 December 1995).

———. "Remarks on Signing the Human Rights Proclamation: December 5, 1995." *Weekly Compilation of Presidential Documents* 31.49 (11 December 1995).

———. "Remarks Prior to a Meeting with Congressional Leaders and an Exchange with Reporters: 28 November 1995." *Weekly Compilation of Presidential Documents* 31.48 (4 December 1995).

———. "Remarks Prior to Discussion wth Balkan Leaders and an Exchange with Reporters in Paris, France: December 14, 1995." *Weekly Compilation of Presidential Documents* 31.50 (18 December 1995).

———. "Remarks to Citizens Involved in Humanitarian Relief Efforts for Bosnia and an Exchange with Reporters: December 12, 1995." *Weekly Compilation of Presidential Documents* 31.50 (18 December 1995).

———. "Remarks to the Committee for American Leadership in Bosnia and an Exchange with Reporters: December 6, 1995." *Weekly Compilation of Presidential Documents* 31.49 (11 December 1995).

———. "Remarks to the Parliament of Ireland in Dublin: December 1, 1995." *Weekly Compilation of Presidential Documents* 31.49 (11 December 1995).

———. "Remarks to the Parliament of the United Kingdom in London: November 29, 1995." *Weekly Compilation of Presidential Documents* 31.48 (4 December 1995).

———. "Remarks to Troops in Baumholder, Germany: December 2, 1995." *Weekly Compilation of Presidential Documents* 31.49 (11 December 1995).

U.S. Department of State, Office of the Spokesman. "Daily Press Briefing: DPC #170." (22 November 1995). Available from U.S. Department of State: http://www.state.gov

———. "Daily Press Briefing; DPC#171." (27 November 1995). Available from the U.S. Department of State: http://www.state.gov

———. "Daily Press Briefing: DPC#179." (12 December-1995). Available from the U.S. Department of State: http://www.state.gov

———. "Daily Press Briefing: DPC#176." (6 December 1995). Available from the U.S. Department of State: http://www.state.gov

———. "Daily Press Briefing: DPC#178." (8 December 1995). Available from the U.S. Department of State: http://www.state.gov

———. "Intervention by Secretary of State Warren Christopher at the Meeting of NATO Foreign and Defense Ministers on Bosnia." (5 December 1995). Available from the U.S. Department of State: http://www.state.gov

———. "Intervention by Secretary of State Warren Christopher at the North Atlantic Council." (5 December 1995). Available from the U.S. Department of State: http://www.state.gov

———. "Interview of Secretary of State Warren Christopher by Jim Lehrer—PBS-TV 'News Hour with Jim Lehrer.'" (27 November 1995). Available from the U.S. Department of State: http://www.state.gov

———. "Interview of Secretary of State Warren Christopher on ABC-TV 'This Week with David Brinkley.' (3 December 1995). Available from the U.S. Department of State: http://www.state.gov

———. "Interview of Secretary of State Warren Christopher on CNN—'Larry King Live.'" (27 December 1995). Available from the U.S. Department of State: http://www.state.gov

———. "Interview of Secretary of State Warren Christopher on National Public Radio—Robert Siegel 'All Things Considered.'" (27 November 1995). Available from the U.S. Department of State: http://www.state.gov

———. "Press Availability: Secretary of State Warren Christopher on European Issues." (8 December 1995). Available from the U.S. Department of State: http://www.state.gov

———. "Press Conference Following the Initialing of the Balkan Proximity Peace Talks Agreement." (21 November 1995). Available from U.S. Department of State: http://www.state.gov

———. "Remarks by U.S. Secretary of State Warren Christopher and President Milosevic of Serbia, President Tudjman of Croatia, President Izetbegovic of Bosnia-Herzegovina and Representatives of the European Union, the Contact Group and Negotiating Team Members at the Initialing of the Balkan Proximity Peace Talks Agreement." (21 November 1995). Available from the U.S. Department of State: http://www.state.gov.

———. "Statement by Secretary of State Warren Christopher before the Senate Committee on Foreign Relations." (1 December 1995). Available from the U.S. Department of State: http://www.state.gov

———. "Statement by Secretary of State Warren Christopher before the House Committee on International Relations." (30 November 1995). Available from the U.S. Department of State: http://www.state.gov

———. "U.S. Department of State Daily Press Briefing." (4 December 1995). Available from the U.S. Department of State: http://www.state.gov

White House, Office of the Press Secretary. "Background Briefing by Senior Administration Official." (22 November 1995). Available from the White House: http://www.whitehouse.gov

———. "Background Briefing by Senior Administration Official." (14 December 1995). Available from the White House: http://www.whitehouse.gov

———. "Press Briefing by Mike McCurry." (21 November 1995). Available from the White House: http://www.whitehouse.gov

———. "Press Briefing by Mike McCurry." (29 November 1995). Available from the White House: http://www.whitehouse.gov

———. "Press Briefing by Mike McCurry." (30 November 1995). Available from the White House: http://www.whitehouse.gov

———. "Press Briefing by Mike McCurry." (6 December 1995). Available from the White House: http://www.whitehouse.gov

———. "Press Briefing by Mike McCurry." (8 December 1995). Available from the White House: http://www.whitehouse.gov

———. "Press Briefing by Mike McCurry." (12 December 1995). Available from the White House: http://www.whitehouse.gov

———. "Press Briefing by Mike McCurry." (13 December 1995). Available from the White House: http://www.whitehouse.gov

———. "Press Briefing by Mike McCurry." (14 December 1995). Available from the White House: http://www.whitehouse.gov

———. "Press Conference by the President and Prime Minister Shimon Peres of Israel." (11 December 1995). Available from the White House: http://www.whitehouse.gov

———. "Remarks by the President during Interview with Joe Garvey, U.S. Army Europe, Armed Forces Network." (2 December 1995). Available from the White House: http://www.whitehouse.gov

———. "Remarks by the President in Meeting with Democratic Governors." (8 December 1995). Available from the White House: http://www.whitehouse.gov

———. "Remarks by the President in Satellite Feed to Florida Democratic Party's Convention." (10 December 1995). Available from the White House: http://www.whitehouse.gov

New York Times

Apple, R. W., Jr. "Flimsy Bosnia Mandate." *New York Times* 14 December 1995: A1.

Bonner, Raymond. "'The Abandoned': Elderly Serbs in Region Retaken by Croatia." *New York Times* 12 December 1995: A10.

———. "Bosnian Serb Leader Signals Acceptance of Peace Plan." *New York Times* 25 November 1995: A3.

———. "Croaion Forces Razing Serb Villages as They Withdraw." *New York Times* 10 December 1995: A14.

———. "In Reversal, Serbs on Bosnia Accept Peace Agreement." *New York Times* 24 November 1995: A1

———. "In Suburbs of Sarajevo, Serbs Firm on Leaving." *New York Times* 30 November 1995: A10.

———. "Muslims and Croats Seek Home." *New York Times* 13 December 1995: A16.

———. "Rising Serb Leader Offers Accord Rare Praise." *New York Times* 26 November 1995: A12.

———. "The Serbs' Hopes Rise as the Sanctions Fall." *New York Times* 28 November 1995: A15.

"Bosnia and Serbia Plan Ties, But Not Croatia and Serbia." *New York Times* 14 December 1995: A14.

Brooke, James. "Army Stress Control Unit Mobilizes, Too, to Seek Out Peacekeeping's Hidden Toll." *New York Times* 7 December 1995: A6.

Clines, Francis X. "Balkans 101: Not with a 10-Foot Pole." *New York Times* 29 November 1995: A18.

———. "Clinton Gets Wary Backing from His Rival, Dole." *New York Times* 14 December 1995: A15.

Clymer, Adam. "The Silent Opposition." *New York Times* 28 November 1995: A1.

Cohen, Roger. "Christopher Suggests 'Sensitivity' to Needs of the Bosnian Serbs." *New York Times* 7 December 1995: A7.

———. "France to Rejoin Military Command for NATO Alliance." *New York Times* 6 December 1995: A1.

———. "French Deadline Passes with No Word from Serbs on Pilots." *New York Times* 11 December 1995: A10.

———. "An Imperfect Peace." *New York Times* 22 November 1995: A1.

"Congress Must Vote on Bosnia. " Editorial. *New York Times* 20 October 1995: A34.

Cowell, Alan. "Army Children Express Their Doubts." *New York Times* 2 December 1995: A5.

———. "For Some Bosnians, Return Is Just a Dream." *New York Times* 8 December 1995: A1.

———. "G.I. Gets Support from Shunning U.N. Insignia." *New York Times* 24 November 1995: A14.

Crossette, Barbara. "Squabble at the U.N." *New York Times* 14 December 1995: A14.

————. "Talking Tough, U.N. Condemns Bosnian Serbs." *New York Times* 30 November 1995: A11.

Engelberg, Stephen. "Bosnian Croat Sought by the Tribunal Is Freed Despite Pledge." *New York Times* 8 December 1995: A18.

————. "War Crimes Panel Orders Suspect Released." *New York Times* 11 December 1995: A10.

"Force and Diplomacy in Bosnia. " Editorial. *New York Times* 31 August 1995: A24.

"France Gives Serbs Deadline on Lost Pilots." *New York Times* 9 December 1995: A5.

"Germans to Send 4,000 Troops." *New York Times* 29 November 1995: A18.

Hedges, Chris. "Bosnian Serbs Take Vote, and Pact Takes Battering." *New York Times* 13 December 1995: A16.

————. "Bosnia Town Prepares for G.I.'s and Switch from War to Peace." *New York Times* 1 December 1995: A1.

————. "Foreign Islamic Fighters in Bosnia Pose a Potential Threat for G.I.'s." *New York Times* 3 December 1995: A1.

————. "For Milosevic, a Chance at a New Lease on Political Life." *New York Times* 22 November 1995: A10.

————. "In Sarajevo Suburbs, Talk of Resistance." *New York Times* 27 November 1995: A1.

————. "Vanguard Forces Arriving in the Balkans." *New York Times* 5 December 1995: A8.

Johnson, Dirk. "Along a Missouri Highway, Worries and a Sense of Duty to Help Bosnians." *New York Times* 4 December 1995: A10.

"Keep It Simple on Bosnia." Editorial. *New York Times* 11 December 1995: A16.

Kinzer, Stephen. "Hungarian Town Mobilizes for G.I.'s Bound for Bosnia." *New York Times* 4 December 1995: A1.

"The Larger Patriotism. " Editorial. *New York Times* 10 January 1992: A24.

"Making the Case on Bosnia." Editorial. *New York Times* 28 November 1995: A22.

Mitchell, Alison. "Clinton Lays Out his Case for U.S. Troops in Balkans; 'We Must Do What We Can.'" *New York Times* 28 November 1995: A1.

————. "Clinton Seeks Public Support on Bosnia Plan." *New York Times* 26 November 1995: A1.

————. "Clinton's Next Task Will Be to Sell Plan to the U.S. Public." *New York Times* 22 November 1995: A1.

O'Conner, Mike. "Refugees Returning to Bosnia." *New York Times* 11 December 1995: A10.

"Peace and Peacekeeping in Bosnia. " Editorial. *New York Times* 6 October 1995: A30.

"Peace in Bosnia." Editorial. *New York Times* 22 November 1995: A22.

Perlez, Jane. "Bosnia: Proving Ground for NATO Contenders." *New York Times* 9 December 1995: A5.

————. "Serbs Free 2 Pilots, Clearing an Obstacle to Signing of Accord." *New York Times* 13 December 1995: A16.

————— "Serbs Say Captive French Pilots Are to Be Released Today." *New York Times* 12 December 1995: A10.

Purdum, Todd S. "Clinton Invokes British-American Link in Speech to Parliament." *New York Times* 30 November 1995: A9.

—————. "Clinton Rallies Edgy Troops for Bosnia." *New York Times* 3 December 1995: A1.

—————. "For Buoyed Clinton, Down to Business." *New York Times* 4 December 1995: A11.

"The Republican Split on Bosnia." Editorial. *New York Times* 14 December 1995: A30.

Roane, Kit R. "For Bosnian Schoolgirl, an Uneasy Homecoming." *New York Times* 9 December 1995: A5.

—————. "In Weary Bosnian Capital, Joy, and Tears for the Dead." *New York Times* 22 November 1995: A10.

—————. "More Muslims Evicted from Homes Despite Pact." *New York Times* 8 December 1995: A18.

—————. "A Town Feels Betrayed by Milosevic and Talks of Fighting On." *New York Times* 23 November 1995: A12.

Schmitt, Eric. "Bosnian Serbs Balk at Pact, Imperiling U.S. Troop Plan." *New York Times* 23 November 1995: A12.

—————. "High-Tech Maps Guided Bosnia Talks." *New York Times* 24 November 1995: A14.

—————. "In U.S. Peacekeeper Arsenal, Weapons Honed for Bosnia." *New York Times* 5 December 1995: A1.

—————. "Key Bosnia Question: Where Are Exits?" *New York Times* 2 December 1995: A5.

—————. "Pentagon Confident, But Some Serbs 'Will Fight.'" *New York Times* 27 November 1995: A1.

—————. "20,000 G.I.'s Will Face Challenges and Risks." *New York Times* 22 November 1995: A11.

Sciolino, Elaine. "Accord Reached to End the War in Bosnia; Clinton Pledges U.S. Troops to Keep the Peace." *New York Times* 22 November 1995: A1.

—————. "Dole Backs Plan to Send U.S. Force on Bosnia Mission." *New York Times* 1 December 1995: A1.

————— "To Confront the Call-In Critics, U.S. Aides Take to the Airwaves." *New York Times* 7 December

Sciolino, Elaine, Roger Cohen, and Stephen Engelberg. "In U.S. Eyes, 'Good' Muslims and 'Bad' Serbs Did a Switch." *New York Times* 23 November 1995: A1.

Seelye, Katherine Q. "Anguished, Senators Vote to Support Bosnia Mission; Clinton Off to Paris Signing." *New York Times* 14 December 1995: A1.

—————. "Clinton Gives Republicans Pledge on Arming Bosnians." *New York Times* 13 December 1995: A16.

—————. "Congress and White House Barter over Support for U.S. Mission." *New York Times* 5 December 1995: A7.

—————. "G.O.P. Opposition Forces Dole to Delay Vote on Bosnia." *New York Times* 6 December 1995: A14.

————. "Legislators Get Plea by Clinton on Bosnia Force." *New York Times* 29 November 1995: A1.

————. "Nearly Half of House Members Sign Letter Opposing Bosnia Deployment." *New York Times* 8 December 1995: A18.

————. "Some G.O.P. Senators Refusing to Back Dole on Bosnia Mission." *New York Times* 7 December 1995: A5.

Shennon, Philip. "Main Peril for G.I.'s in Bosnia Lies Just Beneath the Surface." *New York Times* 10 December 1995: A1.

————. "U.S. Troops in Bosnia Find a 'Shellshocked' People." *New York Times* 11 December 1995: A10.

Smothers, Ronald. "In Gingrich Country, Bosnia Is a Hard Sell." *New York Times* 29 November 1995: A19.

Stevenson, Richard W. "Talks on Rebuilding Bosnia Become Squabble over Bill." *New York Times* 10 December 1995: A14.

"Stirring of a New NATO." Editorial. *New York Times* 7 December 1995: A30.

"25 Countries Offer to Join Bosnia Force." *New York Times* 24 November 1995: A15.

"U.S. Plea for French Pilots." *New York Times* 10 December 1995: A14.

Wald, Matthew L. "700 U.S. Troops on the Way." *New York Times* 4 December 1995: A10.

"War by Default. " Editorial. *New York Times* 16 December 1991: A14.

"Where is Congress on the Gulf?" Editorial. *New York Times* 3 January 1991: A20.

Whitney, Craig R. "Despite U.S.-NATO Tensions, Troops Get Ready for Bosnia." *New York Times* 30 November 1995: A10.

————. "Europe Has Few Doubts on Bosnia Force." *New York Times* 5 December 1995: A8.

————. "Moscow and NATO in Accord on Russian Troops in Bosnia." *New York Times* 29 November 1995: A18.

————. "Success Has Many Fathers among Allies." *New York Times* 23 November 1995: A11.

"Who Can Declare War?" Editorial. *New York Times* 15 December 1991: I26.

Wren, Christopher S. "Resettling Refugees: U.N. Facing New Burden." *New York Times* 24 November 1995: A15.

————. "U.N. Begins to List the Embargoes on Balkans." *New York Times* 23 November 1995: A12.

————. "U.N. Votes to Make Hast Slowly in Retreat from Balkans." *New York Times* 1 December 1995: A15.

Washington Post

"Answering the Bosnian Serbs. " Editorial. *Washington Post* 31 August 1995: A22.

Atkinson, Rick. "French Pledge Greater Role in NATO." *Washington Post* 6 December 1995: A28.

————. "Military Families Battle the Stress of Separation." *Washington Post* 5 December 1995: A16.

————. "Mines Weigh Heavily on Minds of Troops." *Washington Post* 12 December 1995: A27.

————. "Moscow Accepts NATO Troop Plan." *Washington Post* 29 November 1995: A27.

————. "Peace Force Poses Major Test for NATO." *Washington Post* 22 November 1995: A20.

————. "Perry Declares Troops Bosnia-Ready." *Washington Post* 25 November 1995: A1.

————. "Perry Sets Deadline for Arming Bosnia." *Washington Post* 30 November 1995: A31.

————. "U.S. Bound for Bosnia by Train, Truck, Air." *Washington Post* 4 December 1995: A21.

————. "'We Go Where We're Sent. We Don't Choose the Mission.'" *Washington Post* 7 December 1995: A37.

Balz, Dan. "As Dole Equivocates on Troop Deployment, Most GOP Rivals Oppose Plan." *Washington Post* 28 November 1995: A9.

Barbash, Fred. "British Force Finds NATO Role Less Risky Than Service with U.N." *Washington Post* 4 December 1995: A24.

————. "Diplomats, Aid Officials Grapple with Plans for Rebuilding Bosnia." *Washington Post* 10 December 1995: A32.

————. "'I Don't Fit There.'" *Washington Post* 9 December 1995: A19.

"Bosnia Opportunity." Editorial. *Washington Post* 29 November 1995: A24.

"A Bosnia Peace Force. " Editorial. *Washington Post* 24 September 1995: C6.

"Budget Chairmen on Hill Won't Fight Bosnia Funds." *Washington Post* 4 December 1995: A25.

"Congress and Bosnia." Editorial. *Washington Post* 15 December 1995: A24.

"Congress and War. " Editorial. *Washington Post* 11 January 1992: A20.

Devroy, Ann. "Clinton Defends Sending Troops to Bosnia." *Washington Post* 2 December 1995: A15.

————. "Clinton Lobbies for Troops." *Washington Post* 26 November 1995: A29.

————. "Clinton Reassures Bosnia-Bound Forces Mission Is 'Safe as It Can Be.'" *Washington Post* 3 December 1995: A32.

————. "President Authorizes Deployment to Bosnia." *Washington Post* 4 December 1995: A1.

Devroy, Ann, and Helen Dewar. "Clinton Challenged on Plan for Troops." *Washington Post* 22 November 1995: A21.

————. "U.S. Troops Vital to Bosnia Peace, Clinton Says." *Washington Post* 28 November 1995: A1.

Dewar, Helen. "Bush, Ford Endorse Plan; Lott Opposes." *Washington Post* 6 December 1995: A28.

————. "Dole Predicts Split Senate Will Allow Bosnia Mission." *Washington Post* 13 December 1995: A35.

————. "Senate Set for Debate on Bosnia." *Washington Post* 12 December 1995: A27.

————. "Senate Sets Bosnia Vote; 184 in House Object to Troop Plan." *Washington Post* 8 December 1995: A47.

Dewar, Helen, and Guy Gugliotta. "Senate Backs Troops to Bosnia; House Retreats on Fund Cutoff." *Washington Post* 14 December 1995: A1.

Dewar, Helen, and Michael Dobbs. "Dole Supports U.S. Troop Plan for Bosnia Peace." *Washington Post* 1 December 1995: A1.

Dobbs, Michael. "After Marathon Negotiations, An Extra Mile to Reach Peace." *Washington Post* 23 November 1995: A1.

————. "Balkan Leaders Approve Bosnia Pact." *Washington Post* 22 November 1996: A1.

————. "Bosnia Crystallizes U.S. Post-Cold War Role." *Washington Post* 3 December 1995: A1.

————. "Congress Raising Questions about Bosnia Exit Strategy." *Washington Post* 30 November 1995: A32.

————. "In Selling Policy to the Public, State Dept. Enters a New Stage." *Washington Post* 13 December 1995: A35.

————. "Three Shaped Pact." *Washington Post* 22 November 1995: A20.

————. "U.S. Gains Assurances on Troops." *Washington Post* 24 November 1995: A1.

Dobbs, Michael, and Dana Priest. "Refugees, Elections Pose Tough Challenges in Bosnia." *Washington Post* 8 December 1995: A1.

Drozdiak, William. "European Governments Respond with Relief." *Washington Post* 22 November 1995: A22.

————. "French NATO Forces Face Sensitive Mission." *Washington Post* 4 December 1995: A21.

————. "French Seek Balkan Pact Setting Ties." *Washington Post* 14 December 1995: A37.

————. "NATO Votes to Start Bosnia Deployment." *Washington Post* 2 December 1995: A14.

"Extra Pay Granted to Bosnia Troops." *Washington Post* 14 December 1995: 39.

"4 Units in D.C., Md., Va. Get Call." *Washington Post* 5 December 1995: A12.

Goshko, John. "U.N. Report on Croatia Is Withdrawn." *Washington Post* 14 December 1995: A38.

Goshko, John M., and John F. Harris. "U.N. Votes to Withdraw Sanctions on the Balkans." *Washington Post* 23 November 1995: A1.

Graham, Bradley. "Advice to an Incoming General: Be Firm, Friendly." *Washington Post* 12 December 1995: A28.

————. "Deployment of U.S. Troops Goes Slowly." *Washington Post* 7 December 1995: A31.

————. "Small Advance Team, Large Media Army Set Up Shop in Tuzla." *Washington Post* 10 December 1995: A32.

Gugliotta, Guy. "Balkan Pact Is Final, Administration Says." *Washington Post* 27 November 1995: A16.

————. "Bosnia Situation Changed; Few House Freshmen Have." *Washington Post* 13 December 1995: A35.

Harris, John F. "President Has Long-term Task of Reassurance." *Washington Post* 28 November 1995: A1.

Harris, John F., and Eric Pianin. "Clinton Accepts Hill's Defense Spending Bill." *Washington Post* 1 December 1995: A1.

Harris, John F., and Helen Dewar. "Clinton Bargains Defense Funds for Support on Bosnia." *Washington Post* 15 December 1995: A24.

Pomfret, John. "Bosnia Croats Defy Peace Pact, Loot Town." *Washington Post* 10 December 1995: A1.

———. "Bosnian Serbs Back Pact, Belgrade Says." *Washington Post* 24 November 1995: A1.

———. "Dayton Pact Presidents All Face Challenges." *Washington Post* 8 December 1995: A46.

———. "Once-Red Carpet Is Out for NATO." *Washington Post* 30 November 1995: A1.

———. "Plan Legitimizes Years of 'Ethnic Cleansing.'" *Washington Post* 22 November 1995: A1.

———. "Serb Denies Guilt in War Crimes." *Washington Post* 4 December 1995: A1.

———. "The Dayton Hurrahs vs. Bosnian Reality: Can Serbian Leader Deliver Peace?" *Washington Post* 23 November 1995: A35.

———. "U.S.-Led NATO Force Faces Risky Mission." *Washington Post* 28 November 1995: A1.

———. "Wanted Man Tests NATO's Mission." *Washington Post* 14 December 1995: A37.

Priest, Dana. "Fear of Casualties Drives Bosnia Debate." *Washington Post* 2 December 1995: A1.

———. "For Bosnia Pilots, Virtual Reality Is Reality." *Washington Post* 12 December 1995: A3.

———. "Foreign Muslims Fighting in Bosnia Considered 'Threat' to U.S. Troops." *Washington Post* 30 November 1995: A33.

———. "1,400 U.S. Troops Part of Advance Group." *Washington Post* 28 November 1995: A9.

Priest, Dana, and John E. Young. "Reservists Called Up for Training." *Washington Post* 5 December 1995: A12.

"Resolution 678. 1990. " Editorial. *Washington Post* 30 November 1991: A28.

Schork, Kurt. "Bosnian Serbs Protest Peace Accord." *Washington Post* 26 November 1995: A29.

———. "Bosnian Troops Loot U.N. Base in Bihac." *Washington Post* 25 November 1995: A18.

Smith, R. Jeffrey, and Dana Priest. "Troops Given Wide Range of Authority." *Washington Post* 23 November 1995: A1.

Spolar, Christine. "Bosnian Serb Commander Demands Peace Accord Be Modified." *Washington Post* 3 December 1995: A32.

———. "Bosnians Promise to Oust 'Volunteers,' Protect Serb Rights." *Washington Post* 9 December 1995: A19.

———. "Contingent of 22 Marines Arrives in Sarajevo for Peacekeeping." *Washington Post* 11 December 1995: A20.

———. "In Sarajevo, Peace Can't Defeat Skepticism." *Washington Post* 27 November 1995: A1.

————. "Sarajevo Serbs Find No Peace in Dayton Pact." *Washington Post* 6 December 1995: A1.

————. "Serbs Reassured on Safety after Sarajevo Is Unified." *Washington Post* 28 November 1995: A10.

————. "First NATO Units Arrive in Bosnia." *Washington Post* 5 December 1995: A12.

————. "Serbs Release 2 French Pilots Held 3 [and one-half] Months." *Washington Post* 13 December 1995: A36.

————. "Tuzla Anxiously Awaits NATO Troops and Peace--At Last." *Washington Post* 1 December 1995: A34.

————. "Yule Lights Brighten Bosnia Post." *Washington Post* 12 December 1995: A27.

"U.S. Admiral Says NATO Troops Will Respond Firmly if Challenged." *Washington Post* 13 December 1995: A35.

"U.S. Jets Start Shuttle to Tuzla." *Washington Post* 9 December 1995: A19.

"U.S. Seeks to Reassure Bosnian Serbs." *Washington Post* 7 December 1995: A35.

"U.S. Officers Say Bosnia Resembles the Blue Ridge." *Washington Post* 6 December 1995: A29.

HAITI

Presidential Sources

Office of the President-elect. "Statement of President-elect Bill Clinton on the Crisis in Haiti." (14 January 1993). Available from Clinton@Marist Newsgroup [Internet]: /.data/politics/pres.clinton/haiti.115.

U.S. Department of State. "Exchange with Reporters on the Situation in Haiti: October 4, 1991." *Weekly Compilation of Presidential Documents* 20 (7 October 1991).

————. "Exchange with Reporters Prior to a Meeting with Secretary General Manfred Woerner of the North Atlantic Treaty Organization: March 2, 1993." *Weekly Compilation of Presidential Documents* 29.9 (8 March 1993).

————. "Exchange with Reporters Prior to a Meeting with White House Fellows: June 17, 1993." *Weekly Compilation of Presidential Documents* 29.24 (21 June 1993).

———— "Exchange with Reporters Prior to Discussions with President Hosni Mubarak of Egypt: October 25, 1993." *Weekly Compilation of Presidential Documents* 29.43 (1 November 1993).

————. "Executive Order 12775—Prohibiting Certain Transactions with Respect to Haiti: October 4, 1991." *Weekly Compilation of Presidential Documents* 20 (7 October 1991).

————. "Interview with Radio Reporters: October 18, 1993." *Weekly Compilation of Presidential Documents* 29.42 (25 October 1993).

————. "Letter to Congressional Leaders on Economic Sanctions against Haiti: July 12, 1993." *Weekly Compilation of Presidential Documents* 29.28 (19 July 1993).

————. "Letter to Congressional Leaders on Haiti: November 13, 1993." *Weekly Compilation of Presidential Documents* 29.46 (22 November 1993).

————. "Letter to Congressional Leaders on Haiti: October 20, 1993." *Weekly Compilation of Presidential Documents* 29.42 (25 October 1993).

————. "Message to the Congress Reporting on the Continuation of the National Emergency with Respect to Haiti: September 30, 1992." *Weekly Compilation of Presidential Documents* 28.40 (5 October 1992).

————. "Notice on the Continuation of Haitian Emergency: September 30, 1993." *Weekly Compilation of Presidential Documents* 29.39 (4 October 1993).

————. "The President's News Conference: April 23, 1993." *Weekly Compilation of Presidential Documents* 29.16 (26 April 1993).

————. "The President's News Conference: October 14, 1993." *Weekly Compilation of Presidential Documents* 29.41 (18 October 1993).

————. "The President's News Conference: November 10, 1993." *Weekly Compilation of Presidential Documents* 29.45 (15 November 1993).

————. "The President's News Conference with Prime Minister Brian Mulroney: February 5, 1993." *Weekly Compilation of Presidential Documents* 29.5 (8 February 1993).

————. "Proclamation 6569—Suspension of Entry as Immigrants and Nonimmigrants of Persons Who Formulate or Implement Policies That Are Impeding the Negotiations Seeking the Return to Constitutional Rule in Haiti." *Weekly Compilation of Presidential Documents7* 29.22 (7 June 1993).

————. "Question-and-Answer Session in Miami, Florida: October 23, 1992." *Weekly Compilation of Presidential Documents* 28.44 (2 November 1992).

————. "Remarks and an Exchange with Reporters on Haiti: October 23, 1993." *Weekly Compilation of Presidential Documents* 29.43 (1 November 1993).

————. "Remarks and an Exchange with Reporters Prior to a Meeting with Members of Congress: October 22, 1993," *Weekly Compilation of Presidential Documents* 29.42 (25 October 1993).

————. "Remarks and an Exchange With Reporters Prior to Discussions with President Jean-Bertrand Aristide and Prime Minister Robert Maval of Haiti: December 6, 1993." *Weekly Compilation of Presidential Documents* 29.49 (13 December 1993).

————. "Remarks at a Town Meeting in Detroit: February 10, 1993." *Weekly Compilation of Presidential Documents* 29.6 (15 February 1993).

————. "Remarks and Question-and-Answer Session with the Mount Paran Christian School Community in Marietta: May 27, 1992." *Weekly Compilation of Presidential Documents* 28.22 (1 June 1992).

————. "Remarks in an Interview with the Southern Florida Media: March 13, 1993." *Weekly Compilation of Presidential Documents* 29.11 (22 March 1993).

———— "Remarks Prior to Discussions with President Jean-Bertrand Aristide of Haiti and an Exchange with Reporters: July 22, 1993." *Weekly Compilation of Presidential Documents* 29.29 (26 July 1993).

————. "Remarks with President Jean-Bertrand Aristide of Haiti and an Exchange with Reporters: March 16, 1993." *Weekly Compilation of Presidential Documents* 29.11 (22 March1993).

————. "Statement by the Press Secretary on the President's Meeting with President Jean-Bertrand Aristide of Haiti: July 22, 1993." *Weekly Compilation of Presidential Documents* 29.29 (26 July 1993).

————. "Statement on Sanctions against Haiti: June 4, 1993." *Weekly Compilation of Presidential Documents* 29.22 (7 June 1993).

————. "Teleconference Remarks on Community Policing Grants and an Exchange with Reporters: December 20, 1993," *Weekly Compilation of Presidential Documents* 29.51 (20 December 1993).

————. "White House Statement on Haitian Migrants: May 24, 1992." *Weekly Compilation of Presidential Documents* 28.22 (1 June 1992).

White House, Office of the Press Secretary. "Background Briefing by Senior Administration Official." (March 16, 1993). Available from Clinton@ Marist Newsgroup [Internet]/.data/politics/pres.clinton

————. "Background Briefing by Senior Administration Official." (4 June 1993). Available from Clinton@Marist Newsgroup [Internet]/data/politics/ pres.clinton

————. "Background Briefing by Senior Administration Official." (30 August 1993). Available from Clinton@Marist Newsgroup [Internet] /.data /politics/pres.clinton12, 1993). Available from Clinton@Marist Newsgroup [Internet] /.data/politics/pres.clinton

————. "Executive Order; Blocking Property of Persons Obstructing Democratization in Haiti." (18October 1993). Available from Clinton@Marist Newsgroup [Internet]/.data/politics/pres.clinton

———— "Interview of the President with Radio Reporters." (October 18, 1993). Available from Clinton@Marist Newsgroup [Internet] /.data/politics/ pres.clinton

————. "Prepared Remarks of President William J. Clinton to the American Society of Newspaper Editors 'A Strategic Alliance with Russia Reform,' Annapolis, Maryland." (1 April 993). Available from Clint on@Marist Newsgroup [Internet] /.data/politics/pres.clinton

————. "Press Briefing by Dee Dee Myers." (17 January 1993). Available from Clinton@Marist Newsgroup [Internet] /.data/politics/pres.clinton

————. "Press Briefing by Dee Dee Myers." (15 March 1993). Available from Clinton@Marist Newsgroup [Internet] /.data/politics/pres.clinton

————. "Press Briefing by Dee Dee Myers." (16 March 1993). Available from Clinton@Marist Newsgroup [Internet] /.data/politics/pres.clinton

————. "Press Briefing by Dee Dee Myers." (28 March 1993). Available from Clinton@Marist Newsgroup [Internet] /.data/politics/pres.clinton

————. "Press Briefing by Dee Dee Myers." (29 April 1993). Available from Clinton@Marist Newsgroup [Internet] /.data/politics/pres.clinton

————. "Press Briefing by Dee Dee Myers." (7 June 993). Available from Clinton@Marist Newsgroup [Internet] /.data/politics/pres.clinton

————. "Press Briefing by Dee Dee Myers." (9 June 993). Available from Clinton@Marist Newsgroup [Internet] /.data/politics/pres.clinton

———. "Press Briefing by Dee Dee Myers." (23 June 1993). Available from Clinton@Marist Newsgroup [Internet] /.data/politics/pres.clinton

———. "Press Briefing by Dee Dee Myers." (22 July 1993). Available from Clinton@Marist Newsgroup [Internet] /.data/politics/pres.clinton

———. "Press Briefing by Dee Dee Myers." (16 September 1993). Available from Clinton@Marist Newsgroup [Internet] /.data/politics/pres.clinton

———. "Press Briefing by Dee Dee Myers." (12 October 1993). Available from Clinton@Marist Newsgroup [Internet] /.data/politics/pres.clinton

———. "Press Briefing by Dee Dee Myers." (13 October 1993). Available from Clinton@Marist Newsgroup [Internet] /.data/politics/pres.clinton

———. "Press Briefing by Dee Dee Myers." (18 October 1993). Available from Clinton@Marist Newsgroup [Internet] /.data/politics/pres.clinton

———. "Press Briefing by Dee Dee Myers." (19 October 1993). Available from Clinton@Marist Newsgroup [Internet] /.data/politics/pres.clinton

———. "Press Briefing by Dee Dee Myers." (20 October 1993). Available from Clinton@Marist Newsgroup [Internet] /.data/politics/pres.clinton

———. "Press Briefing by Dee Dee Myers." (22 October 1993). Available from Clinton@Marist Newsgroup [Internet] /.data/politics/pres.clinton

———. "Press Briefing by Dee Dee Myers." (1 November 1993). Available from Clinton@Marist Newsgroup [Internet] /.data/politics/pres.clinton

———. "Press Briefing by Dee Dee Myers." (9 November 1993). Available from Clinton@Marist Newsgroup [Internet]/.data/politics/pres.clinton

———. "Press Briefing by Dee Dee Myers." (7 December 1993). Available from Clinton@Marist Newsgroup [Internet] /.data/politics/pres.clinton

———. "Press Briefing by George Stephanopoulos." (27 January 1993). Available from Clinton@Marist Newsgroup [Internet] /data/politics/pres.clinton

———. "Press Briefing by George Stephanopoulos." (1 February 1993). Available from Clinton@Marist Newsgroup [Internet] /.data/politics/ pres.clinton

———. "Press Briefing by George Stephanopoulos." (15 February 1993). Available from Clinton@Marist Newsgroup [Internet] /data/ politics/pres.-clinton

———. "Press Briefing by George Stephanopoulos." (1 March 1993). Available from Clinton@Marist Newsgroup [Internet] /.data/politics/pres.clinton

———. "Press Briefing by George Stephanopoulos." (9 March 1993). Available from Clinton@Marist Newsgroup [Internet] /.data/politics/pres.clinton

———. "Press Briefing by George Stephanopoulos." (March 16, 1993). Available from Clinton@Marist Newsgroup [Internet] /.data/politics/ pres.clinton

———. "Press Briefing by George Stephanopoulos." (13 April 1993). Available from Clinton@Marist Newsgroup [Internet] /.data/politics/pres.clinton

———. "Press Briefing by George Stephanopoulos." (14 April 1993). Available from Clinton@Marist Newsgroup [Internet] /.data/politics/pres.clinton

————. "Press Briefing by George Stephanopoulos." (19 April 1993). Available from Clinton@Marist Newsgroup [Internet] /.data/politics/pres. clinton

————. "Press Briefing by George Stephanopoulos." (22 April 1993). Available from Clinton@Marist Newsgroup [Internet] /.data/politics/pres. clinton

————. "Press Briefing by George Stephanopoulos." (4 May 1993). Available from Clinton@Marist Newsgroup [Internet] /.data/politics/pres. clinton

————. "Press Briefing by George Stephanopoulos." (13 May 1993). Available from Clinton@Marist Newsgroup [Internet] /.data/politics/pres. clinton

————. "Press Briefing by George Stephanopoulos." (26 May 1993). Available from Clinton@Marist Newsgroup [Internet] /.data/politics/pres. clinton

————. "Press Briefing by George Stephanopoulos." (2 June 1993). Available from Clinton@Marist Newsgroup [Internet] /.data/politics/pres.clinton

————. "Press Conference by the President." (23 April 1993). Available from Clinton@Marist Newsgroup [Internet] /.data/politics/pres.clinton

————. "Press Conference by the President." (17 June 1993). Available from Clinton@Marist Newsgroup [Internet] /.data/politics/pres.clinton

————. "Press Conference by the President." (14 October 1993). Available from Clinton@Marist Newsgroup [Internet] /.data/politics/pres.clinton

————. "Press Conference by the President." (15 October 993). Available from Clinton@Marist Newsgroup [Internet] /.data/politics/pres.clinton

————. "Press Conference by the President." (10 November 1993). Available from Clinton@Marist Newsgroup [Internet] /.data/politics/pres.clinton

————. "Press Conference by the President and the Prime Minister Kim Campbell of Canada." (9 July 1993). Available from Clinton@Marist Newsgroup [Internet] /.data/politics/pres.clinton

————. "Remarks by the President and President Aristide of Haiti." (16 March 1993). Available from Clinton@Marist Newsgroup [Internet] /data /politics/pres.clinton

————."Remarks by the President at Press Availability." (23 October 993). Available from Clinton@Marist Newsgroup [Internet] /.data/politics/ pres.clinton

————. "Remarks by the President in Conference Call with Mayors." (20 December 1993). Available from Clinton@Marist Newsgroup [Internet] /.data/politics/pres.clinton

————. "Remarks by the President in Press Roundtable." (12 November 1993). Available from Clinton@Marist Newsgroup [Internet] /.data/politics/ pres.clinton

————. "Remarks by the President on 'Meet The Press.'" (7 November 1993). Available from Clinton@Marist Newsgroup [Internet] /.data/politics/ pres.clinton

————. "Remarks by the President to the Pool." (23 October 1993). Available from Clinton@Marist Newsgroup [Internet] /.data/politics/pres.clinton

————. "Remarks by the President Upon Departure." (12 October 1993). Available from Clinton@Marist Newsgroup [Internet] /.data/politics/ pres.-clinton

————. "Statement by George Stephanopoulos." (2 March 1993). Available from Clinton@Marist Newsgroup [Internet] /.data/politics/pres.clinton

————. "Statement by the Director of Communications." (14 October 1993). Available from Clinton@Marist Newsgroup [Internet] /.data/politics/ pres.clinton

————. "Statement by the Director of Communications." (16 October 1993). Available from Clinton@Marist Newsgroup [Internet] /.data/politics/ pres.clinton

————. "Statement by the President on Sanctions against Haiti." (4 June 1993). Available from Clinton@Marist Newsgroup [Internet] /.data/politics/ pres.clinton

————. "Statement by the Press Secretary." (1 July 1993). Available from Clinton@Marist Newsgroup [Internet] /.data/politics/pres.clinton

————. "Statement by the Press Secretary." (12 October 1993). Available from Clinton@Marist Newsgroup [Internet] /.data/politics/pres.clinton

————. "Statement by the Press Secretary." (18 October 1993). Available from Clinton@Marist Newsgroup [Internet] /.data/politics/pres.clinton

————. "To The Congress of the United States." (30 June 1993). Available from Clinton@Marist Newsgroup [Internet] /.data/politics/pres.clinton.

New York Times

Apple, R.W., Jr. "In Shift, U.S. Plans to Limit Penalties to Rulers in Haiti." *New York Times* 2 November 1993: A1.

————. "President Orders Six U.S. Warships for Haiti Patrol." *New York Times* 16 October 1993: A1.

————. "U.S. Concludes Aristide Can't Return by Deadline." *New York Times* 27 October 1993: A1.

Berke, Richard L. "Mulroney Offering Troops to Help Blockade Haiti." *New York Times* 3 June 1993: A10.

Binder, David. "Clinton Urges Haitian Leader to Appoint a New Premier." *New York Times* 23 July 1993: A8.

"Brazil Prolongs Haiti's Agony." Editorial. *New York Times* 18 June 1993: A26.

Clymer, Adam. "Foreign Policy Tug-of-War: Latest in a Long String of Battles." *New York Times* 19 October 1993: A18.

"A Defensible Foreign Policy." Editorial. *New York Times* 1 November 1993: A18.

"Embargo Adds to Old Woes." *New York Times* 18 October 1993: A6.

"For Haitians, Cruelty and Hope." Editorial. *New York Times* 17 January 1993: E16.

French, Howard W. "Alliance by Anti-Aristide Forces and Flight by Fearful Lawmakers May Doom Pact." *New York Times* 27 October 1993: A10.

————. "An Aristide Signs Pact to End Crisis." *New York Times* 4 July 1993: A1.

———. "Aristide Team, with Help, Blocks the Sale of Gasoline." *New York Times* 22 October 1993: A10.

———. "Aristide Urges Big U.N. Observer Team for Haiti." *New York Times* 14 January 1993: A3.

———. "As Aristide Fails to Return, His Foes Celebrate in Haiti." *New York Times* 31 October 1993: A12.

———. "As Sanctions Bite, Haiti's Poor Feel the Pinch." *New York Times* 15 November 1993: A7.

———. "As Streets Empty." *New York Times* 19 October 1993: A18.

———. "As U.S. Ships Arrive, Haiti General Refuses to Budge." *New York Times* 18 October 1993: A6.

———. "Despite Plans, U.S. Refugee Processing in Haiti Is Said to Lag." *New York Times* 2 March 1993: A13.

———. "Envoy Says Haiti's Military Agrees to Allow a U.N. Observer Force." *New York Times* 18 January 1993: A5.

———. "Envoys Flee Port as Their Cars Are Struck." *New York Times* 12 October 1993: A1.

———. "Fearful Rural Haitians Yearn for Aristide's Return." *New York Times* 25 October 1993: A3.

———. "Ferry Disaster Underlines Haiti's Everyday Needs." *New York Times* 21 February 1993: A8.

———. "Few Haitians Test U.S. Sea Barricade." *New York Times* 21 January 1993: A8.

———. "Haitian Army Aide Sees Progress toward Accord." *New York Times* 2 July 1993: A7.

———. "Haitian Dissident Loses Plea for U.S. Refugee Visa." *New York Times* 7 March 1993: K19.

———. "Haitian Military Is Said to Accept Plan to End Crisis." *New York Times* 3 July 1993: A1.

———. "Haitian Military Leaders and Aristide Sign Pact to End Crisis." *New York Times* 4 July 1993: A1.

———. "Haitians' Advocates Admit Some Feelings of Betrayal." *New York Times* 15 January 1993: A2.

———. "Haitians Express Sense of Betrayal." *New York Times* 17 January 1993: 3.

———. "Haiti Army Celebrates U.S. Withdrawal." *New York Times* 13 October 1993: A12.

———. "Haiti Removes Obstacles to U.N. Observer Mission." *New York Times* 10 February 1993: A14.

———. "Haiti's Premier and General Meet as Drive to Settle Crisis Intensifies." *New York Times* 26 October 1993: A13.

———. "Haiti's Premier Says He Will Stay at His Post." *New York Times* 29 October 1993: A6.

———. "Hundreds Are Lost as Crowded Ferry Capsizes Off Haiti." *New York Times* 19 February 1993: A1.

———. "In Haiti, There is No Shortage of Fear." *New York Times* 20 October 1993: A5.

————. "In Haiti's Army, Business Is the Order of the Day." *New York Times* 12 November 1993: A12.

————. "Prostrate Haiti Looking to Foreign Aid for a Lift." *New York Times* 11 July 1993: A3.

————. "Restoring Stability to Haiti Is Seen as the Next Big Test." *New York Times* 5 July 1993: A4.

————. "Study Says Haiti Sanctions Kill Up to 1,000 Children a Month." *New York Times* 9 November 1993: A1.

————. "Tension Is Rising as Haiti Military Tightens Its Grip." *New York Times* 17 October 1993: A1.

————. "Two Sides in Haiti Meet on Impasse." *New York Times* 24 October 1993: A7.

————. "U.S. Tells Haitians of Embargo Terms." *New York Times* 21 October 1993: A7.

————. "U.N. Approves Ban on Shipments of Oil to Haitian Military." *New York Times* 17 June 1993: A1.

————. "U.N. Aides Warn Haiti It Could Face Total Blockade." *New York Times* 23 October 1993: A3.

————. "U.N. Envoy Proposes Talks to End the Impasse in Haiti." *New York Times* 30 October 1993: A5.

————. "U.S. Advisor Meets Haitian But Sees No Breakthrough." *New York Times* 16 October 1993: A4.

————. "U.S. Move Angers Diplomats in Haiti." *New York Times* 14 October 1993: A8.

————. "Violence Spreading: Few Expect the Army to Honor a Pact to Yield to Aristide Today." *New York Times* 15 October 1993: A1.

Friedman, Thomas L. "Clinton's Foreign Policy: Top Advisor Speaks Up." *New York Times* 31 October 1993: A8.

————. "Clinton Vows to Fight Congress on His Power to Use the Military." *New York Times* 19 October 1993: A1.

————. "Dole to Offer Bill to Limit President on G.I. Role in Haiti." *New York Times* 18 October 1993: A1.

————. "Envoys Press Aristide." Editorial. *New York Times* 21 October 1993: A7.

————. "Leaders in Haiti Wrong to Think They Can Tell U.S., Clinton Says." *New York Times* 29 October 1993: A6.

Gordon, Michael R. "Failure of Haiti Operation Backs Initial Pentagon Skepticism." *New York Times* 15 October 1993: A8.

Greenhouse, Linda. "Court Is Asked to Back Haitians' Return." *New York Times* 3 March 1993: A16.

Greenhouse, Steven. "Clinton Defends Aristide." *New York Times* 24 October 1993: A7.

"Haitian Radio Host, Backer of Aristide, Is Killed in Miami." *New York Times* 26 October 1993: A13.

"Haiti: The Secret of Success." Editorial. *New York Times* 7 July 1993: A14.

Hilts, Philip J. "7 Haitians Held at Guantanamo Unconscious in a Hunger Strike." *New York Times* 15 February 1993: A7.

Holmes, Steven A. "Administration Is Fighting Itself on Haiti Policy." *New York Times* 23 October 1993: A1.

———. "Aristide Holds to Faith." *New York Times* 16 March 1993: A13.

———. "Bid to Restore Haiti's Leader Is Derailed: U.S. Withdraws Ship and Asks Sanctions." *New York Times* 13 October 1993: A1.

———. "Clinton and Aristide Move to Affirm Policy on Haiti." *New York Times* 14 October 1993: A8.

———. "Haitian Leader Calls on Clinton to Set a Deadline for His Return." *New York Times* 5 March 1993: A3.

———. "Haitian Rulers Are Target of New Sanctions by U.S." *New York Times* 5 June 1993: A2.

———. "Large Group of Monitors Is Planned for Haiti, a U.N. Official Says." *New York Times* 22 January 1993: A8.

———. "U.S. and U.N. Tell Haiti Military Must Cooperate." *New York Times* 12 October 1993: A12.

———. "U.S. May Tighten Embargo on Haiti." *New York Times* 28 October 1993: A17.

———. "U.S. Sends Flotilla to Prevent Exodus from Haiti by Sea." *New York Times* 16 January 1993: A1.

"How to Get Tough with Haiti." Editorial. *New York Times* 13 October 1993: A24.

Ifill, Gwen. "Haitian Is Offered Clinton's Support on an End to Exile." *New York Times* 17 March 1993: A1.

———. "U.S. Presses for New Haitian Plan in Effort to Restore Ousted Leader." *New York Times* 15 October 1993: A1.

Krauss, Clifford. "Dole Concedes to Clinton in Fight over Right to Send Troops to Haiti." *New York Times* 21 October 1993: A6.

———. "Dole Weakening Haiti Resolution." *New York Times* 20 October 1993: A5.

Lewis, Paul. "Aristide Asks U.N. to Place a Total Embargo on Haiti." *New York Times* 29 October 1993: A6.

———. "Haitian Military Condemned by U.N." *New York Times* 31 October 1993: A12.

———. "U.N. Again Imposes Sanctions on Haiti after Pact Fails." *New York Times* 14 October 1993: A1.

"Mr. Dole's Bad Idea." Editorial. *New York Times* 19 October 1993: A28.

"Of 800 to 1,200 Aboard Haitian Ferry, 285 Lived." *New York Times* 20 February 1993: A3.

Pierre-Pierre, Garry. "After Talks, Haitian Aides Hope for a Break in the Impasse." *New York Times* 25 October 1993: A3.

———. "Amid Strife, Haiti Parliament Struggles with Itself." *New York Times* 31 October 1993: A12.

———. "Anxious Haitians Start Building Boats Again." *New York Times* 22 October 1993: A1.

———. "Effort to Save Haitian Talks Fails as Military Leaders Shun Meeting." *New York Times* 6 November 1993: A1.

———. "For Haitians, Politics Has Affected Even the Dead." *New York Times* 2 November 1993: A6.

———. "Haiti Is Suffering Under Oil Embargo." *New York Times* 3 November 1993: A7.

———. "Haitian Talks End on a Hopeful Note." *New York Times* 4 November 1993: A10.

———. "One More Shortage in Haiti: News." *New York Times* 19 October 1993: A18.

———. "Port-au-Prince: City of Many Divides." *New York Times* 17 October 1993: A14.

———. "Rights Monitors Are Pulled Out of Haiti." *New York Times* 16 October 1993: A4.

———. "Terror of Duvalier Years Is Haunting Haiti Again." *New York Times* 18 October 1993: A6.

"President on Haiti: U.S. Interests at Stake." *New York Times* 16 October 1993: A4.

"The Refugee Panic Act of 1993." Editorial. *New York Times* 23 July 1993: A26.

Rohter, Larry "At Haiti-Dominican Border: Barrier or Loophole?" *New York Times* 10 November 1993: A3.

———. "Haitian General Begins a Selling Job." *New York Times* 5 July 1993: A4.

———. "Haitian Hijacks a Missionary Plane to Miami." *New York Times* 19 February 1993: A8.

———. "Haitians Remain Skeptical of Accord." *New York Times* 4 July 1993: A12.

"Same Haiti Policy, Still Illegal." Editorial. *New York Times* 4 March 1993: A24.

Sciolino, Elaine. "Christopher Spells Out New Priorities." *New York Times* 5 November 1993: A8.

———. "Clinton Says U.S. Will Continue Ban on Haitian Exodus." *New York Times* 15 January 1993: A2.

———. "3 Players Seek a Director for Foreign Policy Story." *New York Times* 8 November 1993: A1.

———. "U.S. Offers 350 Troops to U.N. Force for Haiti." *New York Times* 22 July 1993: A5.

———. "With Foreign Policies under Fire, Top State Dept. Deputy Is Ousted." *New York Times* 9 November 1993: A1.

"Shell Delivering Gasoline in Haiti." *New York Times* 17 November 1993: A9.

Sontag, Deborah. "Haiti Arrests Man on Way to Asylum in the U.S." *New York Times* 14 March 1993: A8.

———. "White House Again Defends Bush's Policy on Haitians." *New York Times* 9 March 1993: A16.

"Tighten the Sanctions on Haiti." Editorial. *New York Times* 29 October 1993: A28.

Treaster, Joseph. "Drug Flow through Haiti Cut Sharply by Embargo." *New York Times* 4 November 1993: A7.

"U.S. Freezes Assets of 41 Haitians." *New York Times* 22 October 1993: A10.

Weiner, Tim. "C.I.A. Formed Haitian Unit Later Tied to Narcotics Trade." *New York Times* 14 November 1993: A1.

———. "Key Haiti Leaders Said to Have Been in the C.I.A.'s Pay." *New York Times* 1 November 1993: A1.

Washington Post

"Another Chance for Haiti." Editorial. *Washington Post* 5 July 1993: A18.

Biskupic, Joan. "Administration to Defend Bush Haitian Policy in Court." *Washington Post* 1 March 1993: A9.

———. "Court Hears Administration Defend Bush Haitian Policy." *Washington Post* 3 March 1993: A1.

Booth, William. "Children Long Resident in U.S. Are Caught in Frightening Haitian Limbo." *Washington Post* 27 October 1993: A27.

———. "Despite Embargo, Wealthy Haitians Can Obtain Gasoline Easily." *Washington Post* 26 October 1993: A21.

———. "Navy, Coast Guard to Surround Haiti." *Washington Post* 16 January 1993: A1.

———. "Pro-Army Haitians Ask New Vote: U.N. Envoy, Seeking to Save Fraying Accord, Accedes to More Talks." *Washington Post* 30 October 1993: A17.

———. "Truth or Dare, Haitian Style." *Washington Post* 24 January 1993: A1.

"Clinton Applauds Haiti Agreement: U.S. Back Plan on Restoring Aristide to Power 'to the Fullest.'" *Washington Post* 5 July 1993: A5.

"Congress vs. President." Editorial. *Washington Post* 20 October 1993: A28.

Devroy, Ann, and Douglas Farah. "Clinton Weighs Response to Haiti Minister's Slaying: U.S. Warships May Be Used to Enforce Trade Embargo." *Washington Post* 15 October 1993: A1.

Devroy, Ann, and R. Jeffrey Smith. "Clinton Reexamines a Foreign Policy under Siege." *Washington Post* 17 October 1993: A1.

Dewar, Helen. "Clinton and Congress Cease Fire." *Washington Post* 22 October 1993: A26.

———. "Lawmakers Seek New Methods to Handle Post-Cold War Crises." *Washington Post* 16 October 1993: A18.

———. "Move to Curb Clinton on Troops Is Rejected." *Washington Post* 20 October 1993: A32.

———. "Now It's the GOP Asserting Role for Congress on Foreign Policy." *Washington Post* 26 October 1993: A20.

———. "Senators Act to Rewrite Resolution on Troop Deployment Policy." *Washington Post* 23 October 1993: A5.

———. "Senators Approve Troop Compromise: Clinton Authority Is Left Unrestricted." *Washington Post* 21 October 1993: A1.

Duke, Lynne. "Haitians Hope Strike Will Open Safe Haven." *Washington Post* 11 February 1993: A4.

———. "U.S. Ordered to Free HIV-Infected Haitians." *Washington Post* 9 June 1993: A1.

———. "White House to Obey Order to Admit HIV-Infected Haitians." *Washington Post* 10 June 1993: A30.

Farah, Douglas. "Aristide's Supporters Faltering: Haiti Embargo Adds to Despair." *Washington Post* 21 October 1993: A1.

———. "Class Strife Clouds Haiti's Future: Fear Motivates Elite to Thwart Aristide's Return." *Washington Post* 31 October 1993: A1.

———. "Coast Guard Patrols, Clinton's Switch on Repatriation Delay Haitian Exodus." *Washington Post* 21 January 1993: A14.

———. "Duvaliers' Backers Return to Fight: Ex-Dictators' Supporter, Home from Exile, Ally with Army." *Washington Post* 16 October 1993: A1.

———. "Elections Sought by Haiti Group: Army-Allied Parties Defy U.N. Threat of Wider Embargo." *Washington Post* 1 November 1993: A1.

———. "Generals Said to Gamble Haiti Has Enough Oil." *Washington Post* 18 June 1993: A27.

———. "Haiti: More than a Refugee Issue." *Washington Post* 17 January 1993: A45.

———. "Haiti's Army Accepts Plan for Talks." *Washington Post* 18 January 1993: A14.

———. "Haiti's Embargo Is Shifted into Fast Forward: Premier Cuts Off Car Owners from Gasoline Stored in Capital." *Washington Post* 23 October 1993: A17.

———. "Haitian Legislators Stay Away from Crucial Session, Citing Fear for Lives." *Washington Post* 27 October 1993: A30.

———. "Haitian Rulers Scramble to Forestall U.N. Embargo." *Washington Post* 18 October 1993: A12.

———. "Haitians Preparing Boats Denounce Policy Shift by Clinton." *Washington Post* 16 January 1993: A19.

———. "Haitians Weigh New Plan to End Political Impasse." *Washington Post* 25 October 1993: A12.

———. "Premier of Haiti Steers 'Opposition Government': From Resident, Malval Struggles for Aristide." *Washington Post* 22 October 1993: A25.

———. "Prospects for Prompt Resolution of Haitian Crisis Begin to Dim." *Washington Post* 24 January 1993: A24.

———. "212 Haitians Returned by Coast Guard Cutter." *Washington Post* 17 January 1993: A41.

———. "U.S. Ships Set for Embargo, Haiti Process at 'Dead End.'" *Washington Post* 17 October 1993: A1.

———. "U.S. Shares Anti-Drug Data with Haiti's Military: Aristide, Others Accuse Army of Massive Trafficking." *Washington Post* 24 October 1993: A27.

———. "U.S. Tightens Sanctions on Regime in Haiti." *Washington Post* 5 June 1993: A18.

Farah, Douglas, and William Booth. "Efforts to Restore Aristide Tottering: Haiti's Army Fends Off Pressure." *Washington Post* 28 October 1993: A31.

———. "U.N. Envoy Invites Carter to Haiti; Former President, Other World Leaders Would Act as Protectors." *Washington Post* 26 October 1993: A19.

Farah, Douglas, and Ruth Marcus. "Haiti's Army Rulers Remain Defiant." *Washington Post* 19 October 1993: A18.

————. "U.S. Pulls Troop Ship Back from Haiti: Clinton Seeks Sanctions after Defiant Host Fails to Assure Safety of Force." *Washington Post* 13 October 1993: A1.

Farah, Douglas, and Michael Tarr. "Haitians Block U.S. Troop Arrival." *Washington Post* 12 October 1993: A1.

Gellman, Barton, and R. Jeffrey Smith. "Hesitant by Design: Aspin's Style at Pentagon Often Leaves Important Decisions in Hands of Others." *Washington Post* 14 November 1993: A1.

Goshko, John M. "Aristide Denies CIA Report of Treatment for Mental Illness." *Washington Post* 23 October 1993: A19.

———— "Blacks Criticize Clinton on Haiti: Multilateral Military Action to Return Aristide Suggested." *Washington Post* 11 November 1993: A46.

————. "Monitors Could Be in Haiti by Month's End." *Washington Post* 22 January 1993: A25.

————. "Pullback Is New Setback for Clinton: Effort to Demonstrate Coherent Policy Hurt." *Washington Post* 14 October 1993: A24.

Goshko, John M., and R. Jeffrey Smith. "U.N. Envoy to Go Ahead on Haiti Talks Despite Military's Silence." *Washington Post* 3 November 1993: A16.

"Handling Global Trouble Spots: Mistakes and Lessons." Editorial. *Washington Post* 17 October 1993: A29.

Harrison, Lawrence E. "Haiti's Overseas Resources." *Washington Post* 9 July 1993: A21.

Kamen, Al, and Ruth Marcus. "Clinton to Continue Forcible Repatriation of Fleeing Haitians." *Washington Post* 15 January 1993: A16.

"Laying It Off on Clifton Wharton." Editorial. *Washington Post* 10 November 1993: A26.

Lippman, Thomas W. "U.S. Relaxes Its Drive for Haitian Democracy: No Humanitarian Problems Seen Imminent." *Washington Post* 17 November 1993: A36.

————. "U.S. Willing to Send Military, Police Trainers to Haiti." *Washington Post* 23 July 1993: A24.

————. "Wharton Resigns at State Dept.: Deputy Secretary First Top Member to Quit Foreign Policy Team." *Washington Post* 9 November 1993: A1.

Marcus, Ruth. "Clinton Backs Aristide Return to Power, But Sets No Date." *Washington Post* 17 March 1993: A28.

————. "Clinton Besieged about Policy Shifts." *Washington Post* 15 January 1993: A1.

————. "A 'Pretty Good Beginning': That's How Clinton Rates Foreign Policy Record." *Washington Post* 15 October 1993: A1.

Marcus, Ruth, and Barton Gellman. "U.S. Sends Ships to Enforce Embargo: Human Rights Monitors Evacuated from Haiti." *Washington Post* 16 October 1993: A1.

Marcus, Ruth, and Helen Dewar. "Clinton Tells Congress to Back Off: President Asserts Authority on Military Moves in Haiti, Bosnia. " *Washington Post* 19 October 1993: A1.

McGrory, Mary. "Haiti Scrambles Clinton Options." *Washington Post* 14 October 1993: A2.

"Mr. Aristide's Opportunity." Editorial. *Washington Post* 27 October 1993: A24.

"Mr. Clinton and the Haitians." Editorial. *Washington Post* 16 January 1993: A22.

"Navy Is Said to Interdict Soy Milk and Baby Cribs." *Washington Post* 23 October 1993: A19.

"Next Steps in Haiti." Editorial. *Washington Post* 18 October 1993: A18.

"No One Else Will Do for Haiti." Editorial. *Washington Post* 21 October 1993: A2.

"On the Dock in Haiti." Editorial. *Washington Post* 12 October 1993: A18.

Preston, Julia. "Aristide Asks U.N. for Total Haiti Cutoff: Exile Indicates Military Prevents Return Saturday." *Washington Post* 29 October 1993: A29.

———. "Gen. Cedras Accepts U.N. Pact on Haiti." *Washington Post* 3 July 1993: A13.

———. "Haiti Agrees to Monitoring by U.N., OAS." *Washington Post* 10 February 1993: A28.

———. "Haiti Embargo Revived." *Washington Post* 14 October 1993: A1.

———. "U.N. Votes to Clamp Oil Embargo on Haiti." *Washington Post* 17 June 1993: A1.

Priest, Dana. "Administration Aides Defensive on Foreign Policy Strategies." *Washington Post* 11 October 1993: A1.

———. "U.S. Use of Force in Haiti 'Not Ruled Out.'" *Washington Post* 18 October 1993: A13.

Sawyer, Kathy. "Gore Defends Aristide, Whose Prospects for Return Seem Brighter." *Washington Post* 25 October 1993: A14.

"Shake-up in Haiti." *Washington Post* 6 June 1993: A32.

Smith, R. Jeffrey. "CIA Profile of Aristide Debated: GOP Lawmakers Accuse Christopher of Trying to Gloss Over Report." *Washington Post* 5 November 1993: A34.

———. "CIA's Aristide Profile Spurs Hill Concern." *Washington Post* 22 October 1993: A26.

———. "Hill Briefing about Aristide Renews Debate on CIA Role." *Washington Post* 24 October 1993: A28.

"Strategy in Haiti." Editorial. *Washington Post* 16 February 1993: A12.

"Support of Aristide Defended." *Washington Post* 24 October 1993: A28.

Tarr, Michael. "Attempt to Resume Haiti Talks Collapses: Army Leader Boycotts International Session, Leaving U.S. and U.N. Generals in Lurch." *Washington Post* 6 November 1993: A14.

———. "Haiti's Cedras Hints Delay on Rights." *Washington Post* 10 July 1993: A20.

———. "Haitian Capital Is Calm as Embargo Takes Hold." *Washington Post* 20 October 1993: A32.

———. "Haitian Prime Minister Quits After Loss of Military Backing." *Washington Post* 9 June 1993: A21.

———. "Observers Arrive in Haiti." *Washington Post* 15 February 1993: A35.

"U.N. Presses Haiti Army to Comply." *Washington Post* 31 October 1993: A26.

"U.S. Allies Agree to Seek Oil Embargo against Haiti." *Washington Post* 10 June 1993: A29.

Williams, Daniel. "Christopher Lists Six Goals of Clinton's Foreign Policy." *Washington Post* 5 November 1993: A29.

———. "An Opening on Foreign Policy." *Washington Post* 10 November 1993: A21.

Williams, Daniel and Ann Devroy. "U.S. Warns Haiti's Military to Yield." *Washington Post* 29 October 1993: A32.

Index

About the Author

JIM A. KUYPERS is Senior Lecturer and Director of the Office of Speech, Dartmouth College. He has written on rhetoric and communications in journals such as *Eastern Communication Journal* and *Southern Communication Journal.*